KB234598

인생의 고난에
고개 숙이지 마라

THE RICH MAN'S WILL
Mark Fisher 2010

Represented by Cathy Miller Foreign Rights Agency, London, England.
All rights reserved. Korean translation rights arranged with Cathy Miller Foreign Rights
Agency, through EYA (Eric Yang Agency).

백만장자 아버지의 마지막 가르침

인생의 고난에 고개 숙이지 마라

마크 피셔 **지음** | 배영란 **옮김**

진성북스

<s> 차 례 </s>

한국어판 서문 • 06

어느 날 갑자기 닥친 시련 • 09
또 하나의 비통한 소식 • 24
수상한 거지 • 38

다시 만난 아버지 • 61
네 스스로 위대하다고 생각하라 • 84
네가 하는 일을 뜨겁게 사랑하라 • 108

한 우물을 파라 • 118
매일매일 새로워져라 • 126
끈기를 가져라 • 132

호기심을 가져라 • 146
장애를 이용하라 • 163
가장 중요한 걸 잊지 마라 • 172

예기치 않은 수표 한 장 • 176

프러포즈 • 196

어린 시절의 중요함 • 203

중요한 결심 • 213

아버지의 서재에서 무언가를 발견하다 • 218

아버지와의 이별 • 231

클라라의 고백 • 249

수수께끼의 실마리가 풀리다 • 257

할머니에게서 얻은 힌트 • 266

샤를 레니에, 다시 아이가 되다 • 279

운명의 실현 • 292

예언의 실현 • 300

역자 후기 • 304

런던의 캐시 밀러 에이전시 측으로부터 이 책의 한국어판 서문을 작성해달라는 이메일을 확인하던 순간, 저는 LA 한인 타운의 한 호텔에 있었습니다. 정말 놀라운 우연의 일치가 아닐까요?

'이제 드디어《인생의 고난에 고개 숙이지 마라》가 한국에서 출간될 때가 온 거구나'라고 생각했습니다. 이 책이 한국에서 큰 성공을 거둔다면, 한국 독자들에게 인생의 성공을 이룰 수 있도록 도와주었다는 느낌이 들 것입니다.

이 책의 내용은 제게 개인적으로 매우 공감 가는 이야기입니다. 주인공은 아버지를 여의었고 1년 전 저 또한 그랬으니까요. 주인공의 처지가 어쩌면 가혹해보일 수도 있습니다. 부자 아버지는 그에게 아무 것도 남겨주지 않았고, 형과 누나에게만 큰 재산을 물려주었습니다. 아버지는 왜 이런 선택을 했을까요? 이는 주인공 샤를이 고심하며 풀어야 할 문제입니다.

아버지의 빈소에서 주인공은 신비로운 힘을 지닌 거지 한 명을 만납니다. 그는 돌아가신 아버지를 사흘간 다시 만날 수 있도록 아들을 도와줍니다. 이는 주인공에게 놀라운 선물이 됩니다. 아버지에게 왜 그런 선택을 했는지 물어볼 수 있었으니까요.

그 후 두 부자의 특별한 여행이 시작됩니다. 그리고 여행을 통해, 아버지는 아들에게 인생에 관해 무엇과도 견줄 수 없는 소중한 가르침을 전해줍니다.

그 가르침은 아래와 같습니다.

- 비록 과거에 실패했다 하더라도, 어떻게 하면 상처를 회복하고 다시 부자가 될 수 있을까?

- 모든 상황에서 최고의 거래는 무엇이며, 자신에게 유리한 쪽으로 협상하는 방법은 무엇일까?

- 자기 자신에 대한 믿음을 갖고 자신의 이미지와 가치를 새로 만들어내는 방법은 무엇인가?

- 자유롭고 행복하게 살 수 있는 길은 무엇인가? 그리고 이보다 훨씬 더 나은 삶을 사는 길은 어디에 있을까?

제가 추구하는 삶의 자세가 이 책에 고스란히 녹아 있습니다. 두 시간 정도만 투자한다면 독자들의 삶은 영원히 달라진 모습으로 지속될 수 있으리라 확신합니다.

_ 마크 피셔

어느 날 갑자기 닥친 시련

살다가 혹 길을 잃어버린 것 같다는 느낌이 든 적 있는가? 내가 왠지 다른 사람의 삶을 살고 있는 것 같을 때, 어느 날 아침 거울에 비친 내 모습이 나 같지 않고 어색할 때, 더없이 혼란스럽고 도무지 헤어날 수 없는 그런 기분을 느낄 때가 있었는가?

지금보다 어렸을 때 스스로 꿈꿔왔던 그런 삶을 살고 있지 않은 그 누군가, 페이스북 같은 데에서 왠지 친구로 삼고 싶지 않은 그 누군가, 그렇게 초라한 그 누군가가 된 것 같은 기분이 들지는 않았는가?

모든 게 뒤죽박죽 엉망이 된 상태에서, 이것저것 되지도 않는 시도들을 해보며 그 같은 상황을 피해보려 애쓸 수도 있고, 아니면 결국은 여기에서 헤어나지 못하고 힘겨운 30초간의 자기 독백 끝에 이렇게 말할 수도 있다. "자, 앞으로도 잘해봐야지. 오늘도 무사히 잘 보내길 바라면서……."

그런데 밖에서 보면 내 삶은 별다른 문제없는 행복한 삶으로 보일 수도 있다. 주위의 몇몇 친구들이나 직장 동료들, 클라이언트 입장에서 바라보면 내 팔자가 외려 부러워 보일 수도 있다. 나에 대해 제대로 알고 있지 않은 모든 이들, 내게 안부를 물어오면 으레 하는 대답처럼 그저 "나야 물론 잘 지내지. 그러는 자네는 요새 어떤가? 잘 지내나?"라고 형식적인 답변으로 응하고 말아버리는 모든 이들, 그런 이들에게 내 삶은 꽤 괜찮아 보일 수도 있다.

시간이 흐를수록, 우리는 남들의 눈을 모두 감쪽같이 속이는 일에 달인이 되어간다. 하지만 진짜 내가 아닌 모습으로 그냥 '그런 척'을 하며 살아가는 일도 시간이 지남에 따라 점점 더 지치게 마련이고, 하루하루 그렇게 버티는 게 차츰 힘이 들어간다.

그렇게 삶이 힘들어지고, 삶이 고달파진다. 그리고 늘 행복하고 강인한 사람으로 인정받아왔던 만큼, 이 끝이 없는 '쇼'는 스스로를 더욱 부끄럽게 만든다. 주위 사람들에게 나는 늘 모든 시련을 이겨내는 사람이었고, 친구든 자식이든 부모님이든 연인이든 누구나 잠깐 와서 쉬었다 갈 수 있는 편안한 바위 같은 존재였다.

그런데 그렇게 남들 앞에서 쓰고 있던 가면에 조금씩 금이 가기 시작한다. 내가 살아가고 있는 이 삶의 어디에 기쁨이 존재하는 것인지 모르겠다. 미소 짓던 얼굴은 점점 일그러져 가고, 특히 혼자 있을 때가 더더욱 그렇다. 이런 상황이 점점 더 잦아지고, 웃음은 찡그린 얼굴에 조금씩 그 자리를 완전히 내어준다. 하여 사람들에게 둘러싸여 있을 때도, 침대에 있을 때도, 심지어 다정한 연인과 함께 있을 때도 외로움이 느껴진다. 나를 주인공으로 한 '권태'라는 이름의 연극 속에서, 나는 점점 더 자주 외로움을 느낀다.

최소한 내게 일어나는 이 일에 대해 비난이라도 할 수 있다면……. 최소한 이 삶의 괴로움에 대해 그 정체라도 알 수 있다면…….

어쩌면 당신에게는 그저 변화가 필요한 것인지도 모른다. 침대 위에 함께 누워 있는 사람이, 이 사람이 아닌 다른 사람이면 되는 것인지도 모른다. 새로운 곳에서, 새로운 친구들과 만나면 문제는 쉽게 해결될 수 있을지도 모른다. 휴가 때 아무 생각 없이 여행을 떠나볼 수도 있다. 하지만 아무 것도 변하지 않은 채 돌아올 수도 있다. 휴가지에서 정신없이 제대로 잘 놀았다며 항변을 해볼 수도 있겠지만, 그래도 상황이 크게 달라지지는 않는다. 여전히 우울함은 당신 곁을 떠나지 않으며, 더욱이 휴가 때 쓰고 온 카드 값은 아직 청구서가 날아오지도 않은 상태다. 그러다 결국은 체념해버리고 만다. 어른이 되기로 마음먹는 것이다. 어릴 적 꿈들도 그냥 잊기로 하고, 열정과 패기도 마음속 깊은 곳에 묻어두고 만다.

조금은 서글프지만, 도처에서 찾아볼 수 있는 이 같은 초상은 이 이야기의 주인공인 샤를 레니에의 모습과도 비슷하다.

훤칠한 키에 군살 없는 몸매의 소유자인 샤를 레니에는 푸른 눈에 머리는 금발이었으며, 헤어스타일도 최신 유행에 따라 깔끔하게 깎았다. 꽤 괜찮은 대학에서 철학을 가르치는 그는 서른여섯의 나이에도 아직 독신이다. 물론 말은 그렇게 한다. 하지만 실상은 약간 다르다. 클라라 램플링이라는 서른넷의 매력적인 치과 여의사와 3년째 함께 살고 있기 때문이다.

샤를은 왜 굳이 철학이라는 과목을 가르치기로 했을까? 그건 물론 그가 철학 사상을 좋아했기 때문이다. 위대한 사상가들에 대한 관심도 높았다. 하지만 이는 어쩌면 아버지에게 맞서고 싶어서였는지도 모른다. 어쨌든 그는 아버지와 반대의 길을 가고 싶었던 것 같다. 아버지 피에르 레니에는 현실적인 인물이었다. 굉장한 성공을 거두어 예순 세 살의 나이에 어마어마한 갑부가 되었고, 그의 재산 규모는 3억 달러 가까이로 추정됐다. 물론 이보다 더 부자인 사람도 있고, 그보다 훨씬 부자인 사람도 있다. 하지만 그보다 훨씬 더 가난한 사람도 있다. 피에르는 무일푼에서 시작하여 자수성가한 타입이었고, 일찍이 어렸을 때 아버지를 여읜 채 홀어머니 밑에서 자랐다. 물론 어머니는 훌륭한 분이셨지만, 가진 재산은 별로 없었다. 피에르의 인생 역전은 충분히 귀감이 될 만한 사례였다.

아버지의 회사에서 일하던 형, 누나와 달리, 샤를은 정말 아버지의 삶을 비웃으려 했던 것일까? 확실히 그건 아닐 것이다. 그의 아버지는 사업 쪽에 투신하기 전에 먼저 철학을 공부했던 인물이다. 《국가》에서 플라톤은 철학자가 왕이 되어야 한다고, 왕은 무릇 철학적인 왕이 되어야 한다고 주장했다. 이와 마찬가지로 아버지인 피에르 역시 처음 일을 시작하던 시기, 사업가란 이름에 걸맞게 일단 철학자가 되어 사람들과 그 당시 시대에 대해 이해할 수 있어야 한다고 생각했다. 그래야 성공한 사업가가 될 수 있다고 본 것이다.

처음에 사람들은 그런 그를 비웃었다. 사상이라든가 관념이라든가 하는 것들과 거리가 먼 분야에서 사업 구상을 하는 철학 박사라니, 이 얼마나 웃긴 상황인가? 부동산업이라는 세계에서는 벽돌이 책을 대체하고, 철학자들이 있어야 할 자리에 브로커와 은행가, 세입자가 들어온다. 소크라테스의 산파술이나 칸트의 정언명령과는 하등의 상관도 없는 분야인 것이다.

하지만 5년이 지나자, 결단력 있는 이 사나이는 처음으로 백만 달러의 재산을 모으는 데 성공한다. 어느 누구도 피에르에게 관심을 두지 않는 사람이 없었고, 살벌한 라이벌에서 헌신적인 동료에 이르기까지 모두가 그의 주위로 모여들었다. 희대의 추남이라 불려도 손색이 없을 만한 외모로 연애

까지 성공을 거두었다. 그는 자신이 옳다는 사실을 모든 사람들에게 입증하길 결코 멈추지 않았다. 저들에게 이를 몸소 증명해 보이는 것은 결실을 거둔 그의 생애에서 가장 큰 즐거움 중 하나였다.

옳은 길을 가라. 그리하여 돈을 벌라.
그리고 돈을 벌기 위해서는 즐겨야 한다.
그게 바로 피에르 레니에의 좌우명이었다.

피에르는 수많은 사업가들이 생각했던 것 혹은 생각해야 했던 것을 직접적으로 인정하고 받아들였다. 중요한 건 바로 수익이다. 수익이 없으면 함께하는 사람도 없다.

맞는 말이다.

그의 아들인 샤를은 학과 회의에 참석하던 중이었다. 그는 회의 자리가 영 부담스러웠다. 몇 달 전부터 그랬다. 샤를은 자신이 왠지 자기 자리에 있는 것 같지 않았다. 스스로가 영 낯선 이방인처럼 느껴졌다.

수업 중에도 상황은 마찬가지였다. 학생들과의 사이는 무척 좋았고, 때로 그에게 희열감까지 안겨주었다. 하지만 그래도 샤를 자신이 꼭 남의 자리에 들어와 있는 것 같았다.

55세의 학과장 조르주 다미앵 교수는 30분째 무서운 눈초리를 한 채 두꺼운 뿔테 안경 너머로 교수들을 바라보며 이런저런 문제에 대한 이들의 하소연을 들어주고 있었다. 이제 중요한 의결 사항에 대해 결정을 내릴 때가 왔다.

"찬성하시는 분들, 손들어주시지요."

네 명의 교수가 찬성표를 던졌다.

학과장은 이들을 제하고 나서 다시 물었다.

"반대하시는 분?"

네 명의 교수가 손을 들었다.

어느 쪽도 손을 들지 않은 사람은 오직 샤를뿐이었다.

"레니에 교수?"

학과장이 그를 호명했다.

샤를 레니에는 소스라치게 놀랐다. 마치 한잠 들었던 그를 누군가 흔들어 깨우기라도 한 것처럼, 아니면 적어도 깊은 공상에서 그를 갑자기 끄집어내기라도 한 것처럼 놀란 모습이었다. 동료 교수들은 못마땅하다는 듯한 눈초리로 그를 돌아보았다. 이 회의에 관심을 가질 수 없을 만한 이유가 있었다 한들 소용없는 일이었다. 동료 교수들의 눈에는 그런 샤를의 무관심이 거의 경멸에 가깝게 느껴졌다. 누구에게나 문제는 있게 마련이다. 누군들 자기만의 사정이 없겠는가? 그런만큼 그런 그의 행동이 더더욱 받아들이기 힘든 게 아니었을까?

"그게, 저는…… 저……."

"레니에 교수, 자네 의견은 찬성인가, 반대인가? 지금 가부 동수이기 때문에 자네의 한 표가 무척 중요하네."

그는 찬성과 반대 그 어느 쪽으로도 결국 표를 던지지 못했다.

"저…… 저는…… 저…… 정말 죄송합니다. 더 이상은 못 있겠어요……."

그의 눈에서는 눈물이 흘러내렸다. 그는 사람들 앞에서 울고 싶지 않았다. 적어도 자기 동료들 앞에서만큼은 울지 않길 바랐다. 생판 모르는 사람들 앞에서 우는 것도 미칠 노릇인데, 적어도 이 사람들에게만은, 여기 있는 자기 동료들에게만은 자신의 불행에 대해 엿볼 기회를 주고 싶지 않았다.

샤를은 자기 사무실로 달려갔고, 회의가 무산된 후 곧이어 학과장이 그의 사무실을 찾았다. 사무실 벽은 온통 책장의 책들로 뒤덮여 있었고, 학생들의 논문과 얼마 전 손대기 시작한 자작 소설의 원고도 눈에 띄었다. 사실 수년 전부터 그는 작가가 되길 바랐다. 그 외에도 사르트르, 괴테, 볼테르, 프루스트 등 위대한 철학자나 유명한 소설가의 사진, 초상 등이 놓여 있었다.

"학과장님, 정말 죄송해요. 저도…… 저도…… 이 회의가 중요하다는 건 알아요. 하지만 제가…….

"무슨 일인가?"

"처음부터 다 말씀을 드릴까요, 아니면 짧게만 말씀드릴까요?"

반감이나 비아냥거림은 느껴지지 않는 질문이었다. 샤를의 말에서는 그저 좌절감만이 느껴질 뿐이었다. 학과장은 그냥 미소만 지어보였다.

"클라라와 헤어졌습니다."

"저런, 유감이네. 하지만…… 곧 돌아오지 않겠나. 늘 그렇게 헤어졌다가 다시 계속 만나지 않았던가?"

"이번에는 아닙니다. 이번은 심각해요. 저도 알아요. 이미 마지막 기회까지 다 써버렸어요. 한 번도 아니고 두 번이나 그랬으니……."

"하지만 도대체 왜 클라라가 자네 곁을 떠난 겐가? 자네가 뭘 잘못한 게야?"

"클라라가 제 곁을 떠난 건 클라라가 옳고, 제가 틀렸기 때문이죠. 남녀 사이란 게 늘 그런 거 아니겠습니까?"

"그게 아니지. 진지하게 얘기해보게나."

"클라라가 떠난 건 제가 결혼을 거부했기 때문이에요. 사실 클라라는 우리가 3년째 함께 사는 상황에서 나이도 이제 서른네 살이 되어서 결혼도 하고 아이도 갖고 싶어했는데, 제가 결혼은 안 된다고 한 거죠. 클라라는 제가 그녀를 진심으로 사랑하지 않는다고 생각했어요. 내가 자기랑 헤어지고 다른 여자를 만나고 싶어한다고 생각한 거죠. 더욱이 클라라는 내가 자기보다 더 젊은 여자를 찾고 있다고 확신했어요. 제가 가르치는 학생들을 모두 그 대상으로 넣은 거죠."

"클라라의 생각이 맞는 겐가? 자네가 학생들을 이성으로 본다는 거야?"

"클라라 말이 틀린 건 아니에요. 제가 가르치는 학생들이 클라라보다 더 어리긴 하죠. 하지만 저도 잘 모르겠어요. 뭐, 어쨌든 대개는 그래요.”

“자네, 잘도 그런 위험한 말을 하는군…….”

“하지만 아니에요, 학과장님. 분명 세상 모든 남자들처럼 유혹의 순간을 느끼지 않은 건 아니에요. 하지만 한 번도 그런 적은 없었어요. 저는 클라라를 사랑해요. 클라라가 제 곁을 떠난 이후로는 더더욱 그 마음이 간절해요. 그것만은 분명히 말할 수 있어요.”

“그럼 대체 문제가 뭔가? 클라라는 자네를 더 이상 사랑하지 않아서 자네를 떠난 게 아니라, 자신이 원하는 걸 자네가 해주지 않았기 때문에 자네 곁을 떠난 게 아닌가? 클라라도 아직 자네를 사랑하고 있지 않은가. 서로 그렇게 사랑했던 애틋한 마음이, 빨간 신호등 앞에서 멈추는 자동차처럼 그렇게 멈춰지는 거라고 생각하는 겐가? 자네가 아직 그녀를 사랑한다면, 가서 클라라가 원하는 걸 해주도록 하게. 더욱이 이해가 가지 않는 게, 자네 나이에 사랑하는 여자와 결혼을 해서 함께 아이를 낳는 게 그렇게 이상한 일도 아니지 않은가? 자유로운 삶에 대한 환상이 그렇게 끌리던가? 자네 세대의 사람들이 그토록 열망하는 자유라는 것에 대해 나는 별로 관심이 가질 않는다네. 내가 지금 25년째 결혼 생활을 하고 있는데, 내가 결혼의 굴레에 예속되어 있다는 느낌을 받은 적은 한 번도 없었어. 내게 결혼은 보들레르의 12음절 시구 같은 느낌이었네. 근대 문학의 수많은 사이비 시인들이 자유시로 졸작을 만들어냈지만, 12음절이라는 정형화된 틀은 그가 훌륭한 걸작을 써내는 데 아무런 제약도 되지 않았지.”

샤를은 자신의 철학적 고찰에 대해 뭐라고 늘어놓을 만한 시간이 없었다. 바로 그 때, 그의 휴대폰 벨소리가 울렸기 때문이다.

학과장의 얼굴에서는 승자의 미소가 스쳤지만, 친절하고 호의적인 표정에는 변함이 없었다.

“내 얘기 무슨 말인지 알겠나? 이제 두 사람 사이의 사랑싸움은 끝난 걸세.”

샤를이 보기에도 학과장의 말은 백번 옳았다. 그래서 그는 이 전화가 클라라에게서 온 전화이길 너무나도 바랐던 나머지, 화면에 뜨는 번호도 확인하지 않고, 상대방이 뭐라 말을 하기도 전에 곧바로 소리쳤다.

"클라라?"

삶이란 참 여러 가지 방식으로 하나의 불행을 잊게 만든다. 적어도 한시적으로는 그렇다.

삶의 가장 잔인한 측면은 바로 우리를 더 큰 불행에 처하게 만든다는 점이다.

샤를도 스스로의 쓰라린 경험을 통해 이를 곧 알게 됐다.

"클라라?"

그가 다시 한 번 되물었다.

"아냐, 나야. 지젤……. 안 좋은 소식이 있어……."

지젤은 샤를의 누나였다. 그런데 지젤이 울기 시작했다. 그리고 간신히 다시 말을 이은 뒤, 지젤은 결국 전할 말을 다 전해주었다.

전화를 끊었을 때, 샤를은 거의 망연자실한 상태에 가까웠을 뿐 아니라, 눈물까지 흘리고 있었다. 몹시 걱정스러운 표정으로 학과장이 다가와 물었다.

"무슨 일인가? 클라라에게 무슨 일이 생긴 게야?"

"아뇨…… 저희 아버지께서…… 아버지께서 심장 발작을 일으키셨대요……."

“아니, 그래서 어떻게 되셨다던가?”
“돌아가셨습니다…….”

또 하나의 비통한 소식

아버지께서 돌아가셨다…….

이 지극히 짧은 몇 마디의 말이, 샤를은 도무지 이해가 가지도, 받아들여지지도 않았다. 샤를이 머릿속으로 이 짧은 몇 마디의 말을 삼십 번쯤 되뇌이며 중얼거린 것도, 마치 시 하나를 외울 때처럼 그렇게 계속해서 되뇌인 것도, 아마 그래서였을 것이다. 그렇다. 최소한 삼십 번쯤, 아니면 그보다 더 많이 속으로 이 몇 마디를 되뇌었을 것이다. 누나한테서 아버지의 부고라는 끔찍한 소식을 전해 듣고 난 뒤, 샤를은 셈하는 법조차 잊어버렸다.

아버지께서 돌아가셨다…….

아버지의 연세는 고작 예순세 살이었다. 기력이 넘치는 분이었고, 머릿속에는 사업 계획 구상이 가득했다. 무척 정정해 보였으며, 겉보기에 아무런 문제가 없어 보였다. 그런데 도대체 왜…….

샤를의 머릿속에서 무한 반복되던 말들이 바로 이거였다. 예순셋이라는 나이는 그렇게 많은 나이가 아니다. 적어도 한 아버지의 나이로서, 특히 여든 살까지는 너끈히 살 수 있는 지금과 같은 시대에는 더욱 그렇다. 예순셋에 세상을 떠났다는 건 곧 원래 살 수 있는 기대 수명보다 20년이나 더 빨랐다는 말이 된다.

이런 그의 불만이 괜한 건 아니었다. 불행이 남의 일이 아닌 정말 우리 일이 되어버린 상황에서, 주어진 수명대로 다 살지 못하고 일찍 세상을 떠난 게 어떻게 납득이 되겠는가?

그런데 아버지를 잃은 고통에 더해 또 하나의 충격적인 사실이 있었다. 고인의 유지를 담은 유언장이 장례식 전에 공개되었는데, 이에 따르면 샤를은 아버지의 유산을 단 한 푼도 받지 못하게 되었던 것이다. 그의 앞으로 남겨진 건 단지 낡

은 양복 한 벌과 밑창 뚫린 구두 한 켤레 그리고 아버지가 평
생을 차고 계셨던 시계 하나가 전부였다. 생전에 아버지는 단
한 순간도 시계를 손목에서 끌러 놓는 법이 없었다. 매우 근
사하고 멋진 이 금시계 하나의 값만 해도 몇 천 달러는 족히
나가는 물건이었다. 스위스에서 가장 유명한 시계장인 가운
데 한 사람의 공방에서 제작한 시계였기 때문이다. 그래도 이
러는 법이 어디 있는가…….

샤를은 이 모든 상황이 그저 놀라울 따름이었다.

물론 아버지의 죽음이라는 상황이 고통스러운 건 사실이었
다. 그에게는 더 없이 큰 고통이었다. 하지만 샤를은 아버지
에 대한 반발심이 느껴졌고, 분노와 함께 모멸감에 사로잡혔
다. 그렇다. 이건 분명 치욕스러운 모멸감이었다. 그의 마음을
장악하고 있는 건 바로 그 느낌이었다. 그는 처음엔 심술궂은
공증인이 기분 나쁜 농담을 하는 줄 알았다. 아니면 아버지의
장난이든가. 세상에 어떤 공증인이 자식 하나의 이름을 빠뜨
리는 이런 엄청난 실수를 할 수 있단 말인가? 사실 샤를의 부
친은 살아생전 온갖 종류의 농담을 다 즐기는 사람이었고, 때
로는 짓궂고 심한 농담도 서슴지 않는 인물이었다. 어쨌든 당

하는 사람의 입장에서는 그랬다.

샤를은 씁쓸한 미소를 지었다. 마흔 살의 나이에 이미 머리카락이 듬성듬성 빠진 키 크고 무미건조한 공증인은 조금의 동요도 없이 침착함을 유지하고 있었다. 그의 처지가 안 됐다는 듯이 입가에 힘을 주며 딱하다는 입모양을 지어 보이고는 샤를의 어깨를 토닥여주었다. 그제야 제대로 사태를 파악한 샤를은 자리에서 일어나 형인 시몬과 누나인 지젤에게로 향했다.

샤를과 함께 유언장이 발표되는 자리에 동석한 두 사람은 말없이 침묵을 지켰다. 입은 열지 않았지만, 이 같은 상황에 대해 아무 생각이 없는 건 아니었다. 건장한 체격에 구릿빛 피부를 가진 금발의 남성 같은 스타일인 시몬은 아버지가 동생에게 아무런 재산도 남겨주지 않고 떠나자, 뛸 듯이 기쁜 기색을 감추기가 힘들었다. 동생은 늘 아버지를 경멸했고, 형인 자신에 대해서도 마찬가지였다. 자기는 똑똑한 지식인인 양 굴고 아버지 사업에 뛰어드는 건 한사코 거부했다. 부동산업이라는 게 천박하고 상스러우며 더러운 일이었기 때문이다. 자신이나 지젤같이 대학도 안 나온 촌뜨기나 하는 일이라고 생각하는 듯했다.

그래도 아버지가 동생에게 재산 한 푼 남겨주지 않은 걸 알
았을 때, 그는 무척 놀라고 당황스러웠다. 아버지는 동생에게
땡전 한 푼, 회사의 주식 한 장 안 물려주셨다. 웨스트마운트
의 근사한 별장 한 채도, 멤프레마고그 호수의 호화 빌라 한
채도 동생 차지는 아니었다.

동생에게는 정말 재산 한 푼 안 돌아갔다. 아버지의 호주머
니 푼돈조차, 단 만 달러도 동생의 것은 아니었다. 말도 안 되
는 다 낡아빠진 양복 한 벌과 해진 구두 한 켤레, 별 쓸모없는
금시계 하나를 제외하고 아버지 재산 가운데 동생 소유로 넘
어간 건 아무 것도 없었다. 금시계는 이제 시간도 제대로 맞지
않을 뿐 아니라, 동생이 두 눈 뜨고 손에서 놓친 금을 떠올리
게 만드는 역할을 해줄 터였다. 동생은 그 시계를 당장이라도
공중인 사무실 벽에다 집어던지고 싶은 심정이었을 것이다.

그렇다. 두 형제 사이에는 수년 전부터 알게 모르게 경쟁의
식이 자리 잡았고, 그것이 지극히 평범한 물질적 욕구를 계기
로 막 겉으로 폭발한 셈이었다. 사실 샤를은 형을 좋아했다.
적어도 형이 자기를 싫어하는 것보다는 덜 싫어했다. 시몬은

아버지의 유산을 셋이 아닌 둘이 나누게 된 것에 대해 속으로 쾌재를 부르고 있을 터였다. 귀엽고 통통한 타입의 금발머리 지젤은 시몬 같이 승리자의 마음은 아니었다. 하지만 그렇다고 굳이 나서서 오빠 시몬에게 정당한 재산 분배를 제의할 마음은 없었다. 어쨌든 아버지의 뜻은 따라야 하는 것 아니겠는가? 그게 지젤의 속내였다.

샤를은 자리에서 일어났다. 그리고 공증인의 손에서 유언장을 낚아챘다. 빠른 속도로 아버지의 유언장을 읽어 내려가는 샤를의 모습은 흡사 미친 사람 같았다. 아버지의 죽음에 더해 가정에 불화를 불러온 이 일에 대해 유감스러워하면서 지젤은 고개를 떨구었다. 시몬은 위선을 떨며 거짓 한숨을 내쉬었다. 공증인은 그저 고개만 끄덕끄덕했다. 아무리 화목하고 단합이 잘되는 최고의 가족이라도, 유언장 앞에서는 모든 게 무너져버릴 수 있다는 걸 수백 번도 더 봐온 그였다.

샤를은 정신 나간 사람처럼 유언장을 읽어 내려갔다. 하지만 자신과 관련한 내용은 너무나도 짤막한 한 단락 뿐이었다.

"내 아들 샤를에게는 내가 맨 처음 백만 달러를 벌었을 때 입고 있던 옷과, 그때 차고 있던 시계와, 그때 신고 있던 구두 한 켤레를 남긴다."

이게 전부였다. 고작 이게 다였다.

물론 백만장자가 되던 날 아버지가 입었던 옷, 그때 신었던 신발, 그때 차고 있던 시계를 물려준 것에 대해 샤를 자신은 아버지의 의미심장하고 시적이며 상징적인 관심에 감동을 받았을 수도 있다. 하지만 다른 유산이 있을 때 적용되는 얘기다. 형평성 있게 재산이 분배된 상황에서, 즉 아버지가 남겨준 다른 재산도 있을 때 이 세 가지 유산이 끼어 있어야 감동도 가능한 것이다. 하지만 이건 아니다. 자식이 세 명이면, 재산 분배도 3등분이 되어야 하는 것 아니겠는가?

샤를은 아버지가 한 달 전 자신과의 사이에서 있었던, 말다툼까지는 아니어도 격렬한 논쟁이 오고 갔던 일 이후 유언장 내용을 고친 게 아닐까하고 생각했다. 그날 아버지는 샤를에게 지금 괜한 시간낭비를 하고 있다고, 대학에서 쓸데없이 재능을 썩히고 있다고 꾸중했다. 그날 전화 통화에서 샤를은 아버지의 전화를 매몰차게 끊었다. 아버지가 샤를을 당신의 회사로 집어넣기 위해 벌이는 새로운 수작이라고 생각했기 때문이다. 여기까지 생각이 미친 샤를은 공증인에게 허겁지겁 물어봤다.

"아버지께서 최근 유언장을 고치신 일이 있습니까?"

"음…… 예……. 그러긴 하셨죠. 한 달 전에……. 아시다시피, 심장 발작이 한 번 있었던 직후였죠."

"네? 심장 발작이 있었다고요?"

시몬과 샤를, 지젤 세 사람 모두가 놀라 소리쳤다.

"심장 발작이 있었다니요?"

시몬이 물었다.

"모르셨나보군요. 저는 알고 계실 거라고……."

공증인도 놀라긴 마찬가지였다.

"그러고 보니 건강 부분은 늘 일부러 말씀을 안 하셨던 것 같네."

곰곰이 생각하며 지젤이 말했다.

"그러긴 하셨지."

시몬이 수긍했다.

샤를은 설마했던 의혹을 확인시켜주는 공증인의 말에 아

연실색했다.

자신에게 닥친 불행의 원인이 스스로에게 있음을 알게 될 때, 이는 가장 끔찍한 확인 사살이 된다. 그런데 이 부분은 샤를도 좀 더 확인해봐야 하는 사실이었다. 그래서 샤를이 다시 공증인에게 물었다.

"마지막 유언장에서, 아버지가 저와 관련된 부분을 다시 고치라고 말씀하셨나요?"

"그건 말씀드릴 수 없습니다. 이전 유언장의 내용은 늘 클라이언트와 공증인 사이의 직업상 기밀에 해당합니다!"

샤를은 자리에서 벌떡 일어나 불쌍한 공증인의 멱살을 잡으며 소리쳤다.

"직업상 기밀이라니, 망할! 내 아버지가 나와 관련된 부분을 바꿨소, 안 바꿨소?"

공증인은 시몬과 지젤의 동의를 구하기 위해 이들의 눈치를 살폈다. 이에 곧 두 사람 곁으로 시몬과 지젤이 다가왔다. 지젤은 입가에 미묘한 미소를 지으며 자신은 아무 것도 모르겠다는 듯이 어깨를 으쓱해보였고, 어딜 봐도 기쁜 기색이 완연한 시몬은 경계의 눈빛이라기보다는 도발적 분위기로 두 눈을 동그랗게 뜨며 무언의 메시지를 전했다. '녀석에게 얼른 진실을 말해줘. 이제 어찌됐든 상관없어. 녀석은 땡전 한 푼 못 받는 신세가 됐으니까.'라고 말하는 듯했다.

조금 주저하던 공증인은 결국 어쩔 수 없다는 듯한 제스처를 취하고 옷깃을 바로 잡으며 이야기했다.

"그렇소. 아버님께서 당신과 관련한 부분을 바꾸신 건 사실이오."

"이전 유언장에서는 내 몫으로 얼마를 남겨주셨던 거요?"

"아버님 재산의 3분의 1이었소."

진실이, 알고 싶지 않던 끔찍한 진실이 밝혀진 순간이었다.

샤를은…… 말하자면 아버지에 대한 불효의 책임을 지게 된 것이었다.

바보였다. 자신은 너무나도 어리석은 바보였다. 하지만 이건 지나치게 부당한 처사다.

그는 스스로 어리석고 계산도 불분명한 인간에 지나지 않는다고 느꼈지만, 이 뿐만 아니라 너무도 끔찍한 죄의식을 떨쳐버릴 수가 없었다. 자신의 파멸을 자초한 것도 그렇지만, 아버지와 다툰 못된 자식이었기 때문이다. 어찌됐든 그로서는 너무도 암담하고 서글픈 상황이었다.

샤를은 마지막으로 아버지와 이야기를 나누던 때를 생각해 봤다. 아버지와 서로 욕을 하며 격렬하게 싸우기도 했고, 심한 말도 많이 했다. 하지 말았어야 할 말도 내뱉었다. 상식을 넘어서는 수준까지 나아갔다. 술을 너무 많이 마셨기 때문일 수도 있고, 클라라와 다퉜기 때문일 수도 있다. 학교 동료와의 불화 때문일 수도 있다. 우리의 행동을 정말 최악으로 치닫게 만드는 최후의 무언가, 삶에서 가장 후회스러운 행동으로 치닫게 만드는 것이 무엇인지는 아무도 모르는 일이다.

샤를은 아버지에게 최악의 아버지라는 말도 서슴지 않았고, 아버지를 사랑하지 않는다고, 심지어 당신을 싫어하기까지 했다고, 진실일 리 없는 거짓말까지 내뱉으며 광기 어린 질주를 멈추지 않았다. 아버지는 백만금을 가졌으나, 초라하기 짝이 없는 인간이라고, 단지 돈에 미친 천박하고 비천한 사람에 지나지 않는다고까지 이야기했다.

그렇다. 샤를이 자신의 아버지에게 내뱉은 말은 더없이 끔찍했다. 그리고 이제 샤를은 아버지에게 더 이상 아무 말도 할 수가 없다. 자신의 잘못을 인정하고 용서를 빌 수도 없게 됐다. 자신이 말한 게 진심은 아니었다고, 자신은 아버지를 사랑할 뿐 아니라 존경하고 있었다고, 그렇게 모든 진실을 말씀드릴 수 있는 기회는 영영 돌아오지 않을 터였다. 아버지는 돌아가셨기 때문이다. 말단 공무원이셨던 할아버지와 마찬가지로, 심장발작을 일으켜 세상을 떠났기 때문이다. 같은 질병으로 아버지를 여읜 뒤, 피에르는 고작 열여섯 살의 나이에 집안을 책임져야 하는 가장이 됐다. 할아버지가 아버지에게 남긴 유산이라고는 보잘 것 없는 연금과 엄청난 빚더미뿐이었다.

그럼에도 샤를의 아버지는 자기 능력으로 손수 돈을 벌어 대학을 다녔고, 자신의 형제들과 나이 어린 여동생들도 먹여 살렸다. 이어 맨손으로 그 자신의 제국을 건설했다. 물론 그런 아버지가 한심하고 보잘 것 없는 사람일 수는 있다. 하지만 이러한 환경 속에서 소설가가 되겠다는 꿈을 포기한 채 무위도식하다가 '가짜' 지식인이 된 게 바로 샤를이었다.

왜 그랬을까?

그 이유는 샤를 자신도 몰랐다. 그저 하릴없이 수년의 세월이 흘렀다. 샤를 스스로 제대로 학문에 매진하지 못한 채 다른 데 정신이 팔렸던 그럴 듯한 이유를 찾아 헤맸다. 그건 자신에게 해야 할 일이 있다는 뜻이었다. 그에게는 해결해야 할 미천한 숙제 같은 게 있었다. 작으나마 아파트도 마련해야 했고, 허름한 차도 한 대 장만해야했다. 하지만 삶의 흥분이 느껴질 만한 무언가는 아무 것도 없었다. 물론 사실이긴 했다. 하지만 누구나 다 자신의 게으름을 정당화하기 위해 내뱉는 핑계가 아니던가?

그런데 이제는 너무 늦었다. 모든 게 너무도 늦어버렸다.

하지만 아버지가 그렇게 일찍 세상을 뜨게 되리란 걸 그가 어떻게 예상할 수 있었겠는가? 그것도 이렇게 갑자기 이렇게 예기치 못한 순간에, 느닷없이 돌아가실 줄은 전혀 상상도 하지 못했다. 그리고 마지막으로 둘째 아들과 나눈 대화에서 상처를 받은 아버지가 분한 마음에 아들에게 이렇듯 재산을 한 푼도 남겨주지 않으리란 것도 상상하지 못했다. 시간이 흐르면 아버지와의 관계를 다시 회복할 수 있을 거라고, 아버지와 다시 이야기를 해보면 자신의 생각을 아버지에게 이해시키고, 또 용서를 구할 수도 있을 거라 생각했던 것이다.

그런데 아버지께서 돌아가셨다.

아버지께서…… 돌아가셨다……. 이제 다시는 아버지와 화해를 할 수가…… 없다…….

샤를의 머릿속에서는 이 같은 생각이 무한 반복되었다.

그는 자리에서 일어나 아무런 인사도 없이 문을 향해 걸어갔다. 얼이 다 빠져버린 사람 같았다.

"당신 유산으로 남은 몫은 가져가지 않을 셈이오?"

공증인이 물었다.

샤를은 대꾸조차 하지 않았다.

"아버지 빈소에서 봅시다……."

이 말 한 마디만 남긴 채 샤를은 밖으로 나갔다.

수상한 거지

빈소 입구에 거지 하나가 서서 조문객에게 손을 내밀고 있었으나, 별다른 소득은 없어보였다. 괴로움에 잠도 제대로 못 이뤄 마치 몽유병 환자처럼 넋이 나가 있던 샤를이지만, 빈소에 들어오는 다른 사람과 비슷한 기분이었다. 이런 곳에서 구걸을 하고 있는 거지의 모습이 눈에 거슬렸다. 구걸을 하기에는 너무나도 부적절한 곳이 아니던가? 이곳은 시신이 안치된 빈소다. 거지들은 이렇게 엄숙하고 신성한 곳까지 와서 돈을 달라고 조를 만큼 상식이 없는 작자들이란 말인가?

샤를이 비록 제정신은 아니었으나, 그럼에도 제일 먼저 눈에 띈 건 바로 거지가 내밀고 있는 손이었다. 거지의 손은 무척 하얗고 예뻤으며, 기품이 느껴질 정도였고, 꽤 젊은 사람의 손 같았다. 대부분의 거지처럼 지저분하고 여기저기 갈라진 다 튼 손이 아니라, 매끈매끈하게 뭐라도 칠해둔 것처럼 완벽하게 깨끗한 손이었다. 10대 청소년의 손과도 같은 뽀얀 손에는 반지 두 개가 끼워져 있었다. 조잡한 싸구려 반지 같이 보이지는 않았다.

일단 샤를은 거지를 향해 팔을 들어 올려 보이며 위협적인 행동을 취했다. '저리 안 꺼져?'라는 무언의 협박이었다. 이에 대해 거지는 별 반응을 보이지 않았다. 어쩌면 그는 이런 행동에 익숙해져 있을 터였다. 거지는 다만 고개를 숙이며 입가에 살짝 미소를 띠었다. 그 바람에 눈에 띈 건 정말 너무나도 하얗고 고르게 난 이였다. 역시 어딘가 범상치 않은 인물이었다.

거지의 곁을 지나 빈소 입구로 향하는 계단을 세 개 정도 오른 샤를은 갑자기 생각을 바꾸었다. 자신의 신세를 비꼬고 빈정거릴 심산이었던 건지, 아니면 아버지에 대한 반항심에서였는지, 샤를은 '어차피 무일푼 신세가 될 바에는 차라리 이 거지에게 내가 가진 걸 다 줘버리자'라는 생각이 들었다.

그래서 샤를은 올라갔던 계단을 도로 내려와 지갑을 꺼낸 뒤, 가진 돈의 전부를 꺼내어 거지에게 내밀었다. 거지는 무척 놀란 표정이었다.

"옜소. 이제 난 정말로 빈털터리요."

샤를은 마치 자신에게 하는 말처럼 그렇게 내뱉었다.

그러고는 거지가 고맙다는 인사를 전할 겨를도 주지 않았다. 발길을 돌려 빈소 안으로 들어간 샤를은 불편한 심기에도 워낙 상황이 상황인지라, 아버지에게 마지막 애도의 인사를 전하러 온 조문객의 위로를 받아줄 수밖에 없었다. 물론 형과 누나가 같이 도와주기는 했다. 그러나 이들의 냉담한 분위기로 봤을 때, 아버지의 유지를 다르게 바꿀 의도는 없어보였다. 말하자면 땡전 한 푼 없이 지내야 할 샤를의 상황에는 변화가 없을 거라는 점이다.

끝도 없이 밀려드는 조문객을 상대하느라 샤를은 제정신을 차리지 않을 수 없는 상황이었다. 거의 2백 명에 가까운 사람들이 줄줄이 조문을 와서 샤를과 시몬, 지젤, 그 외 여러 친척 어른들, 엘레오노르 할머니 등 고인의 가족들에게 애도의 인사를 전하고 갔다. 그렇다. 거의 2백 명 가량이 조문을 온 것이다.

빈소에는 정말 많은 사람들이 찾아왔는데, 이들은 갑작스런 고인의 죽음에 진심으로 충격을 받은 분위기였다. 이전 직원들과 현재 직원들, 주주들, 고객들, 어린 시절 친구들, 학창 시절 같은 반 친구들은 물론 집주인의 대소사에 대해서는 별로 관심을 두지 않는 세입자들 같은 의외의 조문객들까지 찾아와서 고인의 죽음을 애도했다.

끊임없이 몰려드는 사람들……. 인사를 받고 또 받아도 끝이 날 줄 몰랐다.

여러 사람들이 샤를의 떨리는 손을 잡고 눈물을 흘렸다. 저들은 마치 샤를의 손이 아닌 그 아버지의 손을 마지막으로 한 번 더 잡고 악수를 하는 듯했다. 고인의 아들을 통해 마지막으로 아버지에게 감사를 표하고 싶은 것 같았다. 조문객들은 샤를의 아버지가 자신들의 삶을 어떻게 바꾸어 놓았는지, 어떻게 자신들을 도와주었으며 어떻게 다시 희망을 불어넣어 주었는지 설명했다. 또 건물주로서는 보기 드문 인내심을 보여주며 자신들에게 기회를 주었던 것이나, 예기치 않게 돈을 빌려주거나 은행에 결정적인 지불 유예 허가를 받아줌으로써 자신들을 도산의 위기에서 구해준 것 등에 대해 이야기했다.

고인의 시신이 안치된 관 앞에서 주저앉아 통곡하는 사람들 가운데는 여자들도 있었는데, 그 가운데 몇몇은 상당히 젊고 미인이었다. 이들은 한때 고인의 삶에 함께했던 혹은 함께했다고 생각하는 여자들이었다. 샤를의 어머니가 돌아가신 뒤에 만난 여자들일 것이나, 개중에는 아마 어머니가 살아계실 때 만난 여자들도 있을 것이다. 물론 아들의 입장에서 이런 여자들의 출현이 반가울 리 만무했다. 다른 가족들도 마찬가지로 한 번도 본 적 없는 낯선 여자들의 등장에 눈살을 찌푸렸다.

언뜻언뜻 서로를 바라보는 적대적인 눈빛이나 놀란 기색으로 보건대, 여자들도 서로를 모르긴 마찬가지였다. 이들은 마치 자기가 제일 고통스럽고 슬프다고 경쟁이라도 하는 모습이었으며, 죽은 자를 앞에 두고 온갖 질투심을 내보이며 위선을 떨었다.

어쨌든 사람들이 아버지께 표하는 진심 어린 애도의 마음으로 미루어보아, 샤를로서는 아버지가 나름의 방식으로 존경받는 위대한 인물이었음을 인정하지 않을 수가 없었다. 어쨌든 아버지는 비범한 존재였으며, 일부는 거의 숭배에 가까울 정도로 아버지를 좋아하는 것 같았다. 단지 아버지가 부자였다는 이유만으로는 설명되지 않는 상황이었다.

이러한 사실은 전날부터 샤를의 머릿속을 괴롭히던 문제를 더욱 부각시키며 그를 고통스럽게 만들었다. 이 때문에 그는 점점 더 머리가 지끈지끈 아파왔다. 도대체 이렇게 훌륭한 분이었던 아버지가, 남들에게는 그토록 관대함을 발휘했던 아버지가, 아무리 전화 통화로 말도 안 되는 언쟁을 벌였다한들 어떻게 아들에게는 재산을 한 푼도 물려주지 않는 잔인함을 보일 수 있단 말인가? 삶에 대한 폭넓은 식견으로 봤을 때, 아버지는 당신의 아들이 정말 그렇게 지껄인 대로 생각하지는 않을 거라는 사실을 응당 알고 있어야 했다. 그렇게 말하면서도 실은 아버지를 사랑했다는 점을, 한 번도 겉으로 내색은 하지 않았지만 속으로는 진심으로 존경하고 있었다는 점을 깨닫고 있어야 했다. 아무리 아들이 그 반대로 이야기했다 해도 말이다. 세상의 모든 자식들은 다들 머리가 크고 나면 부모한테 그런 식의 객기도 부리고 하는 것 아니겠는가?

그런데 도대체 아버지는 왜 그런 것인가?

우리에게서 소중한 존재를 앗아가는 죽음은 때로 우리에게 또 다른 존재를 되찾아주기도 하는 법이다. 바로 클라라가 빈소를 찾은 것이다.

클라라…….

너무도 아름답고 분위기 있는 여자, 클라라…….흔히들 생각하는 치과 여의사에 대한 고정적인 이미지가 있다고 가정한다면, 클라라에게서는 그런 분위기가 전혀 풍기지 않았다. 그런 이미지로 클라라가 인식되는 건 그녀를 직접 보지 않은 채, 직업에 대한 고정관념으로만 그녀를 떠올리는 사람들의 머릿속에서뿐이다.

그래서 클라라가 자기 직업에 대해 밝히고 나면 대개는 늘 놀라게 마련이다. 클라라는 거의 영화배우에 가까운 외모와 몸매의 소유자였기 때문이다. 게다가 능력도 있는 여자였다. 이 직업이 얼마나 능력이 뛰어나야 하는지는 치과의사라는 직업으로 성공을 꿈꾸는 사람이라면 알 것이다. 샤를도 그렇게 작은 편은 아니었지만, 그런 샤를보다도 약간 더 키가 클 정도로 장신인 클라라는 곱슬곱슬한 긴 갈색머리의 소유자로, 눈동자도 연한 갈색이었다. 더욱이 (최근에는 좀 달랐지만)

평소에 늘 즐겁게 살아가는 사람이었다. 오뚝 선 콧날은 지나치게 크지 않았고, 아주 약간 끝이 들린 형태였으며, 입술은 도톰했다. 한마디로 클라라는 아름다운 여성이 가진 모든 특징들을 다 갖추고 있었으며, 주위 사람들을 돌아보게 만드는 정말 멋지고 근사한 여자였다.

모두들 그런 클라라와의 관계를 공식화하고 결혼을 망설이는 샤를을 의아하게 생각했다. 최소한 그녀와의 사이에서 아이라도 먼저 만들어야 하는 것 아닌가? 이미 1년 전부터 클라라가 그토록 아이를 원하는 상황인데 말이다.

클라라는 아버지의 빈소에 기꺼이 와줬을 뿐만 아니라, 샤를에게도 무척 다정한 모습을 보여주었다. 마치 샤를의 곁을 떠나지 않았던 사람처럼, 둘 사이에는 아무 일도 없었던 것처럼 클라라는 힘든 시련을 겪고 있는 샤를의 어깨를 어루만져주었다. 샤를의 부친이 그에게 유산 상속을 거부한 일에 대해서는 몰랐던 그녀였기에, 샤를이 어느 정도로 힘들고 괴로운지까지는 세세히 모르고 있었지만 말이다. 죽음이란 사실 사소한 다툼 따위는 정말 대수롭지 않은 것으로 만들어버린다. 그리고 연인들은 자신들도 모르게 이전의 모습으로 되돌아간다. 마음과 의식이 함께 길을 찾아 나아가며, 질병이나 죽음 등 극심한 불행 앞에서는 무기를 내려 놓는다. 엄청난 삶의 시련이 다시금 두 사람의 제국에 암운을 드리우게 될 때까지. 두 사람이 나중에 다시 다툼을 벌이고, 삶이 다시 정상적인 수순을 밟게 될 때까지.

하지만 샤를은 아직 그럴 때가 아니었다. 아직은 아니었다.

샤를은 계속해서 조문객들을 맞이했고, 그런 그의 곁은 클라라와 엘레오노르 할머니가 지켜주었다. 고인의 모친인 엘레오노르 여사는 올해 85세의 노파로, 자식이 세상을 떠난 상황에 대해 정말로 슬퍼하는 것 같진 않았다. 샤를의 할머니가 자신의 아들을 사랑하지 않았기 때문이 아니라, 몇 년 전부터 알츠하이머병을 앓고 있어서 몸 상태가 별로 좋지 않았기 때문이다. 사실 할머니는 지금 무슨 일이 일어나고 있는지조차 알지 못했으며, 자신의 아들이 죽었다는 사실도 모르고 있었다. 손자인 샤를의 곁에 있으면서 조문객이 건네는 연민의 말이 그저 재미있고 기분 좋을 뿐이었다.

오랜 기간 고인의 운전사로 일해왔던 외젠 역시 마치 가족의 일원인 것처럼 눈물을 흘렸다. 외젠이 그렇게 슬피 울던 것은 사실 그가 레니에 가족의 일원이나 다름없었기 때문이다. 그는 자신의 친아버지가 돌아가신 것처럼 울었다. 외젠은 아들이 자기 아버지랑 보내는 시간보다 더 많은 시간을 피에르와 함께 보냈다. 그래서 고인에 대한 애착이 남달랐고, 그래서 그렇듯 가슴 아파하고 있는 것이었다. 그의 비통함은 주위 사람들에게로 금세 옮겨갔다. 지구라는 신비로운 별 위에서, 눈물이란 쉽게 다른 사람에게 전달되기 때문이다.

이윽고 밤 10시를 알리는 종이 울렸고, 이미 사람들도 어느 정도 빠져나간 상태에서 마지막 남은 조문객들마저 집으로 돌아갔다. 샤를의 형과 누나는 심지어 그에게 잘 자라는 인사조차 건네지 않은 채, 쫓기는 사람마냥 허둥지둥 돌아갔다. 일부러 그런 건 아니었을지 모르지만…….

"당신 괜찮아요?"

클라라가 샤를에게 물었다.

지극히 평범한 한 마디이고, 살아오면서 수백 번도 더 들어왔던 말이지만, 샤를은 이 말이 너무나도 감격스러웠다. 클라라가 마치 둘 사이에 아무 일도 없었던 것처럼 말을 건넸기 때문이다. 둘은 여전히 보통의 연인 같았고, 단지 약간의 다툼이 있었다가 화해한, 그런 일반적인 연인의 모습이었다. 샤를이 "조금 더 있다가 갈게."라고 말하자, 소울메이트처럼 그의 마음을 읽어낸 센스 있는 클라라는 아버지와 단 둘이 있고 싶은 그의 심정을 이해했다. 그래서 클라라는 이렇게 덧붙였다.

"집에서 기다릴게. 너무 늦지 않게 와요."

그러자 샤를이 느꼈던 조금 전의 안도감이 괜히 더 미화되는 듯했다.

클라라는 비통함과 술기운에 젖어 붉어진 샤를의 두 눈을 바라보며 그의 입술에 입맞춤을 해주었다 비참한 그의 상황을 봤을 때, 두 눈이 벌게질 정도로 술을 마실 만한 이유는 충분히 되지 않던가? 클라라의 입맞춤에, 샤를은 정신이 혼미해질 정도였다. 이 가벼운 한 번의 입맞춤이 너무나도 다정하고 감미로웠으며, 그 안에는 깊은 사랑의 마음이 담겨 있었다. 클라라의 입맞춤은 곧 '저, 돌아왔어요. 예전처럼 당신을 사랑해요'란 의미였다. 적어도 비통한 상황으로 얼룩진 그의 머릿속에는 그렇게 믿고 싶은 마음이 가득했다.

결국 샤를은 혼자만 남게 됐다. 그는 먼저 조문객의 발길이 닿기 시작한 이후부터 미치도록 하고 싶었던 행동을 실행에 옮겼다. 아버지의 관 가까이에 가서 묵상을 하는 것이다. 샤를은 기도대 위에서 무릎을 꿇고, 본능적으로 성호를 그었다. 질병과 마찬가지로 죽음이란 우리 안에서 형이상학적인 기질을 부추기는 경향이 있다. 교회라고는 한 번도 간 적 없는 샤를도 예외는 아니었다.

샤를은 아버지를 바라봤다. 조문객들이 하는 말을 가만히 들어보면, 저들은 '아버지의 외관을 아주 깔끔히 다듬어주기도 하고 아름답게도 만들어놓았다'고 했으나, 샤를이 본 아버지의 모습은 끔찍하기 짝이 없었다. '끔찍하다'는 말이 다소 과한 표현일 수는 있다. 하지만 어쨌든 파운데이션으로 두껍게 얼굴을 칠해놓아 도무지 누군지 알아보지도 못할 정도였다. 입은 너무나도 꼭 다물게 한 상태였으며, 두 손은 마치 기도라도 드리는 듯 가슴 위에 곱게 포개져 있었다. 살아생전 기도 한 번 안 드리던 아버지였으며, 성직자들의 위선이나 교회의 퇴보적 철학에 대해서는 대놓고 반발하던 아버지였다.

죽은 자 앞에서 늘 그렇게 생각하듯이, 샤를 역시 비슷한 생각을 하며 다들 하는 얘기를 속으로 되뇌었다. '이제 다 끝났다. 아버지는 결코 다시 돌아오지 않을 거야. 다시는……'

생각이 여기까지 미치자, 샤를은 크게 오열하며 울기 시작했다. 그래서 샤를은 자기 뒤로 들리는 발자국 소리도 미처 듣지 못했다.

조심스럽게 다가온 남자의 정체는 건물 관리인이었다. 40대 정도로 보이는 남자는 이미 머리가 조금씩 벗겨지고 있는 상태였다. 그는 으레 그러하듯 정장과 검은색 넥타이를 착용하고 있었다.

"지금 시각이 밤 10시라서요. 이제 빈소를 닫아야 할 시간입니다."

"밤 10시요?"

몽유병자가 갑자기 잠에서 깨어나듯 소스라치게 놀란 샤를은 남자에게 부탁하며 물었다.

"몇 분 만 더 있게 해주시면 안 될까요?"

마치 어린아이가 어머니에게 간절한 청을 할 때와도 같이, 샤를이 너무나도 간절한 마음으로 부탁을 했기에, 건물 관리인도 그의 청을 들어줄 수밖에 없었다. 다만 그는 "단 5분 만이오."라고 못 박았다. 이에 샤를은 "알겠습니다."라고 대답했다.

샤를은 너무나도 기뻤던 나머지, 자기도 모르게 무심코 주머니에 손을 넣어 지갑을 꺼내려고 했다. 관리인에게 팁이라도 주고 싶었던 것이다. 하지만 샤를에게는 땡전 한 푼 없었다. 빈소 입구에서 만난 거지에게 모든 걸 다 내어주었기 때문이다. 샤를은 다소 멋쩍은 웃음을 지어보였고, 조금 실망한 듯한 기색의 관리인은 다시 자리를 피해주었다.

샤를은 다시금 아버지와 단 둘이 남게 됐다. 그는 아버지의 손을 만져보았다. 아버지의 손은 늘 곱고 기품이 흘렀으며, 그와 동시에 근육과 힘줄이 뚜렷이 드러나는 굳센 느낌이었다. 하지만 이제는 싸늘하고 뻣뻣하게 굳은 망자의 손이었다. 샤를은 아버지가 시계를 차고 있지 않다는 사실을 깨달았다. 늘 손목에 차고 있던 시계였는데 말이다. 그리고 잠시 후 그 이유를 생각해냈다. 당신께서는 샤를에게 시계를 물려주었기 때문에, 이제 더는 시계를 손목에 차고 있을 수 없었다.

이에 샤를은 자기 시계를 아버지께 채워드리고 싶다는 엉뚱한 생각을 하게 됐다. 물론 자신의 시계는 아버지가 차던 시계보다 훨씬 값이 싸긴 했지만, 왠지 그렇게라도 보답을 해야 짐이 덜어지는 것 같았다.

아버지의 손목에 자신의 시계를 채운 샤를은 다시금 눈물을 흘렸다. 그리고 그때 뒤에서 발자국 소리가 들려왔다. 샤를은 당연히 건물 관리인의 발자국 소리라고 생각했다. 자신에게 약속한 5분의 시간이 다 되었음을 말하려는 것인 줄 알았다. 어쩌면 마지막 순간까지도 이렇게 방해를 한단 말인가? 아버지가 돌아가셔서 이제 더는 볼 수 없게 됐는데, 그까짓 몇 분 더 주는 게 뭐가 그리 어렵단 말인가?

샤를은 당당히 한바탕 붙어보려는 심산으로 확 일어서며 뒤를 돌아봤다. 하지만 몇 발짝 뒤에 서 있던 건 관리인이 아니었다. 거기에는 예상과 달리 빈소 입구의 거지가 서 있었다. 샤를이 객기에 지갑을 다 내어줬던 바로 그 거지였다.

샤를에게서 다섯 발짝 떨어진 곳에서, 거지는 말없이 그 자리에 서서 미소를 지어보였다. 상가집에서 나올 법한 표정은 결코 아니었다. 즉, 고통이나 연민의 감정이 나타나지 않는 얼굴이었다는 뜻이다.

거지는 그저 미소를 짓고 있을 뿐이었다. 식료품가게 주인이나 무도회장에 참석한 누군가의 얼굴에서 보일 수 있는 표정이었다. 사실 이 거지가 고인과 혹은 그 가족과 친분이나

면식이 있을 리 만무했다. 그래도 고인의 빈소에 온 사람으로서 최소한의 기본 예의라는 게 있는 것 아닌가? 샤를은 거지의 웃음이 불쾌하게 느껴졌다.

"제게 무슨 용건이라도⋯⋯?"

"그저⋯⋯ 고맙다는 말씀을 드리고 싶어서요⋯⋯. 아까는 너무 급하게 자리를 뜨셔서⋯⋯."

"그거라면 됐습니다."

샤를은 냉랭하게 잘라 말했다.

"고맙다는 의미로 제가 뭐라도 해드릴 만한 건 없을까요?"

"없습니다."

"정말이신가요?"

"제가 원하는 건 그 누구도 들어줄 수 없는 소원입니다. 당신뿐 아니라 미국 대통령이 와도, 교황이 와도, 하물며 신이 와도 들어줄 수 없는 소원이죠."

"그래도 한 번 말씀을 해보세요."

"무언가⋯⋯ 무언가 끔찍한 일이 제 인생에서 일어나고 만 겁니다. 제 아버지가⋯⋯."

"돌아가셨지요. 저도 압니다."

"그래요. 하지만 아버지께서는 제게 한 푼도 유산을 남겨주지 않으셨어요. 그리고 도무지 그 이유를 모르겠어요. 뭐, 사실 얼마 전에 아버지와 다툼이 있기는 했어요. 하지만 벌이라고 하기에 이건 너무 심하지 않나요? 내가 완벽한 아들이 아니었다는 건 나도 알아요. 그렇다고 내가 무슨 범죄자도 아니고, 약을 한 것도 아니고, 인생을 실패한 사람도 아닌데, 도대체 왜 저는 유산을 못 받은 거죠? 무덤에서 제 얼굴에 침이라도 뱉고 싶으셨던 걸까요? 저는 아들도 아니에요?"

"무슨 말인지 잘 알아들었습니다."

거지는 이렇게만 이야기했다.

하지만 샤를이 보기에 거지가 그냥 자신을 이해해주는 척하는 것 같지는 않았다. 진심으로 자기 맘을 알아주는 듯한 분위기였다. 거지는 이렇게 덧붙였다.

"그럼 제가 선생의 관대한 행동에 대해 어떻게 보답하면 좋을까요?"

그러자 샤를이 흥분하며 소리쳤다.

"사람 말귀를 못 알아들으시는군요. 제가 원하는 건 제 아버지가 살아 돌아오시는 거예요. 그래서 아버지와 이야기를 나누는 거죠. 마지막으로 아버지와 대화를 해보는 거라고요. 전 아버지의 설명이 듣고 싶어요. 아버지께서 제게 왜 그러신 건지 그 이유가 궁금하다구요! 제 말 못 알아들어요? 저는 너무도 슬퍼요. 정말 너무나도 슬퍼서 눈물이라도 흘리지 않고서는 이 끔찍한 상황을 견딜 수가 없다고요!"

그리고 샤를은 정말로 울기 시작했다. 거지는 샤를에게로 다가와 그의 어깨 위에 부드럽게 손을 올린 뒤, 귀에 대고 속삭였다.

"제가 선생님의 청을 들어드릴 수 있을 것 같군요."

"무슨 청 말이요? 당신 미친 거요? 우리 아버지는 돌아가셨어요. 이 세상 사람이 아니라고요. 내일이면 차가운 땅 속에 묻히실 분이란 말이요!"

샤를은 거지가 자신의 어깨 위에 올려놓았던 손을 잡아 매몰차게 뿌리쳤다. 거지는 뭐라 반박하지 않은 채, 다만 한 걸음 뒤로 물러섰다. 거지는 챙이 넓은 모자를 쓰고 있었지만, 마침내 얼굴이 드러나 샤를은 처음으로 똑똑히 그 얼굴을 볼 수 있었다. 특히 그의 눈도 확실히 보게 됐다. 샤를은 그런 눈은 여지껏 처음 보았다. 무척 맑고 투명한 푸른색의 두 눈은 눈동자가 매우 작고 예리했으며, 그 때문에 사람을 꼼짝 못하게 할 정도로 위엄이 느껴졌다. 마치 마음속 깊은 곳까지 꿰뚫어보는 눈초리였다. 눈빛 한 번만으로도 모든 걸 간파할 수 있을 것 같았고, 그 앞에서는 무엇도 숨길 수 없을 것 같았다. 그때 거지가 샤를에게 말했다.

"아마 내가 하는 말을 믿지 않으실 겁니다. 말도 안 되는 일이라고 생각하실 것 같으니까요. 하지만 제게 몇 초의 시간만 주시면 직접 보여드리겠습니다. 겉으로는 비록 제가 젊은 사람처럼 보이겠지만, 실은 당신보다 나이는 한참 많은 사람입니다. 우주에서의 제 위치가 꽤 되니, 당신이 원하는 걸 들어드릴 수 있을 것 같군요."

"무엇을 말이오?"

"당신의 아버님을 살아 돌아오시게 만드는 거요. 하지만 그 전에 몇 가지 허락을 구할 게 있습니다."

거지는 주머니 안에서 사과 한 알 크기의 작고 검은 유리 구슬 하나를 꺼냈다. 거지는 몇 초간 이를 뚫어지게 쳐다봤고, 이미 빛이 나던 그의 두 눈이 더욱 반짝이기 시작했다. 그러자 신기한 일이 벌어졌다. 구슬에서 무언가 조화가 일어나더니 연기 같은 게 생겼다가 흩어지고, 생겼다 흩어지더니 마침내 하나의 형체가 나타났다.

의구심을 품고 가까이로 다가간 샤를에게 그 형체는 자신이 아는 사람처럼 보였다. 검은 양복에 넥타이를 한 남자. 그렇다. 샤를은 그 남자를 알아보았다. 샤를은 감격이 북받쳐 올라왔다.

"아버지!!"

깜짝 놀란 샤를이 소리쳤다.

남자는 바로 샤를의 아버지였다. 샤를은 아버지를 곧바로 알아보지 못했다. 신기하게도 아버지의 모습이 돌아가신 당시보다 훨씬 젊어보였기 때문이다. 아버지는 지금 샤를의 나이인, 약 서른다섯 살 때의 모습으로 다시 살아 돌아온 것이었다. 아버지가 그렇게 잘생긴 모습은 아니었다. 그는 얼굴이 못생긴 축에 속했기 때문이다. 그런데 지금의 아버지는 잘생겼을 뿐만 아니라 젊음까지 느껴졌다. 어쨌든 샤를은 한 번도 자신의 아버지가 못생겼다고 생각한 적이 없었다. 아버지에 대해 못생겼다고 하는 주위 얘기를 들으면서 샤를은 도무지 그게 무슨 소리인지 알 수가 없었고, 그래서 늘 가슴이 아팠다.

거지는 여전히 정신을 집중한 채 구슬을 바라보고 있었다. 그리고 구슬 속 샤를의 아버지 곁에 새로운 형체가 하나 더 나타났다. 적어도 쉰 살가량은 되어 보이는 나이 든 얼굴이었다. 남자는 밤색의 긴 수도승복을 입고 있었다.

이어 거지는 두 남자와 이야기를 나누었다. 아니, 한 사람과 이야기를 하는 것인지도 몰랐다. 구슬 안에서 사람들이 뭐라고 말을 하는지 입술의 움직임을 볼 수 없었기에, 샤를로서는 무슨 이야기를 하는지 알 수 없었다. 게다가 거지는 고대의 언어인지, 아르메니아어인지, 그 외 다른 언어인지, 도무지 알아들을 수 없는 신기한 언어를 구사하고 있었다. 20초가량 이어졌던 대화가 끝나고 난 뒤, 샤를의 아버지는 신비로운 구슬 안에서 자취를 감추었다. 이에 샤를은 아연실색했다.

"아니, 이게 도대체 어떻게 된 일이죠? 저희 아버지는 남아 계셔야죠! 그래야 아버지께 제가 말씀을 드릴 수 있죠! 아버지께서 왜 사라지신 거죠?"

거지는 웃으며 설명했다.

"당신의 소원이 곧 이뤄질 겁니다. 당신 아버지께서는 앞으로 사흘간 살아 돌아오시게 됩니다."

"사흘이요?"

거지의 설명에 깜짝 놀란 샤를이 물었다.

"예, 사흘이요."

"하지만 제 눈에는 아버지가…….."

"저길 보세요."

반지를 낀 둘째손가락으로 빈소 한 쪽 구석을 가리키며 거지가 말했다.

샤를은 즉각 주위를 돌아봤다. 하지만 그의 눈에는 사랑하는 아버지를 위해 조문객들이 놓고 간 꽃더미 밖에 보이지 않았다.

"하지만 제 눈에는 아무 것도 보이지 않는걸요."

"잘 살펴보세요."

그러자 아주 작은 푸른 점 같은 게, 점점 빛을 발하며 커지기 시작했고, 곧 사람의 형체로 바뀌었다. 그건 바로 샤를의 아버지였다. 머리숱도 많고, 사자의 웃음을 띤 35세 젊은 아버지의 모습이었다. 사업을 하실 때면 늘 끼고 다니셨던 아

버지 특유의 트레이드마크인 두꺼운 뿔테 안경도 빠지지 않
았다.

"아버지! 다시 돌아오셨군요!"

샤를은 이렇게 소리친 뒤, 아버지를 향해 달려가 와락 껴
안았다.

다시 만난 아버지

　샤를은 아버지의 품에 안겼다. 아버지는 두 팔을 벌려 그를 껴안아주었다. 살아있을 때보다도 더 화려한 미소를 입가에 머금은 채, 그렇게 샤를을 끌어안았다. '살아있을 때'라……. 말하자면 그렇다는 것이다. 그리고 지금은 진정 새로운 삶의 세계로 들어간 상태다. 하지만 거의 모두가 그 세계로 들어가길 두려워한다. 무지함에서 비롯된 그릇된 결과다.

　샤를은 당혹스러움을 느꼈다. 자신의 아버지가 지금 유령과도 비슷한 혼령의 상태로 있다는 걸 잠시 망각했기 때문이다. 단지 흔히 상상하던 유령보다는 더 많이 빛나고 반짝이는 상태였고, 형체는 더욱 뚜렷했다. 어쨌든 보이는 건 평소의 모습과 거의 비슷했다.

물론 샤를은 아버지가 살아있던 때처럼 그를 껴안을 수 없었다. 게다가 생각해보니 아버지가 자신을 품 안에 꼭 껴안아주던 게 이미 수년 전의 일이었다. 솔직히 마지막으로 아버지 품에 안겼던 게 언제였는지 정확히 기억나질 않았다. 분명 아주 오래전 일이었을 것이다.

곰곰이 생각해보니, 아버지 품에 안겼던 마지막 기억은 자신이 여섯 살 때였던 것 같다. 당시 샤를은 학교에서 1등한 성적표를 아버지에게 보여드렸고, 당신의 아들이 자랑스러우셨던 그는 아들의 눈높이에서 두 팔로 샤를을 껴안아주었다. 그리고는 10달러짜리 지폐 한 장을 꺼내며, 다음 달에도 또 다시 1등을 하면 두 배를 주겠다고 말씀하셨다.

각자 나름의 자녀교육법이 있겠지만, 샤를 아버지의 이 같은 교육법에도 샤를은 돈에 눈이 트이지 않았다. 오히려 샤를은 공부에 눈이 트인 철학 박사가 되었다.

어쨌든 실제로 아버지를 꼭 껴안을 수 없다는 사실을 깨달은 샤를은 몇 걸음 뒤로 물러나 눈물을 흘리며 아버지를 바라봤다. 샤를은 기쁨과 불신의 감정이 교차함을 느꼈다.

"아버지, 저는 이 상황이 도저히 믿기지 않아요. 아버지는 분명……."

"죽었다고?"

아버지는 아들의 뒷말을 어렵지 않게 알아 맞혔다. 샤를은 뚜껑이 열린 채 아버지의 시신이 놓여 있던 관을 돌아보며 말했기 때문이다. 그 안에서 피에르는 다른 고인들과 마찬가지로, 싸늘한 시신이 되어 전혀 움직임이 없는 상태로 누워 있었다. 아버지의 말에 샤를은 그렇다고 대답했다.

"모든 사람들이 그렇게 생각하긴 하지. 자신이 죽을 때까지는 말이야……."

아버지는 유령처럼 그렇게 말했다. 그러고는 고개를 끄덕거리며 말없이 아버지의 말에 동조하는 거지 쪽을 바라보았다.

그런데 그때, 아버지와의 뜻하지 않은 상봉에 기쁨과 놀라움이 교차하던 샤를은 마음이 약간 가라앉고, 잠시 잊고 있던 분노의 마음이 조금 되살아나는 걸 느꼈다.

"사실 아버지 때문에 저는 무척 상처를 받았어요. 어떻게 제게 그러실 수 있죠?"

"네 앞에 다시 나타난 것 말이냐?"

"아뇨. 그게 아니라……. 그게…… 저한테 유산을 물려주시지 않은 그 일 말이에요. 그거…… 제가 바보같이 아버지랑 말도 안 되는 다툼을 했기 때문에 생긴 일이잖아요. 사실 전화 끊고 나서 바로 후회했거든요……."

"그게 아니란다. 내가 너에게 유산을 물려주지 않은 건 너를 사랑하기 때문이야."

"저를 사랑하셔서 그런 거라고요? 지금 저를 놀리시는 거예요?"

"아니다, 샤를. 너를 놀리는 게 아니야. 내가 너 말고 네 형과 누나에게 모든 재산을 물려준 이유는……."

"두 사람은 저 같이 아버지에게서 등을 돌리지 않았기 때문이잖아요."

참을 수 없는 분노에 어찌할 줄 몰라 하던 샤를은 당돌하게 아버지의 말을 끊으며 말했다.

"그 둘은 아버지의 회사 일을 함께 봐왔지만, 저는 아니었어요. 결국 아버지께서는 제가 미웠던 거예요. 제가 저 하고 싶은 대로만 하고, 그 둘처럼 회사에 가는 게 아니라 학교에서 철학 따위나 가르치고 있었으니까, 그래서 제가 미웠던 거라고요."

"그게 아니란다. 넌 아무 것도 모르는구나. 너는 내 세 자식들 가운데 내가 가장 사랑하던 아이였어. 물론 부모가 된 입장에서 할 말은 아니라는 거, 잘 안다. 하지만 이제 나도 이 세상 사람이 아니니, 그런 건 중요한 일이 아니라고 생각해. 전에는 그렇게 중요하다고 생각했던 일들도, 이제는 그렇지 않게 됐지. 시간이 지나면 너도 알게 되겠지만, 죽는다는 건 굉장히 놀라운 일이며, 사람들이 생각하는 것보다 더 편하단다. 사실 사람들이 죽은 자를 위해 흘리는 눈물만큼, 죽음은 우리에게 기쁨을 가져다주지. 어쨌든 이건 별개의 문제이니 나중에 다시 생각해보자꾸나. 우리에게는 사흘의 시간밖에 주어지지 않았잖니? 그래, 샤를. 난 정말로 너를 사랑한단다. 널 보면 마치 나 자신을 바라보는 것 같아. 내가 젊었을 때, 내가 스스로의 삶을 짊어져야 했을 때, 그때의 나 같았지. 내가 내 아버지에게 대들었던 것처럼, 그렇게 너는 내게 대들었어. 네게 차마 그 얘기를 해줄 수는 없었단다. 남자들이란 바보 같은 수치심을 갖고 있기 때문이지. 심지어 그게 아버지와 아들

사이라면 상황은 더욱 심하게 마련이고……."

아버지는 잠시 멈췄다가 다시 말을 이었다.

"나도 아버지 말을 들으려하지 않았어. 말단 공무원이셨던 아버지의 직업에 대해, 나는 사실 아무런 반감이 없단다. 그렇게 안 좋게 생각하는 것도 아니고……. 하지만 그게 아버지의 직업이었지. 미미한 직업에 대해 나는 별로 대수롭지 않게 생각했고, 이를 직업으로 삼고 있는 사람들에 대해서는 더더욱 그랬지. 저마다 자신이 겪어야 할 경험을 겪는 거고, 각자 배워야 할 교훈을 배워가며 그렇게 사회에서 자기 자리를 차지하는 것이란다. 크게 포부를 갖지 않은 사람들에게 내가 할 수 있는 유일한 반박은 이들이 자신들과 다르게 커다란 포부를 갖고 살아가는 사람들을 용인하지 않는다는 점이야. 저마다에게 각자 나름의 삶이 있듯, 누구나 자신의 꿈을 가질 권리가 있지. 비록 나중에 가서 그 꿈이 산산조각 물거품이 될지라도 말이야. 하지만 그래도 최소한 저들은 그 꿈을 위해 노력할 것이고, 그렇게 계속 꿈을 꿀 것이며, 그에 따른 떨림도 느낄 수가 있지. 이들은 여생 동안 한 곳에 묻혀서 지내길 바라지 않아. 내가 사랑해 마지않던 내 아버지께서 너무 일찍 세상을 뜨는 바람에 나는 내 삶에 대해 아버지와 함께 이 야기를 나눌 겨를이 없었단다. 그때 내 나이가 열여섯 살이었으니까. 만일 내가 퇴직할 날이나 손꼽아 기다리며 살아갔다면, 내 삶은 죽은 삶이나 다름없었을 게다. 나는 어쩌면 내 아버지를 그렇게 일찍 돌아가시게 만든 게 바로 그런 마음가짐이 아니었을까하고 여러 차례 생각했지. 네 할머니께서 아직 제정신이셨을 때 말씀하시길, 내 아버지께서는 당신의 직업을 별로 좋아하지 않으셨다고 하더라고. 단지 의무감이 강한 사람이었기에 그런 직업을 택하셨다는 거야. 네 할머니와 당신의 자식들을 위해, 할 수 없이 그런 직업을 택해서 퇴직 연금을 받을 날만을 기다리다 가신 거지. 존경할 만한 일이기도 하면서, 동시에 좀 서글픈 이야기이기도 하단다."

피에르는 잠시 이야기를 멈추었다. 그는 다정한 눈길로 그저 말없이 자신의 아들을 바라보기만 했다. 그의 눈에서는 뭐라 형언할 수 없는 애정이 느껴졌다. 그리고 다시 말을 이었다.

"그래, 샤를. 나는 늘 네가 자랑스러웠단다. 최근 1년간은 예외였지만……."

샤를의 눈에서는 불현듯 걱정의 기운이 스쳤다. 아버지와의 어리석었던 전화 통화보다도, 어쩌면 그 때문에 아버지는 자신에게 유산을 물려주지 않았던 것인가?

"지난 1년간이라면……."

샤를은 말을 더듬었다.

"그래. 지난 1년간 너는 조금 이상했다. 우리가 서로 자주 보는 사이는 아니었지만, 네 안에서 무언가가 변했다는 사실은 알 수 있었지. 무언가가 깨져 없어져버린 듯한 느낌이야."

샤를은 부끄러움에 시선을 아래로 떨구었다.

아버지 말이 맞았다. 샤를의 마음속에서는 무언가가 깨져 없어져버렸다. 그가 정말로 하고 싶었던 일, 언젠가 모든 걸 내려놓고 정말로 소설가가 되어보겠다는 그 꿈이 사라져버린 것이다.

아버지의 짐작이 맞았다. 아버지가 제대로 본 것이다. 하지만 그리 놀랄 일도 아니었다. 아버지는 사람의 심리에 대해 가장 세밀하고 미묘한 부분까지 정통한 유일한 사람이었기 때문이다. 어쩌면 아버지가 사업에서 엄청난 성공을 거둔 이유도 여기에 있을지도 모른다. 사업이란 결국 동시대 사람들이 필요로 하는 바를 포착해낸 뒤, 그 부족한 부분을 채워주는 것이기 때문이다. 당황한 기색을 감추기 위해 샤를은 서둘러 다음과 같이 말했다.

"아버지께서 절 사랑하시는 마음은 잘 알 것 같아요. 제가 아버지께 했던 어리석은 말들에 대해서도 아버지는 별로 개의치 않으셨죠. 그런데 아무리 그래도 그렇지, 제게 유산을 하나도 물려주시지 않은 걸 아버지께서 저를 사랑하시는 마음의 증거라고 보기는 좀 힘들지 않아요? 제게 유산을 물려주시지 않은 건 곧 '너는 내 아들이 아니다. 너는 우리 가족의 일원이 아니야'라는 말밖에 더 되나요?"

"나는 내가 그에 대해 너에게 설명할 날이 올 줄 알았단다. 그리고 너도 그 얘기를 들으면 이해를 하게 될 거라는 걸 미리 알고 있었고."

"알고 계셨다고요? 말도 안 되는 소리 하지 마세요, 아버지!"

샤를은 거지를 돌아봤다. 거지는 아까부터 두 남자의 말을 조용히 귀 기울여 듣고만 있었다.

"만일 저 거지가 그 자리에 없었다면……!"

"나는 그가 저기에 있게 될 줄 미리 알았지."

"미리 아셨다고요? 어떻게요?"

"한 달 전, 심장에 이상이 생겼을 때, 나는 잠시 이승을 떠나 저 세상에 다녀온 적이 있었단다. 그리고 그곳에서, 네 유산 문제에 대한 결정을 내리기 위해, 조금 전 니로다의 유리구슬에서 봤던 그 사람과 함께 이야기를 나누었지."

"니로다요?"

"그래. 저기 있는 거지가 바로 니로다란다."

"아버지가 아는 사람이었어요?"

"그래."

샤를이 거지가 있는 곳을 돌아보자, 그는 야릇한 미소와 함께 고개를 끄덕이며 긍정의 표시를 전했다.

"하지만 제가 니골라에게 돈을 주지 않았더라면……"

"니골라가 아니고 니로다입니다!"

거지가 바로 잡아주었다.

"알겠어요, 니로다. 어쨌든 그건 별로 중요하지 않고…… 제가 말하고 싶은 건…… 만일 저 자가 내게 감사의 뜻을 전하러 오지 않았고, 스스로 특별한 능력을 갖고 있다는 걸 모르고 있었으며, 제가 아버지와 다시 만나게 해주는 이런 특별한

호의를 제게 베풀어주지 않았더라면, 저는 남은 평생을 답도
안 나오는 끔찍한 물음 속에서 헤매며 살아가야 했을 거예요.

…하고 말이에요."
"그 시계가 맘에 들지 않더냐?"
"그런 말이 아니라……,"
"시계를 차고 있지 않느냐?"
"네……."
"하긴, 그럴 수도 있지. 넌 네 시계도 차지 않았으니……."
"아니에요. 제 시계는……."
샤를은 아버지에게 당신 손목에 채워진 자신의 시계를 보
여주었다. 물론 자기 눈앞에서 환하게 빛나는 모습으로 신이
나서 서 있는 철학자 같은 혼령의 손목이 아니라, 관 속에 누

워 있는 시신의 손목에 채워진 시계를 가리키는 것이었다. 다만 확실히 그의 눈앞에 있던 아버지는 정말로 살아 있을 때 그 모습 그대로였다.

이어 샤를이 말했다.

"어쨌든, 도무지 영문을 알 수 없는 지금 같은 상황을, 저 니로다라는 사람이 제게 선물해주지 않았더라면……."

그러자 아버지는 다정하게 웃으며 아들에게 설명을 해주었다.

"이건 니로다가 네게 준 선물이 아니라 바로 내게 준 선물이다."

"아버지께 드리는 선물이요?"

어리둥절한 샤를이 물었다.

"맞습니다. 당신 아버지께서 그럴 만한 자격을 얻으셨기 때문에 베풀어드린 선물이지요. 말하자면, 아버님께서 살아계신 동안 선행을 베푸시고 사람들을 도와주셨기 때문에 받으신 선물이랍니다."

거지가 이와 같이 설명하자, 샤를은 거지의 말이 쉽게 수긍이 갔다. 사실 그날 저녁 빈소에서 보았던 수많은 사람들만 해도, 이를 충분히 증명하고도 남았다. 아버지에게서 받은 은혜에 대해 이야기하는 사람들이 얼마나 많았던가?

샤를은 그런 아버지에 대해 감동을 받았으나, 일단은 상황에 대해 좀 더 반박을 해보고 싶었다.

"만일 니로다가 거기에 있지 않았고, 또 제가 니로다에게 돈을 주지 않았다면요?"

그러자 아버지가 웃으면서 말했다.

"그에게 와달라고 부탁한 게 바로 나였단다. 또 너에게 그 옛날 내가 처음으로 백만 달러를 벌었을 때 입었던 옷차림과 구두 그리고 내 시계만 줬던 건 네가 형제들보다 더 재능을 많이 갖고 있기 때문이지."

"제가 다른 형제들보다 재능이 더 많았기 때문이라고요?"

"그래."

"그렇다면 제게 회사 일을 맡기실 수도 있었을 텐데요?"

"내가 살아 있는 동안 절대 그 일을 원하지 않았던 네가, 나 죽은 뒤라고 해서 그 일을 하고 싶겠니? 그럴 리가 없지. 네게 아무 것도 남기지 않은 건 스스로의 꿈을 실현하도록 하기 위해서야. 네가 싫어하는 일을 하다가 조금씩 삶의 기운을 잃어버리지 않도록 하기 위해서지. 네 재능이 썩어 들어가도록 방치하지 않도록 하기 위해서라고. 나는 네게 재능이 있다는 걸 안다. 아주 엄청나게 큰 재능이지. 조금 전에도 말했듯이, 너는 나를 쏙 빼닮았다. 다만 나는 직접 물속에 뛰어들어 스스로 깨우침을 얻은 것뿐이고. 내가 사흘간의 말미로 여기에 다시 온 건 네게 가르침을 전해주기 위해서란다. 그래. 네 스스로 자아실현을 하는 법에 대해 가르쳐주려고 온 거야. 그리고 이를 실현하는 데는 백만금이 필요치 않단다. 돈이 많으면 오히려 그 역효과를 낼 수도 있지. 돈이 모든 걸 짓이겨버리는 수가 있거든. 인간의 본성이 그렇단다. 돈 앞에서 한없이 작아지고 눌려버리는 게 인간이지. 자신의 역량을 모두 다 발휘하려면 먼저 굶주린 상태여야 한단다. 배가 잔뜩 부른 상태에서는 열정이 나올 수가 없지. 이기겠다는 열의가 있어야 성공을 하고, 승자가 되며, 최고의 자리에 오를 수 있어. 만일 내가 너에게 남은 생애 동안 아무런 걱정 없이 먹고 쓸 수 있을 만큼 충분히 돈을 줬다면, 네 재능은 묻혀버리고 말았을 거야. 편히 지낼 수야 있었겠지. 하지만 저기 관 속에 묻힌 이 애비처럼 그렇게 죽은 자의 삶을 살게 됐을 게다……."

피에르는 관 속에 누워 있는 자신을 가리키며 말했다.

"옷을 잘 입혀놓은 시신의 모습……. 조문객 말마따나 외관을 깔끔하게 다듬어놓은 이 모습과도 비슷하겠지. 하지만 죽은 상태라는 점에는 변함이 없다. 내가 가장 사랑하는 아들에게 바란 모습이 이런 거였겠니? 그것도 자식들 중 가장 재능이 뛰어난 아들한테? 네가 스스로의 삶에서 바랐던 것도 바로 저런 모습이었느냐? 이쯤 되면 내가 왜 그런 결정을 내린 건지 잘 알겠지? 너 또한 내가 그런 결정을 내려준 게 다행이라고 생각하리라 믿는다만……."

"그래서 형과 누나한테만 모든 걸 물려주신 거예요?"

여전히 아버지의 뜻을 완전히 깨우치지 못한 샤를이 놀라서 물었다. 눈앞에서 놓쳐버린 수백만 달러에 대해 미련이 남은 터였다.

"그렇단다. 그 두 사람에게는 너만큼의 특출한 재능이 없어. 게다가 그 아이들은 너나 나처럼 철학을 공부한 것도 아니잖니."

"지금 절 놀리시는 거예요?"

"나는 지금 그 어느 때보다도 진지하단다."

이때 니로다가 말했다.

"그럼 저는 이만 물러가보겠습니다. 사흘 후 밤 열 시에 성 요셉 성당에서 봅시다. 아버지께서는 돔 지붕을 통해 다시 저 세상으로 돌아가실 겁니다."

"돔 지붕을 통해 돌아가신다고요?"

"그렇습니다. 그 길이 가시는 아버지에게나 보내드리는 제 게나 더 편합니다. 그 돔 지붕은 수많은 영혼들이 오고 가는 통행로니까요."

행동이나 말투나 모든 게 신비롭기만 한 니로다가 여전히 신비로운 분위기로 설명했다.

니로다는 양손을 가지런히 모은 다음 공손히 고개 숙여 인 사한 뒤, 발걸음을 돌려 빈소를 빠져나갔다.

"그런데 아버지, 무언가 잊으신 게 있는 것 같은데……. 조 금 전 하신 말씀도 다 좋은 얘기들뿐이고 저에 대한 평가도 모두 지나치게 긍정적인 것 같아요. 하지만 그러다 제가 성공 하지 못하면요? 저는 성공도 못하고, 돈도 못 모으고, 그저 빈 털터리가 될 것 같아요."

"네가 성공을 하지 못할 경우를 말하는 게냐? 하지만 아들아, 그렇게 위험하고 바보 같은 소리는 하는 게 아니란다! 지금부터는 당장 그런 몹쓸 단어들을 네 머릿속에서 완전히 지워버리렴!"

피에르는 믿을 수 없다는 듯이 고개를 좌우로 저으며, 그 자신에게 하는 말처럼 입에 힘을 주어 반복해서 말했다.

"성공하지 못할 경우라……."

이어 그는 아들을 향해 말했다.

"내 생각에 우리에게 주어진 사흘은 네게 가르침을 주기에 충분한 시간이 아닐 것 같구나. 지금도 이미 상당한 시간이 지체됐단다. 내일 아침 일곱 시에 내가 전에 지내던 웨스트마운트 별장에서 보자꾸나. 외젠에게 차를 한 대 준비해달라고 부탁하렴. 단, 그 이유에 대해서는 말하면 안 된다. 너는 곧 네 집으로 돌아가라. 집에서 널 기다리고 있는 한 사람이 있을 것 같구나. 너도 그 사람이 무척 보고 싶을 테지."

"클라라에 대한 일을…… 아세요?"

샤를은 조금 부끄러운 듯 되물었다. 연인과 헤어진 일이라면 누구나 부끄러운 게 당연지사, 심지어 그게 차인 경우라면 더더욱 그러하다.

피에르는 그저 웃음으로 화답했다. 그리고 아들의 곁으로 다가가 다정하게 볼을 톡톡 쳐주었다. 그런 아버지의 손짓에서는 묵직한 기운이 느껴졌다. 마치 살아있을 때와 똑같은 느낌이다. 이에 샤를은 깜짝 놀랐다. 특히 그와 같은 아버지의 애정 표시에 몹시 감동을 받았다.

"자, 그럼 나는 이만 가보도록 하마."

"어디로 가시는 거예요?"

아들의 질문에도 피에르는 답을 하지 않은 채, 그저 웃기만 했다. 그리고 처음 모습을 나타낼 때와 비슷하게, 그러나 그와는 반대로 다시 몸이 작아지기 시작했다. 이에 깜짝 놀란 샤를이 소리쳤다.

"아버지! 대체 아버지께 무슨 일이 일어난 거예요?"

"걱정하지 말거라. 이런다고 내가 다시 죽는 건 아니란다."

피에르는 위트 있게 아들을 안심시켜주었다.

피에르의 몸은 계속 더 작아지더니, 어린아이만한 크기가 되었고, 다시 더 작아지다가 정말로 자그마한 몸집이 되었다. 그러면서도 입가에는 계속 웃음이 비치고 있었다. 그러다 결국 처음 나왔던 작고 푸른 점 속으로 빨려 들어갔다. 이어 그 점은 샤를의 머리 주위를 빠르게 서너 번 돌더니 그의 눈앞에서 멈춰 섰다. 그렇게 인사를 건네고 난 뒤, 그 점은 다시 움직이기 시작하다 처음 빠져나왔던 꽃 더미 속으로 모습을 감추었다.

샤를은 아버지의 무한한 사랑으로 가슴이 벅차오름을 느꼈다. 마치 작고 푸른 별 하나가 자신의 마음속에 아버지의 모든 사랑을 퍼뜨려주는 느낌이었다.

집에 돌아왔을 때, 샤를은 욕실 거울 앞에 있던 클라라를 발견했다. 클라라는 화장을 지우고 잘 준비를 하고 있었다. 이는 곧 클라라가 가지 않고 여기서 지내겠다는 뜻이었다. 샤를은 그동안 클라라가 어디에 가서 지냈는지조차도 알지 못했다. 그 때문에 죽을 만큼 괴로웠다. 이는 둘 사이에 엄청나게 큰 거리를 만들었으며, 둘을 마치 낯선 타인처럼 만들었다. 그것도 무척 빠른 속도로 둘을 멀어지게 만들었다. 이는 상당히 괴로운 일이었다.

집에 돌아온 샤를을 보자, 클라라는 특유의 마법 같은 다정한 미소를 지었다. 하지만 그 미소에는 예전과 다른 슬픔이 배어 있었다. 피에르의 죽음이라는 상황 때문이었다. 클라라는 샤를의 아버지에 대해 늘 애정을 느끼고 있었다. 여자 다루는 법을 알았던 피에르는 늘 클라라가 여자로서 무척 아름답고 비중 있는 존재임을 지각하게 만들었기 때문이다. 클라라는 곧 샤를의 얼굴에 서려 있는 낯선 기운을 포착하고 그에게 말을 걸었다.

"당신…… 어딘가 좀 이상해보여요."

그동안 클라라의 입에서 수도 없이 여러 번 나왔던 단어였다. 여태까지는 늘 무심하게 흘려들었던 '당신'이라는 단어 하나가 이 순간만큼은 얼마나 벅찬 느낌으로 다가왔는지 모른다. 두 사람이 함께해온 판에 박힌 일상 때문에 그 느낌이 퇴색했던 단어를, 클라라는 그저 단순한 습관처럼, 혹은 잠시나마 둘의 별거 상황을 잊게 해주기 위한 연민의 마음에서 말한 것일지도 모르나, 샤를에게는 이 단어가 너무나도 감격스러웠다. 그런 샤를은 흥분 섞인 말투로 대답했다.

"응. 그럴 일이 좀 있었어. 내 말을 안 믿을 지도 모르겠지만…… 내가 정말 미쳤다고 생각할 지도 모르겠지만…… 실은 아버지를 다시 만났어. 아버지와 이야기를 나눴다고!"

"세상에, 당신 지금 무슨 말을 하고 있는 거예요? 제정신이에요? 당신 아버지는 관 속에 누워계시잖아요. 모든 사람들이 다 봤는 걸요."

"그건 나도 봤지. 아버지의 시신이 관 속에 누워 있다는 건 나도 알아. 그런데 아버지께서 내 앞에 다시 나타나셨어. 아버지가 지금 살아계신다고. 돌아가시지 않으셨단 말이야. 빈소 입구에 거지 하나가 있었지? 기억이 날지 모르겠는데, 입구에 거지가 한 명 있었거든……."

"커다란 모자를 쓰고 있던 사람 말예요?"

"응. 그 사람이 마술사인지 마법사인지 모르겠지만, 마치 맥베스에서 같은 상황이었는데, 그 자가 아버지의 혼령을 다시 나타나게 만들었어. 그래서 내가 아버지하고 이야기를 나누었다고. 아버지께서는 젊은 시절의 모습으로 되살아나셨고, 한 서른다섯 살 때쯤으로 보였지. 아버지께서는 모든 걸 다 기억하셨고, 아버지께서 왜 내게 유산을 남겨주시지 않았는지도 말씀해주셨어."

"아버님께서 당신한테 유산을 남겨주지 않으셨어요?"

"응."

"어머, 내가 괜한 소릴……."

"아냐. 괜찮아. 사실 공증인에게서 그 소식을 전해 들었을 때는 화도 많이 나고, 실망도 많이 했는데, 아버지께서 그 이유를 설명해주셨어. 앞으로 사흘간 나는 아버지와 함께 있을 거야."

"사흘 동안이요?"

샤를은 자신이 미치지 않았다는 사실을 조금씩 클라라에게 납득시킬 수 있었다. 자신에게 일어난 일이 실제로 벌어진 사실이었다는 점을 이해시킨 것이다.

솔직한 마음을 나누고 나서야 비로소 둘은 서로에 대한 진실한 사랑을 깨달을 수 있었다. 샤를은 맨 처음 클라라를 만나 사랑에 빠졌던 순간보다도 더욱 벅찬 감정을 느꼈다. 클라라는 정말 아름다웠고, 너무나도 사랑스러운 여자였다. 서로의 진심을 확인한 순간, 클라라는 갑자기 울음을 터뜨렸다. 샤를도 클라라를 따라 울었다. 왜 자꾸 눈물이 흐르는지 이유는 알 수 없었다. 샤를은 클라라를 위로해주려는 듯 따뜻하게 안아 주었다. 자기 스스로에 대한 위안이었는지도 몰랐다. 절박했던 두 사람 사이에서 화해의 시간이 지나고, 마침내 입을 연 클라라가 그 속마음을 이야기했다.

"그렇다고 내가 다시 돌아온 건 아니에요, 샤를……."

네 스스로 위대하다고 생각하라

다음 날 아침, 전날 예고한 대로 다시 떠나는 클라라와 쓰라린 포옹을 나눈 뒤, 샤를은 머릿속이 텅 빈 것 같았지만 나름 일말의 희망을 안고 웨스트마운트를 향해 떠났다. 가는 길이 너무 막혀서 샤를은 그곳에 약속 시간보다 약간 늦게 도착했다.

샤를에게 문을 열어준 건 별장에 있던 가정부였다. 50대의 히스패닉계 가정부는 키가 꽤 컸다. 갑작스런 샤를의 방문에, 가정부도 다른 하인들도 아무런 준비가 되어 있지 않은 상태였다.

“샤를 씨, 아버님 일은 정말 유감이에요.”

“걱정해주셔서 감사합니다. 저는 아버지를 만…….”

샤를은 거기에서 말을 멈추었다. 자신이 여기 온 이유를 설명하자니 너무 길었고, 여차저차 설명하기도 너무 복잡했기 때문이다. 가정부는 무슨 말인지 모르겠다는 듯 눈썹을 실룩거렸다.

“저…… 외젠 있습니까?”

“네, 있어요.”

“이리로 좀 와달라고 전해주실래요?”

“네. 다른 것 뭐 필요하신 거라도……?”

“커피 한 잔 주십시오.”

“알겠습니다, 샤를 씨.”

얼마 안 있어 곧 외젠이 도착했다. 나이는 45세였으나, 여섯 아이를 둔 외젠은 10년 전 피에르의 기사가 되기 전에 이미 서른여섯 개의 직업을 전전했던 탓에 실제 나이보다 더 들어 보였다. 하지만 여전히 열의가 넘치는 운전 기사였다.

아버지가 시킨 대로, 샤를은 그에게 리무진을 준비해달라고 부탁했다.

외젠이 자리에서 물러갔을 때, 샤를은 거실의 오래된 괘종 시계의 시간을 확인했다. 아버지와 약속했던 일곱 시는 이미 지나 있었다. 정확히는 7시 10분이었다.

샤를은 걱정이 됐다. 언제 어디서든 아무 때나 모습을 나타낼 수 있는 아버지가 어떻게 아직 도착을 하지 않을 수 있을까? 아버지는 자기처럼 교통 체증을 겪을 일이 없는 분이다. 그렇다면 이건…….

그렇다. 이건 분명 최악의 상황이 생긴 것이다. 어쩌면 자신은 극심한 고통 속에서 착각에 빠졌던 것인지도 모른다. 클라라가 생각한 게 맞았던 것 같다.

마지막에는 클라라도 결국 자기 말에 수긍해주긴 했지만, 그건 고뇌에 빠진 샤를의 말을 반박하지 않기 위해서, 그저 자신을 기쁘게 해주기 위해서 그런 것이었을 뿐이다.

그렇다. 모든 게 다 자신이 지어내고 만들어낸 것이며, 아버지를 다시 보고픈 마음에 고통 속에서 자신이 꿈꿨던 것에 지나지 않는다. 아버지가 왜 그토록 잔인한 방법으로 자신에게 유산을 물려주지 않은 것인지, 그 이유를 설명하기 위해 모두 자신이 만들어낸 것이다. 아니면 아버지가 정말로 살아 돌아오셨을 수도 있다. 기적처럼 그렇게 몇 분간 살아 돌아오셨던 것일 수도 있다…….

그러다 문득 샤를은 이런 일이 자신의 회계사에게 일어난 적이 있었다는 걸 깨달았다. 회계사의 아버지가 세상을 뜨던 날, 회계사에게 갑자기 아버지의 모습이 보였단다. 환하게 빛이 비추는 멋진 모습으로 아버지는 그가 있던 침실에 나타났다는 것이다. 소스라치게 놀란 회계사는 침대에서 벌떡 일어섰고, 아버지 곁으로 다가가려 했다. 아버지에게로 다가가 안기려고 하자, 아버지는 강압적인 손짓으로 아들을 저지했다. 그때 아버지가 하셨던 짧은 몇 마디를 결코 잊을 수가 없었고, 이후로도 늘 가슴 속에 간직하고 살았단다. 아버지가 한 말은 당신은 잘 지내고 있으니 당신의 죽음으로 슬퍼하지 말라는 것이었다. 이렇게 잘 지낸 적이 없었다고, 당신의 자식인 회계사를 무척 사랑하고 있으며 당신은 또 다른 세계로 옮겨간 것뿐이라고, 근사한 역할이 자신을 기다리고 있는 그 세계로 떠난 것뿐이라고, 아들의 삶에서 모든 게 다 잘 될 거라고 말했단다. 그리고 다시 한 번 사랑한다고, 앞으로 평생 지켜줄 거라고 했단다.

그렇다. 어쩌면 이건 그 회계사에게 일어났던 일이 자신에게도 일어난 환각 현상에 지나지 않을지도 모른다. 여기까지 생각이 미치자 샤를은 미치도록 괴로웠다. 이 얼마나 절망적인 상황인가?

화려한 은쟁반에 하얀 천을 깐 위에 김이 피어오르는 커피 포트와 크림, 설탕, 커피잔을 올려 들고 온 가정부는 샤를의 기분이 가라앉아 있음을 깨달았다. 사실 시간은 이미 7시 15분을 가리키고 있었다. 누군가를 기다리고 있을 때, 혹은 기다리는 사람이 오지 않을 걸 알기에 더 이상 그를 기다리지도 못하게 되었을 때, 시간은 얼마나 속절없이 빨리 가던가.

"샤를 씨, 괜찮으세요?"

"예, 예…… 괜찮아요."

그는 잠시 미소를 지어보인 뒤, 커피 한 잔을 더 갖다달라고 부탁했다. 마치, 운명에 맞서는 듯한 행동이었다. 그는 속으로 '나는 꿈을 꾼 게 아니야. 나는 미치지 않았어. 아버지께서는 오실 거야. 아버지는 절대 헛소리를 하시는 분이 아니니까'라고 생각하는 듯했다.

이런 샤를의 부탁에, 커다란 벽난로 장식이 되어 있는 화려한 거실 안을 둘러보던 가정부는 거기에 샤를 말고 다른 그 누구도 없다는 사실을 확인한 뒤 다시금 무슨 말인지 모르겠다는 듯 눈썹을 실룩거렸다. 하지만 샤를이 클라라나 다른 어떤 손님을 기다리고 있는 중인지도 모르는 일이었다.

"알겠습니다……."

가정부는 고개를 갸우뚱하며 밖으로 나갔다. 슬픔에 젖은 주인집 아들이 엉뚱하게 변덕을 부리는 것인가하고 생각하는 듯하기도 했다.

샤를은 잔에 커피를 따랐다. 커피를 한 모금 마시고 나니, 기분이 한결 좋아졌다. 가정부에게 부족한 면이 없지는 않았지만, 커피 솜씨 하나는 일품이었다.

샤를은 가볍게 떨리는 입술을 커피잔에 갖다 댔다. 잔에서는 아직 김이 피어오르고 있었다. 그런데 그때, 샤를의 등 뒤에서 목소리가 들려왔다.

"내 것은 어딨느냐?"

샤를은 소스라치게 놀란 나머지, 하마터면 커피잔을 떨어뜨릴 뻔했다. 뒤를 돌아보니, 거기엔 아버지가 더없이 인자한 미소를 지으며 서있었다. 이전 날보다 더 멋있어진 모습이었다.

아버지는 늘 커피를 좋아했다. 이 세상 사람이 아니라고 해서, 그의 기호에 변화가 생길 리 만무했다.

"아버지! 깜짝 놀랐잖아요. 어쨌든 다행이에요. 저는 안 오시는 줄……."

샤를이 말을 채 끝마치기도 전에, 그의 생각을 이미 다 알고 있었다는 듯이 아버지가 자초지종을 설명했다.

"늦어서 미안하구나. 하지만 저 세상에서 우리가 해야 될 일이 생각보다 많은 데다, 그곳에서의 시간이 이곳과 완전히 똑같이 흐르지는 않는단다. 그런데 어느 순간, 네가 이 아버지를 무척 강하게 생각하는 게 느껴지고, 또 신기하게도 이 훌륭한 커피 향기가 느껴지기 시작하더구나. 그래서 우리의 약속이 생각나 부랴부랴 여기로 달려온 거란다."

샤를은 아무 말 없이 그저 미소만 지을 뿐이었다. 샤를은 아버지를 보게 되어 무척이나 놀란 상태였다.

놀란 건 가정부도 예외가 아니었다. 샤를이 부탁한 커피를 들고 거실로 돌아오던 가정부는 놀라 비명을 지르며 기절했다. 하지만 다행히도 엄청나게 빠른 속도로 피에르가 (혹은 그의 혼령이) 그녀를 부축해주었고, 또 특히 커피잔을 잽싸게 붙잡았기 때문에, 잔이 대리석 바닥에 떨어져 카펫 위에서 와장창 깨지는 일만은 피할 수 있었다.

혼령으로서 아버지의 모습과 그 재빠른 동작에 감탄한 샤를은 아버지 곁으로 가까이 다가갔지만, 아버지는 손으로 저지하며 샤를이 다가오지 못하게 했다. 그리고 가정부를 바라보며 말했다.

"괜찮아질 거다."

이어 손으로 잔을 든 피에르는 서둘러 테이블로 향한 뒤, 커피를 따라 마셨다. 아니, 목구멍에 털어 넣었다는 표현이 더 맞을지도 모르겠다. 하지만 커피는 피에르의 몸과 광채로 빛나는 옷을 통과하여 그의 발아래 카펫으로 스며들었다. 실망한 피에르가 바닥을 적신 커피를 보며 소리쳤다.

"이거 원, 커피 한 잔 제대로 마실 수가 있나. 헛수고가 되어버렸군."

뜻밖의 사건에 재미를 느낀 샤를이 웃음을 지었다. 하지만 아버지를 생각하면 왠지 서글프기도 했다. 그토록 커피를 좋아하던 아버지가 앞으로는 결코 커피를 마실 수 없는 애처로운 신세가 되지 않았는가.

잠시 후, 피에르가 말했다.

"자, 그럼 이제 슬슬 움직여볼까?"

"아버지 분부시라면……."

샤를은 아버지 쪽을 향해 잠시 기다려달라는 포즈를 취하고는 단숨에 커피를 목에 털어 넣어 잔을 비웠다. 그리고 맛있다는 듯한 표정을 지었는데, 이 때문에 아버지는 또 다시 투덜거렸다.

"리무진은 준비해두었느냐?"

"예."

"그럼, 슬슬 가보자꾸나."

"가정부는요?"

"아, 그렇지……."

그때 가정부가 다시 제정신을 차렸는데, 팔꿈치를 짚어 천천히 몸을 일으키다가 피에르를 발견하고는 다시금 혼절했다. 다행히도 마침 침실 담당 하녀가 와서 혼절한 가정부를 발견하여 정신을 차리게 도와주었고, 이 틈을 타서 레니에 부자는 슬그머니 사라졌다.

운전사 외젠은 자신이 모시던 주인을 다시 보게 되어 무척 놀라고 감격스러웠다. 하지만 외젠은 가정부처럼 혼절하지는 않았다. 외젠은 신비술과 영혼의 존재를 믿기 때문에, 이 상황을 이해시키는 데 그리 많은 설명이 필요하진 않았다.

세 사람이 차에 오른 뒤, 피에르가 운전사 외젠에게 물었다.

"자네는 내가 죽은 뒤에도 평소처럼 차를 청소했나?"

"그렇습니다, 사장님."

외젠은 모르는 사람이 있을 때만 '레니에 씨'라고 부르고, 평소에는 그냥 사장님이라고 불렀다.

"확실한가? 장갑을 넣어두는 칸도 청소한 게 맞는가?"

"그건……."

"안 했군, 확실히. 지금 그곳 청소를 해야 할 것 같군, 그래."

조금 귀찮게 느껴지기도 했고, 뭔가 복잡 미묘한 감정이 일기도 했지만, 외젠은 일단 훌륭하게 도장 처리가 된 마호가니 나무 서랍의 화려한 뚜껑을 열어보았다. 그런데 그 안에는 봉투가 하나 들어 있었다. 이를 집어든 외젠은 겉봉에 자신의 이름이 써 있다는 걸 깨달았다. 외젠이 피에르를 돌아보자, 피에르는 얼른 봉투를 열어보라는 눈짓을 하였다. 봉투를 열어보니 그 안에는 외젠의 이름이 쓰인 25만 달러짜리 수표가 들어 있었다. 깜짝 놀란 외젠이 소리쳤다.

"25만 달러라니요, 사장님! 이러실 필요는……."

"따지고 보면 자네도 내게 그렇게까지 열의를 다할 필요도 없었다네. 자네는 내가 생각하는 것이나, 특히 내게 엉터리 수작을 부리려는 사람들에 대해 솔직히 생각하는 것들을 이야기해줌으로써, 내가 잘못된 길로 들어서는 것을 수십 번도 더 피하게 해주었네. 자네가 그 돈을 받을 필요가 없다면, 과거의 자네 역시 내게 그렇게까지 도움을 줄 필요는 없었던 것 아니겠는가?"

"사장님, 저는 그저 제가 할 일을 했던 것뿐인걸요……."

"자네가 해야 할 일 그 이상을 했지. 어쨌든 자네가 무엇보다도 소중한 여섯 아이들을 훌륭히 교육시키는 데 그 돈이 조금이나마 일조를 했으면 하네. 가능한 한 최고의 교육을 시켜주도록 하게나."

"아이들을 저처럼 키우지는 않을 겁니다. 약속드려요."

"하지만 그렇게 되면, 그 아이들은 평생 25만 달러 수표를 받을 일도 없지 않겠나?"

“이렇게 받는 돈이 결코 필요하지 않을 사람으로 아이들을 키우겠습니다.”

“듣던 중 반가운 소리로군.”

전날 아버지와 대화를 나누지 않았더라면, 완전히 모르는 사람이 아닌, 그러나 가족이라고는 볼 수 없는 타인에게 아버지가 베푸는 관대함에 대해 샤를은 아마도 오해를 했을 것이다. 무언가 부당하고 억울하다고 말했을 것이며, 말하지 않더라도 생각은 했을지 모른다. 고함을 질렀을지도 모를 일이다. 하지만 이제 샤를은 아버지를 이해할 수 있게 되었다. 아버지가 왜 그런 행동을 했는지 받아들일 수 있게 된 것이다.

외젠은 수표를 받아 주머니에 챙겨 넣었다. 그런데 그때, 샤를이 무언가에 생각이 미친 듯 눈을 휘둥그레 뜨며 아버지에게 물었다.

“아버지, 그러고 보니 저기 수표가 있었다는 건 아버지께서 곧 세상을 뜨리란 걸 알고 계셨단 소리잖아요?”

“우리는 누구나 다 언젠가 자신이 죽게 되리란 걸 알고 있단다.”

피에르가 예리하게 받아쳤다.

"하지만 아버지는 언제 죽을지 알고 계셨던 거 아닌가요?"

"만일 내가 가르쳐주려는 걸 네가 깨우친다면, 또 내가 바라는 모습대로의 네가 될 수 있다면, 너 또한 알 수 있을 게다. 언젠가는 네가…….'"

샤를은 가슴이 벅차오르는 걸 느끼고 한동안 말이 없었다. 그러자 피에르가 말했다.

"이봐요, 기사 양반. 뭐하고 계시는 거요? 출발 안 할 겁니까?"

"예! 사장님!"

비록 앞으로 사흘간의 시간밖에 주어지지 않았지만, 외젠은 존경하는 사장님을 다시 모실 수 있게 된 것이 무척이나 기뻤다. 물론 조금 전 받아 챙긴 뜻밖의 선물인 수표 때문에 더 기쁜 것일 수도 있었다.

몇 분 후, 웨스트마운트 언덕에서 내려간 리무진은 몬트리올 간선도로를 탔다. 가는 동안, 샤를은 문득 자신이 아버지의 리무진에 오른 게 난생 처음 있는 일이라는 사실을 깨달았다. 서른여섯의 나이에 그제야 비로소 처음으로 아버지 차를 타게 된 것이다.

빨간 신호등 앞에서 리무진이 멈췄을 때, 피에르는 손가락으로 조심스럽게 길 위의 어느 40대 남자를 가리켰다. 남자는 표정이 매우 심각했으며, 온몸에서 스트레스가 느껴졌다. 이른 아침 시간이었음에도, 말 그대로 진이 다 빠진 상태였다. 이 시대를 살아가는 다른 수많은 사람들과 마찬가지로, 어두운 색깔의 양복을 입고 손에는 검고 작은 서류 가방을 들고 있던 그는 스트레스에 찌든 모습이었다. 그는 자기 곁에서 가볍게 입맞춤을 하는 나이 어린 연인들을 무척 신경질적인 시선으로 바라봤다. 두 연인은 마치 세상에 자기네들 둘밖에 없는 것처럼 굴었고, 어쨌든 그게 진지한 분위기의 남자에게는 꽤 거슬려보였다. 남자는 마치 무슨 근심거리라도 있는 듯했다. 그래서 아침 햇살이 너무나 따사로운 가운데서도 그는 기운을 내지 못하는 것 같았다. 끝나지 않을 것 같은 기나긴 겨울날이 지나가고 모처럼 몬트리올에도 상쾌한 봄 공기가 느껴지고 있었지만, 그는 영 기분이 좋지 않아 보였다.

심각한 표정으로 서류 가방을 들고 있던 남자는 하늘을 올려다보고 입가에 근엄한 주름을 잡으며 신경질적으로 담배를 피우고 있었다. 마치 남자는 '저것들, 할 일도 더럽게 없군. 녀석들이 제대로 뭘 할 생각을 않잖아? 저래가지고 어디 세상 살겠어?'라고 말하는 듯했다. 그 와중에 두 연인은 남자와 같은 버스를 탔다. 그때 피에르가 외쳤다.

"저기 저 회사원과 내 차이점이 뭐겠느냐?"

"음, 저 사람은 사장님보다 스트레스가 더 많아 보이는데요?"

외젠이 대답했다.

"맞네."

"하지만 저 사람에게는 사장님 같이 차를 운전해줄 기사가 없잖아요."

"그것도 맞는 말이네. 그러나 더욱 심각한 문제는 저 친구에게 자네처럼 조언을 건네줄 사람이 없다는 점이지."

외젠은 가지런한 이를 드러내 보이며 기쁨의 미소를 지어 보였다.

"하지만 그건 내가 원하는 진짜 답이 아니라네. 샤를, 넌 어떻게 생각하느냐?"

"음, 확실히 남자는 아버지보다 돈이 더 적어 보여요. 버스를 타고 직장에 출근을 해야 하니까요."

"그것도 맞는 말이다. 하지만 진짜 답을 알려주마. 남자가 저렇게 스트레스에 찌든 모습을 보여주고, 곤란한 표정을 지으며 이 이른 아침 시각에도 피곤에 지친 모습을 보인다면, 그리고 특히, 삶을 정말로 제대로 즐기는 것 같은 분위기가 아니고, 눈앞에서 애정 행각을 보이는 저 나이 어린 커플로 인해 신경이 거슬려 하는 분위기라면, 그건 남자가 잠들어 있는 상태이기 때문이다."

그때, 아주 타이밍도 기가 막히게, 남자가 찢어지게 하품을 했다. 그 모습을 본 샤를은 잠시 웃음을 지었으나, 그 웃음도 그리 오래 가지는 못했다. 이윽고 리무진이 다시 출발하면서 아버지 피에르가 이렇게 덧붙였기 때문이다.

"샤를, 너 역시 아직 깨어나지 못하고 잠을 자는 상태란다. 네가 받아들이든 그렇지 않든 그게 현실이야. 네가 잠들어 있는 상태로 하루하루를 지내는 이유는 몇 년 전부터 네가 그다지 좋아하지 않는 일을 해오고 있기 때문이야. 네가 할 수 있는 것과 맞지 않는 일을 하고 있는 셈이지. 너는 그같은 무기력함이 얼마나 심각한 문제인지 깨닫지 못하고 있다. 네 자신의 능력을 잊고 사는 거야. 네 능력을 생각해보렴. 너는 쳇바퀴 돌듯 일만 하는 일꾼들처럼 네 자신의 능력을 썩히고 있어."

샤를은 이에 반박하지 않았다. 샤를은 그저 눈물을 흘릴 뿐이었다. 아버지의 말씀이 가슴 한가운데로 날아와 꽂혔기 때문이다. 또한 아버지의 말씀이 심하다고는 해도, 그건 아버지의 진심이 담긴 것이었다. 샤를은 자신이 부끄러웠다. 무기력한 자기 자신이 못견디게 창피했던 것이다. 잠시 후, 피에르가 다시 말을 이었다.

"그렇지만 모든 게 다 끝난 건 아니란다. 넌 아직 모든 것에서 실패한 게 아니야. 너는 아직 젊잖니."

"하지만 아버지, 제가 뭘 어떻게 해야 하는 거죠?"

"일단 먼저 시작부터 해야 한다. 우선 수 세기 전부터 이 세상의 토양을 다져놓은 모든 위인들로부터 영감을 얻도록 해라. 위대한 예술가들, 유명한 정치인들, 훌륭한 작가들은 물론이고, 내가 존경해 마지않는 베토벤이나 모차르트 같은 최고의 음악가들도 포함된다. 저들의 삶에 관한 이야기를 살펴보고, 저들의 책을 탐독하며, 저들의 음악을 귀기울여 듣고, 저들의 그림을 감상해보거라. 맨 처음 시작은 대개 미미하고 하찮았을 것이며, 처음에는 그렇게 재능이 뛰어나지 않은 경우도 더러 있었을 게야. 그리고 대부분의 경우 엄청난 결함

앞에서 좌절하기도 했겠지. 어쨌든 이들 모두 처음에는 그렇게 깨어나지 않은 상태였단다. 하지만 이들은 스스로의 달란트를 믿었으며, 그 자신에 대한 믿음을 잃지 않았어. 이 세상 모든 사람들이 모두 똑같지 않다면, 그건 각자 자신에게 내재된 힘을 끌어내는 능력이 동등하지 않기 때문이지. 자신의 재능을 표현하는 법을 몰랐던 거고, 그 자신의 위대함을 발견하지 못했던 거야.

존 F.케네디가 미국의 대통령으로 당선되기 얼마 전, 어느 기자의 질문에 대해 했던 답변을 생각해보렴. 당시 기자가 '미국의 대통령이 되기 위해 필요한 게 무엇이며, 무엇이 가장 중요하다고 생각하는가?'라고 묻자, 케네디는 그저 '하고자 하는 마음'이라고 답했단다. 무언가를 원한다는 건 그걸 원할 만한 재능과 역량이 있다는 말이지. 샤를, 너는 네 자신이 위대하다고 생각하느냐? 네 안에 모든 꿈을 실현시킬 만한 힘이 있다고 생각해? 정말 네 '모든' 꿈을 이룰 수 있을 것 같으냐? 아니면 남은 평생을 그렇게 버스를 기다리던 그 사람 같이, 스트레스 받고 정신 나간 사람처럼 짜증내며 살아갈 테냐? 그 사람은 자신이 즐기면서 살아갈 수 있다는 사실도, 그렇게 즐기며 살아가는 삶이 중요한 문제라는 사실도, 또 성공을 꿈꾼다면 그게 제일 중요한 요소라는 사실도 미처 깨닫지 못하고 있다. 정녕 그 사람처럼 그렇게 살아가길 바라는 것이냐?"

샤를은 아무 말도 하지 않은 채 그저 고개만 떨구었다. 아버지의 말이 옳았다. 그는 버스를 기다리던 남자처럼 그렇게 잠에서 덜 깬 상태의 삶을 살아가고 있었다. 미간에 주름을 잡고, 입을 삐쭉 내민 채 그렇게. 샤를은 자기 삶에서 스스로 즐기는 법을 더 이상 알지 못하는 상태였다. 스스로가 한 말에 자못 흥분의 기색을 감추지 못했던 아버지는 평생 동안 자신을 움직여온 이 열정적인 에너지를 모두 아들에게 전달해주고자 하는 의지로 충만했다. 아버지는 혼잣말을 계속 이어갔다.

"살아 있을 때 내 기억은 괜찮은 편이었는데, 죽고 난 뒤에는…… 아, 그러고 보니 자꾸 이 '죽고 난 뒤에는'이라는 표현이 어색하게 느껴지는구나."

"그건 저도 그래요, 아버지. '죽고 난 뒤에는'이라고 말씀하시는 게 영 적응이 안 돼요."

"그래, 그 마음 알 것 같구나. 하지만 어쨌든 죽음은 인생의 수많은 단계 중 하나에 지나지 않는단다. 인생이라는 위대한 사전에서 잠시 지나가는 한 순간, 한 문장, 한 단어 같은 것이지. 다만, 우리는 그걸 모르고 괜히 걱정하고 고민하는 거고, 떠나간 사람들 때문에 눈물을 흘리는 것이란다. 하지만 그 또한 또 다른 찰나일 뿐이야. 또 다른 한 단어고……. 그런데 내가 지금 무슨 소리를 하고 있는 게냐? 여하튼, 죽고 난 뒤 과거의 기억이 내게 엄청난 기쁨을 선사하는데, 이게 정말 놀라워……. 아마 내가 더 이상 육체적인 피로와 변덕스런 몸 상태로 지치지 않기 때문일 텐데, 나는 정말 환각에 사로잡힌 듯 매우 정확하게 모든 일들을 기억하고, 내가 살아 있는 동안 겪은 일들뿐만 아니라, 살면서 내가 생각했던 것들까지 아주 세세한 일이더라도 모두 생생하게 기억하고 있지. 내가 읽었던 책의 내용도 물론 기억하고 있단다. 문득 내 말에 설득력을 실어주는 레오나르도 다빈치의 선지자적 글귀가 떠오르는구나. 〈새들의 비행에 관하여〉라는 글에서 그는 이렇게 썼단다.”

위대한 새가 곧 체체로 산에서 첫 비상을 시작할 것이다. 온 세상을 경이로움으로 가득 채우고, 온갖 신문 지

면을 그에 관한 명성으로 가득 채우며, 이 위대한 새는
자신이 본디 태어났던 둥지에 영원한 영광을 가져다줄
것이다.

"아, 정말 훌륭한 글귀네요. 몰랐어요, 전……."
"너도 나도 철학을 배웠던 젊은 시절, 철학과 교수들이 하
는 것처럼 해석을 좀 해줘도 괜찮겠니? 그래야 네가 지금과
같은 무기력 상태에서 벗어날 수 있을 것 같구나. 일단 '위대
한 새가 곧 체체로 산에서 첫 비상을 시작할 것'이라는 문장
에서 '위대한 새'는 젊은 시절의 레오나르도 다빈치를 말한단
다. 그러니 지금의 너 같은 상태인 거지. 체체로 산은 피렌체
부근에 있는 산인데, 레오나르도 다빈치는 이곳에서 수년간
을 보냈지. 이는 네가 넘어야 할 산, 네 꿈과 이상을 의미해.
특히 지금 이 순간, 현재 네가 위치한 곳을 가리키지. 너도 알
다시피 철학을 시작하기에 최적의 장소란다. 철학을 하고, 그
럼으로써 행복해지기 시작하고, 이로써 자신의 진정한 위대
함을 펼쳐 보이는 곳인 셈이지. 샤를, 너는 네 자신이 위대하
다고 생각하니? 너 스스로를 위대하다고 생각해?"

무슨 뜻인지 확실히 그 의미가 전해지는 재기 넘치는 이야기에 감명을 받은 샤를은 제대로 답을 하지 못하고 말을 우물거렸다. 이에 아버지가 아들의 말을 끊으며 이야기를 계속했다.

"애야, 네가 네 자신을 믿지 못한다면, 누가 널 믿어주겠느냐? 내가 너에게 유산을 물려주지 않은 건 그만큼 너에 대한 믿음이 크기 때문이다. 그런데 네가 스스로에 대한 믿음을 갖고 있지 않다면, 그런 내 시도가 모두 무용지물로 돌아가지 않겠느냐? 샤를, 네 자신의 위대함을 믿고 있니?"

피에르는 아들에게 충분히 대답할 시간을 주었다. 샤를은 약간 주춤거리며 결국 입을 열어 대답했다.

"네, 믿어요. 제 자신을…… 믿어요……."

피에르는 함박웃음을 지은 뒤, 외젠에게 말했다.

"외젠, 전망대 쪽으로 가주게."

"예, 사장님."

"그리고 베토벤 교향곡 9번을 틀어주게나."

"1악장은 건너뛰고 바로 2악장을 틀어드릴까요?"

"그렇지."

외젠이 2악장을 틀려고 채비하는 동안, 피에르는 근사한 테너 톤으로 이 곡의 유명하고 인상적인 첫 소절을 흥얼거렸다. 이어 음악이 시작되자, 위대한 사업가였던 피에르는 큰 소리로 명령을 내렸다.

"더 크게, 더욱 크게! 소리가 안 들리잖아?"

"예, 사장님!"

외젠은 피에르의 말에 순순히 따랐다.

외젠은 웃음을 지었다. 익살스레 바보짓을 하며 경계를 넘어선 한 어른 앞의 어린아이처럼 좋아했다. 외젠은 이 상황이 무척 즐거웠다. 자신이 모시는 사장을 좋아했기 때문이고, 그렇게 흥분한 모습을 보는 게 좋았기 때문이며, 또 사장의 그 같은 열정적 광기가 좋았기 때문이다.

몇 분 후, 리무진은 산 정상의 웨스트마운트 전망대에서 멈추었다. 피에르가 혼자서 조용히 명상을 하고 중요한 결정을 내릴 때 즐겨 찾던 곳이었다. 이곳에서는 저 멀리 도시 전체를 내려다볼 수 있었다. 멀찍이 떨어진 곳에 있는 도시는 오전 나절의 붉은 황금빛 속에서 찬란하게 빛나고 있었다. 아울러 멀리 생로랑 강줄기와 샹플랭 다리도 보였다.

"그럼 이번에는 네 기억력이 젊은 시절의 내 기억력보다 더 훌륭한지 알아보자꾸나. 젊은 시절 내가 모델로 삼았던 레오나르도 다빈치의 선지자적 글귀가 뭐였는지 다시 한 번 얘기해주겠니?"

피에르는 먼저 첫 문장의 운을 뗐다.

"위대한 새가 곧……."

그리고 아들인 샤를이 그 뒤를 이었다.

"체체로 산에서 첫 비상을 시작할 것이다. 온 세상을 경이로움으로 가득 채우고……."

이어 두 부자는 난생 처음으로 ― 피에르가 죽은 상태이긴 하지만 ― 서로의 눈을 바라보며 환상의 궁합을 자랑하는 만담꾼이라도 된 듯 나머지 글귀를 합창했다.

"온갖 신문 지면을 그에 관한 명성으로 가득 채우며, 이 위대한 새는 자신이 본디 태어났던 둥지에 영원한 영광을 가져다줄 것이다."

두 사람은 서로 말없이 미소를 지었다.

네가 하는 일을 뜨겁게 사랑하라

"동네를 좀 거닐어보자꾸나."

피에르가 제안했다. 두 사람은 리무진에서 내렸다.

"음…… 아버지. 지금 모습이 좀 유령 같아서 사람들 이목을 끌게 될 것 같아요."

샤를이 지적했다.

"그건 좀 그렇지?"

피에르도 그에 수긍했다.

피에르는 어떻게 하면 좋을지 고민했는데, 해결책을 찾은 건 외젠이었다.

“제 재킷을 입고 야구 모자를 쓰시면 어떨까요?”

“그거 좋은 생각이네!”

샤를도 미소로 이에 동의했다. 이어 외젠이 리무진에서 내려 피에르에게 자신의 상의를 입혀주고 모자를 씌워주었다. 그의 유령 같은 몸이 완전히 형체가 없는 건 아니어서 옷가지를 걸치고 있기에는 충분했다. 앞서 쓰러진 가정부를 부축하고 커피잔을 받아낸 그가 아니었던가.

“이제 좀 괜찮은가?”

피에르가 물었다.

“네, 그런데 뭔가가 빠진 것 같아요.”

외젠은 미간에 주름을 잡으며 무언가를 골똘히 생각하는 모양이었다. 이어 외젠은 피에르에게 선글라스를 씌워주었다. 피에르가 미소를 지었다.

“완벽해요, 아버지!”

샤를은 박수를 치며 좋아했다.

“외젠, 쇼팽의 장송행진곡을 틀고 우리 뒤를 따라오게.”

“알겠습니다, 사장님!”

다시 차로 돌아간 외젠은 쇼팽의 장송행진곡을 틀었다. 피아노 솔로 버전이었다.

"소리를 더 키우게."

피에르가 명령했다.

"예, 사장님!"

외젠은 웃으며 사장의 명령을 고분고분 따랐다. 첫 번째 화음이 매우 크게 울려 퍼졌다. 이에 샤를은 얼굴을 찌푸리며 물었다.

"아버지, 이런 상황에서 장송행진곡은 좀 아니지 않아요?"

"아니, 오히려 그 반대란다. 지금 상황에 완전히 딱 맞아 떨어지는 곡이지. 이 곡과 함께 땅 속에 묻는 건 바로 과거의 네 자신이란다. 이전의 네 자신과 함께, 그때의 오랜 습관, 네가 느끼던 두려움 등을 모두 묻어버리렴. 그렇게 해서 과거의 네 모습은 땅 속에 묻히고, 너는 긴 잠에서 깨어나는 거지. 이 곡의 한 소절 한 소절을 들어보렴. 쇼팽이 이 음표들을 통해 우리에게 은밀히 이야기하고자 하는 바가 느껴지지 않니? 이는 삶에 대한 찬가란다. 부활과 소생의 의미를 담고 있는 곡이야. 이 곡에서 느껴지는 힘을 귀 기울여 느껴보렴. 네 안에서 위대함을 깨우는 게 무엇인지 느껴지지 않느냐?"

"네…… 그런 것 같아요……."

아들이 자신의 뜻을 잘 이해했는지 확신을 하고 싶어서였는지, 아니면 단순히 음악의 힘에 이끌려서인지는 모르겠지만, 피에르는 길 위의 나뭇가지들을 주워 모은 뒤, 죽기 전 자신이 후원하던 교향악단에서 했던 것처럼 지휘하는 시늉을 했다. 물론 그의 머릿속에 있는 상상의 교향악단이었다. 하지만 피에르의 몸짓은 너무나도 그럴 듯하고 훌륭해서, 샤를은 정말로 그곳에 교향악단이라도 있는 것 같은 착각이 들었다.

피에르는 목청 높여 장송행진곡 아리아를 부르기 시작했다. 이 또한 샤를을 놀라게 하는 데 부족함이 없었다. 샤를은 아버지의 이런 솔직한 모습을 한 번도 본 적이 없다는 사실을 깨달았다. 알고 보니 아버지는 정말 특이한 분이었다. 실로 레오나르도 다빈치와 베토벤에 심취한 분이었으며, 당신이 처음부터 말해왔던 바로 그런 사람이었다. 즉, 단순한 사업가가 아니라 한 사람의 철학자이자 예술가였던 것이다. 그것도 무척 독창적인 예술가였다.

피에르는 하던 노래를 잠시 멈춘 뒤, 옆에서 걷고 있던 아들을 돌아보며 말했다.

"샤를, 너도 노래를 불러보렴, 어서. 그래야 쇼팽의 신비로운 기운이 네게도 스며든단다. 노래를 부르고, 이 음악과 하나가 되렴! 노래를 해, 어서! 그리고 위대한 네 자신을 잠에서 깨워보렴!"

샤를은 잠시 망설이다가 곧 수줍게 아리아를 입에서 우물거리기 시작했다.

"더 크게 해야지! 더 크게!"

피에르가 명령했다.

결국 샤를은 포기하고 아버지의 말을 따라 좀 더 확신에 찬 목소리로 노래를 부르기 시작했다. 아버지와 자신이 남들 눈에 미친 사람으로 보이리란 생각도 없진 않았다. 근처에 있는 숲속으로 이어지는 오솔길에서 개 한마리가 나와 이들을 뒤따르기 시작했다.

"모차르트의 장송 행렬이라도 되는 것 같구나!"

피에르가 말했다.

"그러네요……."

이들을 따라오던 개는 길을 잃고 헤매던 개가 아니었다. 곧 세 명의 아이들이 개가 있는 곳으로 찾아왔기 때문이다. 세

명 중 두 명은 각각 일곱 살과 여섯 살의 여자아이였고, 나머지 하나는 금발의 정말 귀엽고 예쁜 다섯 살 남자아이였다.

두 어른이 노래 부르는 모습을 보고 흥이 난 아이들은 그게 하나의 놀이라고 생각하고 떨어진 나뭇가지 하나씩을 집어들었다. 그리고 한 줄로 늘어서서 교향악단을 지휘하는 시늉을 했다.

"아이들이 우릴 따라올 게 아니라, 우리가 저 아이들을 따라가야 할 것 같구나."

피에르가 짚어주며 말했다.

"아이들이 바로 비밀의 열쇠를 쥐고 있기 때문이지. 어른이 될 때까지는 그렇다. 내가 떠나고 나면, 바로 이 같은 진리를 떠올리렴."

이어 음악이 그치자, 세 꼬마는 '지휘봉'을 집어던진 뒤, 다시금 개와 함께 오솔길로 사라졌다.

레니에 부자는 계속해서 리무진을 뒤로 한 채, 한 거리에 도착했다. 그 거리에는 무척 화려한 집들이 많이 눈에 띄었다.

"이 사람들이 왜 여기에 사는지 아느냐?"

피에르가 물었다.

"음……. 이 동네를 좋아해서겠죠."

"그야 그렇지. 하지만 내가 말하고 싶은 건 이 사람들이 어떻게 해서 이 동네에 살 수 있게 되었을까 하는 점이다. 답은 무척 간단하지. 유산을 물려받아 여기에 사는 사람들은 제외하고 말이야."

"흠……."

"이 사람들은 모두 자신의 일을 열정적으로 사랑했던 사람들이야. 그리고 샤를, 너도 그렇게 해야 한단다."

이어 시간이 약간 흐른 뒤, 피에르는 아들에게 열정에 대해 이야기했다.

"이런 얘기 들어본 적 있을 게다. '해볼 가치가 있는 일이라면, 제대로 해볼 만하다.' 나는 여기에서 한 발 더 나아가볼까 한다. '해볼 가치가 있는 일이라면, 열정적으로 해볼 만하다'라고 말하고 싶은 게지. 샤를, 내 생각에 가장 중요한 비밀은 바로 여기에 있단다. 네 마음이 원하는 직업을, 네가 열정적으로 사랑할 수 있는 직업을 고르는 거야.

열정적으로 그 일을 사랑할 수 없다면, 다른 직업을 선

만일 네가 그조차도 못한다면, 나는 너를 솔직히 동정할 것 같구나……. 자기 일을 열정적으로 사랑하지 않고서 성공한 사람은 남녀 통틀어 내 평생 한 명도 못봤기 때문이지. 반대로 자기 일을 열정적으로 사랑하는데도 그 일에서 결국 성공을 거두지 못한 사람도 못봤단다. 거의 필연에 가까운 일이다. 수학처럼 답이 확실히 나오는 문제지.

샤를, 인생의 성공이란 것도 결국은 여자 문제랑 비슷하단다. 소심하고 뜨뜻미지근한 사람은 좋아하지 않아. 물론 수줍은 사람만의 매력이 없다고는 볼 수 없지만, 망설이고 주저하며 우물쭈물하는 사람은 눈 밖에 나게 마련이지.

네가 직업을 구할 때, 단지 돈을 벌기 위해, 그저 생계수단으로만 그 직업을 택한다면, 너는 결국 별수 없이 지루하고 불행한 삶을 살게 될 거고, 보잘 것 없고 초라한 생을 보내게 될 게다.

사무실에도 가기 싫은 마음을 누르고 억지로 가게 될 테고,

정신은 영 딴 데 가 있을 뿐 아니라 시간이 길고 지루하게 느껴질 거야. 반면 스스로 하는 일에 대해 애정을 갖고 있는 사람에게는 그 시간이 무척 빠르게 느껴지지. 자기 일에 애정을 갖지 못하면, 점심 때만 되도 벌써 집에 돌아가고 싶어질 거고, 수요일만 되도 이미 금요일 생각이 간절할 게다. 이를 미처 깨닫지도 못한 채, 네 몸 안으로 아주 치명적인 독을 집어넣게 되는데, 그게 곧 네 기분과 건강, 네 삶을 모두 망쳐버리게 되는 거야.

이런 것들을 모두 가볍게 여겨선 안 된다. 이 모든 게 무척 중요한 부분들이니까 말이지. 네 자신을 존중하거라. 그게 네 첫 번째 과제다.

네가 가장 싫어하는 적수에게 억지로 강요할 일을 네 자신에게 강요하지 말거라.

네 재능을 허비하지 말거라. 그러는 동안 네가 결국 허비하게 되는 건 바로 네 자신의 삶이란다.

네가 딱 이 점만 깨달을 수 있다면, 나는 다시 널 찾아온 것에 대해 충분히 만족할 수 있단다.

이처럼 네 일을 미치도록 사랑하고, 네 일과 관련한 모든 것들이 네 관심을 끈다면, 그렇게 네 정신을 번쩍 들게 하고 네게 떨림을 선사하며 너를 매료시킨다면, 무언가 놀라운 일이 네 삶에서 생겨날 게다. 내 삶에서 찾아볼 수 있는 수많은 예처럼 말이지. 샤를, 너도 이 신비로운 현상에 대해 알고 싶지 않으냐?"

한 우물을 파라

이번에는 유명한 '바넘 앤 베일리' 서커스를 만든 설립자 중 한 명인 P. T. 바넘의 조언을 들려줄까 한다. 업계에서는 이미 꽤 알려진 이야기인데, 한 번 들어보렴.

"네 힘을 분산시키지 말라. 일단 어떤 일에 착수하면, 성공할 때까지, 혹은 더 이상 희망이 없어 보일 때까지 그 일에 악착같이 매달려라. 망치로 계속해서 못을 두드리다 보면, 결국 들어갈 수 있는 한 들어가게 마련이다. 한 사람의 관심이 하나의 대상만으로 집중되면, 그 사람은 결국 최선의 방식을 생각해낸다. 열두 개의 프로젝트를 동시에 처리할 때는 결코 생각나지 않을 아이디어가 떠오르는 것이다. 더욱이 그 사람의 손에서는 재산도 술술 빠져나가게 마련이다. 한 번에 두 마리의 토끼를 잡으려 하지 말라고 했다. 백번 옳은 속담이다."

만일 내 조언을 원한다면, 위 내용을 읽어보도록 하거라. 읽고 또 읽어야 한다. 이 안에 상당히 많은 지혜가 담겨 있기 때문이다. 하나의 텍스트에 대해 그 의미를 파악하고 해석하기 위해 대학에서 우리가 어떻게 했는지 기억이 날 게다. 그러니 원하면 그때처럼 그렇게 하도록 하려무나.

네 힘을 이곳저곳 분산시키지 말고, 한쪽 방향만을 집요하게 파고들어라. 같은 못을 계속 두드리되, 현실적으로 넣을 수 있는 못을 두드려야 한다. 못은 결국 들어가게 되어 있다. 단, 두드려서 박힐 수 있는 못이어야 한다. 우리는 알지 못하지만, 때로는 못의 한쪽 끝이 바위나 금속판에 가서 위치할 수도 있다. 그렇게 되면 아무리 여기에 노력을 쏟아붓는다 한들 노력은 온통 헛된 것이 되고 만단다.

사람들은 안 좋은 직업을 고를 때가 있단다. 혹은 안 좋은 이유로 그런 직업을 고르기도 하지. 둘 다 결국은 매한가지 상황이란다.

돈이나 명예, 사회적 인정을 위해, 혹은 부모님을 만족시키기 위해 잘못된 진로 선택을 하는 경우도 있는데, 그런 경우 결국 이 직업을 진심으로 좋아하기 힘들지. 자신이 고른 못을 집요하게 두드려보려 노력하며 우리의 선택이 옳았음을 증명하려 들기도 한단다. 그 일을 잃어버리기 싫기 때문이기도 하고, 돈을 벌고 싶은 절대적 욕구가 있기 때문이기도 하지. 하지만 그건 친구에게서 여자를 뺏기 위해 여자를 유혹하는 경우, 아니면 단순히 그 마을에서 가장 아름다운 여자이기에 여자를 꼬시는 경우와 비슷하다. 그러나 결국 그 여자는 그 사람에게 진심으로 관심을 갖지 않는단다. 그 남자도 여자를 사랑한 게 아니지. 이는 그저 허영심의 문제일 뿐이다.

좀 더 흥미로운 대목을 살펴보지 않겠느냐? 내 생각엔 이게 핵심 문장인 것 같다만…….

"한 사람의 관심이 하나의 대상만으로 집중되면, 그 사람은 결국 최선의 방식을 생각해낸다. 열두 개의 프로젝트를 동시에 처리할 때는 결코 생각나지 않을 아이디어가 떠오르는 것이다."

그렇단다. 이게 바로 인내와 끈기가 만들어내는 마법 같은 힘이란다. 인내와 끈기가 없는 사람은 이를 절대 알 수 없을 게다. 유감스럽긴 하지만, 인내와 끈기가 없으면 진정한 성공은 불가능하단다.

늘 하나의 동일한 목표를 생각하거라. 하루하루, 참을성 있게 전념하고 매진하다보면, 너도 모르는 사이 한없이 빠져 있던 잠에서 조금씩 깨어나게 될 게다.

앞을 제대로 보지 못했던 네 눈은 이제 앞을 보기 시작할 것이다. 지극히 고귀하고 한없이 마법과 같은 의미에서의 '보다'라는 의미를 말하는 것이란다. 너는 이제 선지자가 되었으며, 다른 사람들은 보지 못하는 걸 보게 된다. 너보다 앞서 이 세상을 살아갔던 사람들이 너보다 먼저 보았던 것을 보고, 저들이 무엇을 했는지 이해하고 깨닫는단다. 저들이 성공을 거둔 비결을 이해하고, 저들의 원칙과 저들이 쓰는 기술의 규칙, 저들이 사용했던 수단, 저들의 기교와 술책, 저들이 일할 때의 습관 그리고 저들의 사고방식 등을 모두 깨우친단다. 그래, 이 모든 것들, 이 모든 철학에 대해 네가 알게 되는 것이며, 이를 네 자신의 것으로 만들고, 온전히 네 것으로 만들 수 있는 거야.

철학을 공부했으니 아마도 니체의 《짜라투스트라는 이렇게 말했다》에서 시적으로 묘사된 정신의 세 가지 변화에 대해 알고 있을 테지. 그에 따르면 과거의 너는 낙타의 상태였다. 그리고 이제 너는 사자가 된 상태다. 네가 있는 분야에서 식견 있는 학자가 된 것이지. 네가 다른 사람들로부터 배운 모든 것을, 한 마리의 낙타처럼 등에 짊어지고 있었기 때문에, 너는 기존의 방법을 적용하는 새로운 방식을 깨닫고, 네가 이전의 선배들에게서, 혹은 동시대의 명석한 누군가에게서 무엇을 '훔쳤는지' 알게 된다.

그게 그에게 먹혀 들어갔던 방식이라면, 너에게는 왜 적용되지 않는 것일까? 사람은 대개 실수와 실패에서 배움을 얻는다고 한다. 확실히 그건 맞는 말이다. 그런데 우리는 종종 우리가 성공에서도 상당히 많은 걸 배운다는 사실을 망각하고 만단다. 그 사람이 거둔 성공에서 배움을 얻는 것이지. 처음부터 성공하는 경우가 얼마나 있겠느냐? 그러니 다른 사람들의 성공 사례에서 가르침을 얻어야 한단다. 저들의 성공에 대해 분석하고 이를 샅샅이 파헤치며, 하나하나 뜯어봐야 해. 마치 사자가 자신의 먹이를 헤집어놓듯 그렇게 철저히 파헤쳐야 한다. 혼다 역시 처음에는 오토바이를 분해하는 것에서부터 시작했단다. 그리고 나중에는 경쟁사에서 제작한 자동차를 분해했지. 그렇게 우리도 다른 사람들의 성공 사례에서 교훈을 얻어야 하는 것 아닐까?

한 마디로, 처음 시작할 때는 머리를 잘 써서 '똑똑하게' 카피를 해야 한다. 매번 바퀴를 다시 발명해내려 애쓰며 시간 낭비할 게 뭐 있겠느냐? 하지만 어느 순간에 가면 너는 이를 다시 발명해낼 것이다. 혁신이란 것도 이뤄내야 하고, 기존과는 다른 것도 만들어내야 하며, 독창적인 발명도 해야 하기 때문이지.

네 분야에서 고집스레 한 우물을 파다 보면, 너는 새로운 바퀴를 발명해낼 수 있지. 그리고 넌 아이가 된단다. 니체가 말한 정신의 마지막 변화 단계란다.

그렇게 되면 네 정신은 실로 새롭게 '태어난다.'

네 정신은 창의적이고 풍성해지지…….

더 이상 아이디어를 찾아 헤맬 필요가 없다. 이들이 널 찾아 헤맬 것이기 때문이다.

피카소가 말했듯이, 더 이상 찾아 헤매는 게 아니야. 그저 '발견'하는 것뿐이지. 새로운 생각들, 유익한 생각들을 발견하는 것이다. 네가 손을 뻗는 그 어디에서든 결실을 얻어낼 수 있어. 사막을 건너야 하는 고행은 이제 끝이 났고, 하늘에서는 풍성하게 신이 내린 축복이 떨어진단다.

더 이상 일을 한다는 느낌이 아니라, 그저 즐길 뿐이고, 일이 아닌 놀이를 하는 기분이 들 게야. 네가 다시 어린아이가 된 것이지. 너는 그저 한 사람으로서의 경험만을 갖고 있을 뿐이란다. 너는 남보다 더 이득을 누릴 수 있고, 예전에는 미처 눈에 보이지 않았던 곳에서 기회를 알아볼 수 있으며, 주위의 다른 사람들, 심지어 바로 네 옆에 있었던 사람들이 아직 눈이 트이지 않은 곳에서 너만은 그 기회를 알아볼 수 있게 되지. 저들은 아직 눈이 트이지 않았다. 네가 있는 그 영역에서 말이다.

기회들이 샘솟고, 사람들은 네게로 찾아오며, 은쟁반 위에 놓여진 사업 기회들을 제공한단다. 알리바바의 동굴 속으로 들어가는 것이다. 네가 시선을 두고 있는 방향이 어딘지는 중요하지 않아. 그저 어디서든 보물이 보일 테니까.

그게 바로 재산이란다. 이 모든 게 가능한 건 단 하나의 분야에만 집중했기 때문이야. 네 관심이 그 단 하나의 대상에만 오롯이 집중됐기 때문이지.

매일매일 새로워져라

미국의 국무장관이었던 헨리 키신저는 점진적 외교를 구사했지. 점진적 외교란 협상을 할 때 한발 한발 조금씩 나아가며 실리를 추구하되, 꾸준히 추구하는 방식을 말한단다. 이는 체스를 둘 때, 인내심을 갖고 병사를 앞세워 안정적인 포진을 구축하고 최종 승리를 준비하는 방식과도 조금 비슷하다. 외교의 달인이었던 그는 노련한 체스 고수이기도 했지.

그러니 일에서도 이와 같은 방식을 이용하도록 하거라.

네게 주어지는 매일 매일의 시간 동안, 인내심을 갖고 조금씩 한발 한발 나아가면서 자신을 개선하고 점차 발전된 모습으로 거듭나되, 그러한 과정을 무한정 꾸준히 지속해야 한다.

새로운 것을 배우거라.

예전에 했던 것을 보다 효율적으로 할 수 있는 새로운 방식을 발견하렴.

일에서 돈을 조금 더 버는 방법도 깨우치고.

돈이란 곧 군자금에 해당하는 것임을 절대 잊어서는 안 된다.

그래, 그렇게 매일 조금씩 보다 나은 네가 되도록 해라. 네 분야에서 최고가 되도록 노력하는 것이다.

어느 분야든 최고의 자리에 있는 사람은 있게 마련 아니더냐? 그게 네가 될 수도 있는 일 아니냐? 소설가가 되고 싶다고 했던가? 그럼 자신에게 이렇게 말해보렴. '나는 모든 시대를 통틀어 최고의 이야기꾼이 될 것이다. 가장 재미있고 가장 감동적이며 가장 능수능란한 이야기꾼, 사람들의 심금을 울리고 가장 유익한 이야기꾼이, 그렇게 최고의 소설가가 될 것이다!'라고 스스로에게 말해보렴.

네가 속한 분야에서 최고가 되거라. 그 분야를 독파하고, 밤낮으로 이에 대해 끊임없이 생각하며, 황홀한 강박에 사로잡히면 그리 될 수 있다. 만일 네가 이에 대해 끊임없이 생각하지 않는다면, 조언을 하나 해주도록 하마. 아마 이는 쉽게 따를 수 있으리라 생각한다. 그 조언은 다른 걸 생각하라는 뜻이다. 네가 이 분야에서 성공을 거두지 못할 것이기 때문이다. 사실 너보다 더 굶주린 사람이야 얼마든지 있다. 너보다 더 단호하고 열광적인 사람, 늘 그 일에 대해 생각하며 긍정적인 강박에 사로잡혀 있고, 그래서 결국 너를 뛰어넘을 사람, 결승선에서 너보다 두 배로 더 빨리 도착할 사람, 네가 소심하게 노리던 자리를 빼앗게 될 사람, 그런 사람은 너무나도 많단다.

그러니 과감해지거라.

머릿속에, 단순하지만 놀라운 힘을 가진 이 한 마디를 새겨두도록 해라. 성공한 사람들의 머릿속에는 늘 이 한 마디가 간직되어 있단다. 이 사람들은 문제를 그렇게 복잡하게 이것저것 제기하지 않아. 어쨌든 늘 너무 많은 문제들을 제기하다가 결국은 그 답을 다 찾지 못하고 두 손을 놔버리는 사람들보다는 문제를 제기하는 게 더 적은 편이지.

네 스스로 직접 나서기 전에 제기한 그 '모든' 문제들에 대해 너는 그 '모든' 답변을 결코 찾을 수 없을 것이다. 사실 앉아서 고민만 하고 있는 것보다는 직접 뛰어드는 게 더 낫다.

모험이란 걸 더욱 흥미롭게 만들어주는 것도 '모든 걸 다 예측할 수는 없다'는 사실이지. 모든 걸 다 예상하려는 사람은 결코 직접 일에 뛰어들지 못해. 아니면 무척 두려움에 떨며 그 일에 뛰어들 거야. 그래서 본인의 삶은 물론 주위 사람들의 삶까지도 엉망으로 만들어버린단다. 성공한 사람들은 대개 이 놀랍고 단순한 생각을 늘 염두에 두고 살지. 저들에게 만일 "성공하기 위해 무엇을 하였느냐?"라고 물어본다면, 저들의 대답은 지극히 간단할 거야.

"나도 모른다. 나는 그저 행동을 했을 뿐이고, 직접 뛰어든 게 전부다."

그러니 너도 즉각 실천에 옮기도록 해라. 1년 후, 혹은 한 달 후에 그럴 생각 하지 말고, 지금 당장 움직여야 한다. 지금 당장 이 순간이 늘 최고의 순간이기 때문이지.

이와는 다르게 말하고 다르게 생각하는 사람들은 계속 잘못 생각하고 대부분의 삶을 제자리에 머물러 있으면서 보내다가 주위에서 지나가는 성대한 행렬을 가만히 바라만 보는 게 전부란다. 그리고는 이렇게 말하겠지.

"내가 저걸 했어야 하는데……."

저들의 생각은 틀렸다. 왜 그럴까? 저들이 직접 몸소 뛰어
드는 걸 주저하고 계속 그 자리에만 머물러 있었다면, 그건
과감하게 뛰어드는 모험이 저들의 관심을 끌지 못했기 때문
이야. 저들이 여기에 관심을 갖지 못한다면, 저들이 실패하는
건 당연하다. 수학처럼 답이 분명한 문제이지.

그런데 안달이 난 상태에서 과감히 직접 일에 뛰어들었을
때, 한번 그렇게 뛰어들고 난 후에는 조급함이 네 마음을 어
지럽히고 네 믿음을 좀먹지 않도록 조심해라. 로마는 하루아
침에 세워진 게 아니란다. 그 어떤 위대한 재능이라도, 그 어
떤 굉장한 성공이라도, 여기에서 벗어나는 법이 없지. 시간
과 더불어 천천히, 하루하루 그렇게 조금씩 쌓아가야 한다.

잠들기 전, 네게 솔직하고 분명히 물어보거라.

나는 과연 오늘 하루 동안, 내 목표에 다가가기 위해
무엇을 하였는가? 내가 몰랐던 무언가를 배웠는가?

나는 오늘 아침보다 더 내 목표에 가까워졌는가? 나는 더욱
나아졌는가? 나는 보다 나은 작가가 되었는가?

성공이란 한 그루 나무와도 같은 것이다. 나무에는 수천 개의 이파리들이 있고, 네가 내딛는 한 걸음 한 걸음이 마치 네 성공의 나무에서 새롭게 이파리가 하나 돋아나는 것과 비슷하단다.

네가 들인 노력에 대해 생각해보거라. 네가 삶을 위해 흘리는 그 힘겨운 땀방울을 생각하도록 하렴. 때로 그 노력이, 네게 응당 주어져야 할 성공을 가져다주지 못할 수도 있다. 하지만 결국 마지막에 가서는 머리에서 흘러내리는 노력의 땀방울들이 넘쳐나서 결국은 무릎을 꿇고 네 노력을 광기로 만든 뒤 네게 성공의 결실을 가져다줄 것이다.

꾸준히 가는 걸음에는 실로 마법 같은 힘이 존재한단다. 이에 대해서 좀더 이야기를 듣고 싶지 않니?

끈기를 가져라

"실패하는 사람들의 대부분은 무척 단순한 이유 하나 때문에 실패를 경험한단다. 바로 너무 일찍 포기하기 때문이지. 5년, 1년, 한 달, 하루만 더 참으면 된다는 걸 저들이 알았더라면, 저들의 인생은 아마 크게 달라졌을 지도 모르지.

그래. 정말 아주 약간, 너무 이른 포기 때문에 그 같은 실패를 겪는 거란다. 때로 성공은 무척 가까이에 다가와 있게 마련이지. 그런데 그 낌새를 알아차리지 못해 좀 더 기다리지 못하고, 그래서 결국은 달콤한 결실도 거두지 못하고 마는 것이란다. 그래서 다른 사람이 그 결실을 낚아채 가버리는 것이지. 그것도 바로 눈앞에서…….

어쩌면 그 사람은 재능도 경험도 부족한 사람이었을지 몰라. 심지어 머리도 딸리고 공부도 많이 못했을지도 모르지. 이 얼마나 모순된 상황이냐? 또한 이는 얼마나 멋진 삶의 교훈이란 말이더냐? 그런데 저들은 왜 그렇게 빨리 손을 놔버린 걸까? 그건 이들이 바람직하지 못한 이유로 그 일에 뛰어들었기 때문이다."

"바람직하지 못한 이유요?"

샤를이 물었다.

"그래. 힘들다는 걸 알면서도 그 일에 뛰어드는 사람이 많다는 건 너도 잘 알고 있을 게다. 그렇다면 저들이 그렇게 하도록 만드는 이유 가운데, 바람직하지 못한 이유란 뭐겠느냐?"

"돈과 안정된 생활이요?"

"그렇다. 돈이다. 사회에 첫 발을 내딛으려할 때, 혹은 어떤 새로운 일을 처음으로 시도하려 할 때, 누구나 자신에게 던져봐야 하는 질문이 하나 있다. 매우 가혹하면서도 동시에 많은 걸 알려주는 질문이지. 너라면, 5백만 달러와 네 인생 가운데 뭘 택하겠느냐?

자기 인생을 포기하고 돈을 선택하는 모든 사람들에게, 나는 그 생각을 버리라고 얘기하지. 이는 스스로가 내릴 수 있는 가장 현명한 선택이다. 성공할 수 없기 때문이지. 어쨌든 성공의 기회가 무척 줄어든단다. 왜 그럴까? 바로 그 이유가 바람직하지 못하기 때문이다. 아니면 성공을 하더라도 행복하지 않을 게다. 우리가 뭘 하든 최종적으로 그 이유가 되는 게 바로 행복이기 때문에, 결국은 전체적으로 봤을 때 실패한 것이나 다름없지.

5백만 달러를 택할 것이냐, 자기 인생을 택할 것이냐의 문제에 대해, 너는 물론 수많은 사람들이 평생을 가도 5백만 달러를 벌지 못한다고 생각할지도 모른다. 그리고 이 사람들은 그저 생계비를 벌기 위해 일을 할 수밖에 없는 사람들이라고, 그래서 어떤 직업을 선택할 것인가는 부차적인 문제라고 말이야. 하지만 나는 진정 원대한 꿈을 가진 사람들, 위대한 꿈을 가진 사람들, 대부분이 만족하며 살아가는 판에 박힌 삶을 거부하는 사람들을 말하는 것이란다. 네가 용감히 5백만 달러를 뿌리칠 수 있다면, 그리고 네 일과 꿈을 더 소중히 여길 수 있다면, 그건 아마도 이 일이 내적인 본성과 더 부합하는 일이기 때문일 거야. 지금의 성장 단계에서 네가 가진 자질과 잘 맞는 일인 셈이지.

새에게 더 이상 지저귀지 말라거나, 장미꽃에게 더 이상 그 향기를 내뿜지 말라고 말할 수 있겠니? 그건 불가능한 일이다. 그게 저들 각자의 본성이기 때문이지. 그러니 네 뿌리 깊은 진짜 본성에 부합하는 일을 선택하도록 하거라. 그러면 너는 지속적으로 끈기 있게 그 일을 할 수밖에 없을 게야. 그 일을 멈춘다는 건 곧 네게 죽음을 의미하는 것이나 마찬가지일 테니까…….

끈기를 가져라. 비록 처음에는 사람들이 너를 비웃을 수도 있다. 네 미숙함을 놀릴 수도 있다.

네가 하는 일과 네가 쓴 작품을 헐뜯고 비하할 수도 있고, 소설가로서 생업을 이어간다는 게 불가능하다는 이야기를 할 수도 있으며, 이런 저런 유감스러운 통계치를 한가득 내밀면서 자신들의 생각을 입증할 수도 있다. '만 명 중에 성공한 사람이 아무도 없다. 그러니 네 꿈과 재능 따위는 현명하게 갖다버려라. 합리적으로 생각해보라. 우리처럼 해라. 비록 우리가 흐리멍덩한 눈을 갖고 있고, 위궤양 때문에 고생을 하며 웃는 일도 별로 없고 가짜 웃음을 짓긴 해도, 적어도 우리는 돈은 번다'는 게 저들의 생각이다. 이 얼마나 엄청난 생각이냐? 살아 있어도 죽은 자와 별반 다를 게 없는 저들에게 저들의 생각이 틀렸음을 증명해보이거라. 만 명 가운데 소설가를 생업으로 삼아 성공한 그 한 사람이 바로 네가 될 거라는 사실을 입증해보이거라."

"아버지 말씀에 힘이 나네요. 기운이 생겨요."

"이에 대해 한 마디 더 하자면, 최고가 되라는 것이다. 물론 그렇다고 해서 처음부터 최고가 되라는 소리는 아니다. 그건 현실적으로 불가능할 뿐더러, 사람을 좌절시키는 말이기도 하지.

한국 사람들의 경우를 한 번 생각해보렴. 너는 너무 어려서 잘 모르겠지만, 내가 젊었던 시절, '메이드 인 코리아'라는 마크가 붙은 상품이 곧 최고의 상품을 의미하는 건 아니었단다. 사실 그건 모욕이나 다름없었지. 한국제라는 건 곧 제품의 질이 안 좋다는 뜻이었고, 곧 부서지고 망가질 거란 말과도 같았단다. 하지만 지금의 상황은 어떠하냐? 한국 제품이라는 건 곧 품질이 우수하고 견고하며 정교하다는 뜻 아니냐? 그래, 자동차건 가전제품이건 '메이드 인 코리아'라고 하면, 그건 품질이 뛰어나고 믿을 만하며 기발한 아이디어 상품이란 뜻이다. '메이드 인 코리아'란 단어의 변신이 놀랍지 않느냐? 이 세 단어가 의미하는 바가 완전히 상반되고 정 반대의 뜻을 담고 있다는 게.

아들아, 네 일을 할 때, 한국 사람들이 보여준 엄청난 끈기를 본받으렴. 한국 전쟁 후, 온 나라가 다 폐허가 된 상황에서 이들이 가진 단 하나의 원자재는 바로 '두뇌'라는 자원뿐이었다. 그런 저들의 훌륭한 정신력을 본받아라.

어니스트 헤밍웨이의 끈기는 얼마나 굉장했는지 아느냐? 그는 《노인과 바다》의 첫 페이지를 50번도 넘게 퇴고했단다. 그런 그의 훌륭한 끈기를 본받도록 해라. 몇 번이고 네 첫 장을 계속해서 다시 고쳐 써서 치명적인 매력을 발산하도록 만들어라. 그리고 이야기가 좀 더 진행된 뒤에는 한 장 한 장이 마치 네 첫 번째 페이지인 것처럼, 각 장이 매번 첫 장인 것처럼 그렇게 이야기를 써나가라. 좋은 첫 인상을 줄 기회가 두 번 주어지는 건 아니다.

열심히, 인내심을 갖고 네 작품을 다듬어라. 하지만 그렇다고 도를 넘어서선 안 된다. 완벽주의의 늪에 너무 자주 빠져선 안 된단다. 파스칼이 한 말을 기억하느냐? "우리는 어떤 일을 완성시키는 게 아니라 포기하는 것"이라고…….

네 소설이 백만 달러짜리 영화만큼이나 중요하다고 생각하거라. 네 소설의 부분 부분이, 책 속에 등장하는 각각의 인물과 장면 그리고 대사들이, 모두 중요하다고 생각하거라. 그 무엇도 가볍게 여기지 말되, 그러면서도 마음은 가볍게 작업하거라. 성공의 모순적인 법칙이 바로 여기에 있단다.

처음에는 물론 사람들이 너를 비웃을 수도 있다. 사람들이 한국 사람들을 비웃었던 것처럼 말이지. 네 소설에 대해서도 '샤를표 작품'이라고 말하겠지. 너는 이제 막 작가로서의 삶을 시작한 풋내기일 것이고, 열정은 있지만 어쨌든 막 발을 내딛은 초짜 작가일 테니까.

네게 1년, 3년, 5년의 시간을 주고, 이를 성공하는 데 필요한 시간이라고 생각하거라. 인생에서 5년이란 그렇게 긴 시간이 아니란다. 특히 좋아하는 일을 할 때, 단지 좋아하는 그

하고 있겠느냐? 그 위대함에 대해, 이 나무들이 겪은 엄청난 경험에 대해, 저들의 지혜에 대해 생각해보거라. 그리고 너도 올리브 나무처럼 되었으면 좋겠구나. 계속해서 한 우물을 파다 보면 언젠가는 성공하게 되어 있단다. 이게 내가 오늘 너에게 전해주는 마지막 조언이 될 것 같다."

피에르는 하늘에 뭉게뭉게 피어나는 구름을 뚫어져라 주시하기 시작했다. 이어 그는 아들에게 말을 건넸다.

"이제 저 위로 다시 떠나야 할 때가 된 것 같구나. 뭐라 설명은 할 수 없다만, 왠지 기력이 다한 듯 해……."

그러자 불안해진 샤를이 물었다.

"아버지, 사흘간은 여기 계시는 거 아니셨어요?"

"그야 그렇지. 그건 변함이 없으니 걱정하지 말거라. 나는 다시 돌아올 거란다. 내일 아침 일곱 시에 골프장 로커에서 보자꾸나."

"골프 치고 싶으세요?"

샤를이 놀라며 물었다.

"그렇구나. 마지막으로. 하늘에도 필드는 있는데, 무척 훌륭하긴 하다만 여기랑 아주 똑같지는 않아. 모든 게 너무 쉽고 완벽해서 말이야. 그리고 너와 오랜 기간 헤어져 있기 전 마지막으로 함께 칠 수 있는 시합이 될 텐데…… 안 그러냐?"

"그렇죠……."

그때 샤를은 열흘 전쯤 아버지가 전화로 골프치러 가자고 했던 일이 생각났다. 어쩌면 그게 아버지와 화해를 할 수 있었을 마지막 기회였는지도 모른다. 그런데 그때 샤를은 이를 거절했다. 샤를은 자신이 아버지의 제안을 수락했더라면, 아버지가 자신에게 유산을 물려주지 않는 일은 없었을 거라 생각했다. 하지만 이제는 생각이 달라졌다. 유산을 한 푼도 물려주지 않은 진짜 이유에 대해 자세히 설명을 해준 뒤였어도, 아버지는 그에게 유산을 물려주지 않았을 것이었다.

하지만 샤를은 특히 자신이 경솔했다고 생각했다. 뭐랄까, 우리들 대부분처럼 그렇게 생각이 짧았다고 생각했던 것이다. 샤를은 아버지의 제안을 거절했다. 아버지에게 굉장한 하나의 즐거움을 거절한 셈이었다. 아버지가 자신과 함께 골프치러 가는 걸 좋아한다는 사실을 모르는 샤를이 아니었다. 형은 골프를 치지 않았기 때문이다. 그런데도 그는 싫다고 한 것이다. 아버지가 자신에게 함께 골프를 치러 가자고 부탁했

던 게 마지막이 될 줄은 몰랐다.

이제 아버지와 헤어지기 전 진짜로 마지막 시합이 될 터였다. 신비한 힘의 조화로, 다들 알듯이 기적과 같은 이 일이 벌어지면서 한 번 더 마지막 기회가 주어진 것이다.

피에르는 미소를 지어보인 뒤, 아들과 짧은 작별의 인사를 나누었다.

"내일 또 보자."

그렇게 말하고는 조금 전 뚫어져라 쳐다봤던 구름을 향해 순식간에 날아올랐다.

샤를은 마음이 약간 죄어오는 느낌을 받았다.

'아버지가 내일 정말로 다시 돌아오실까? 내가 아버지를 뵙는 게 이게 마지막은 아닐까?'

그리고 집으로 돌아오면서, 샤를은 자신이 클라라에게도 부정적인 답변을 많이 했었다는 사실을 떠올렸다. 결혼에 대해서도, 아이에 대해서도…….

그리고 여행이나 휴가라든지, 그보다 더 비중이 적은 문제에 대해서도 그랬고, 스탠드 램프 색깔이나 소파 재질, 벽지 색깔 등 보다 소소한 다른 문제에 대해서도 그는 늘 싫다고

만 말했었다.

그렇다. 마치 그게, 싫다고 말하는 게 주특기인 사람 같았다. 자신도 그걸 의식하지 못한 채……

그리고 이제 샤를은 클라라에게 싫다는 말을 할 수 없게 됐다. 그녀가 떠나버렸기 때문이다.

하지만 클라라가 다시 돌아올 수도 있을 것 같은 느낌에 그는 잠시 흐뭇해졌다. 어쨌든 둘이 함께 밤을 보내지 않았던가? 더욱이 무척이나 다정하고 달콤한 밤이었단 말이다!

그는 서둘러 집으로 달려갔다. 하지만 거기에 클라라는 없었다. 당황한 그는 클라라가 아예 자기 짐을 챙겨갔다는 걸 깨달았다. 그녀의 옷장이 모두 비어 있었기 때문이다. 옷장에는 더 이상 아무 것도 남아 있지 않았다. 그를 비웃기라도 하는 듯, 클라라가 안 입은 지 오래된 원피스 한 벌만이 걸려 있을 뿐이었다. 게다가 이 원피스는 클라라가 정말로 좋아하지 않는 옷이었다.

식탁 위에서 샤를은 클라라가 손으로 써서 남긴 짤막한 메모 하나를 발견했다.

"샤를, 모레 아버님 장례식 때 올게요. 모두 다 미안해요. 하지만 언젠가 당신이 대수롭지 않게 내게 말했듯, 'Sic transit gloria mundi(이 세상의 영화로움은 이렇듯 사라진다)'라고 하잖아요. 모든 건 다 지나가게 마련이에요. 아무리 강렬했던 사랑이라도 그럴진대 하물며 그렇지 않은 경우라면……. 클라라가."

이 대목에서 샤를은 클라라가 정말 진심이라는 사실을 깨달았다. 그리고 아마도 전날 미치도록 감성적인 포옹을 나누고 난 뒤, 그녀가 말했던 것처럼, 클라라는 다시 돌아오지 않을 것이었다.

호기심을 가져라

샤를은 끔찍한 하룻밤을 보냈다. 머릿속으로 그는 클라라가 남기고 간 잔인한 몇 마디와 비꼬는 듯한 라틴어 인용구를 수십 번도 더 되뇌었다. 이 세상의 영화로움은 이렇듯 사라진다……. 클라라는 나름의 복수를 한 것이다. 사실 둘이 함께 사는 동안, 클라라가 말을 하거나 글을 쓸 때, 심지어는 논리적으로 반박을 할 때도 샤를은 클라라를 나무라는 경우가 많았다. 아마도 그래서 클라라가 골이 났던 것 같다.

이제 샤를의 곁에는 더 이상 나무랄 사람도, 뭐라 잔소리를 하며 바로잡아줄 사람도 없다. 더욱이 다음날 골프장에서 보기로 한 아버지와의 약속에서, 혹 아버지가 안 오시는 건 아닐까하는 생각에 불안하고 초조했다.

그런데 이번에는 아버지도 정시에 도착했다. 아버지의 모습은 전날 본 것보다 더 훌륭하고 멋있었다. 마치 죽음이 아버지를 더욱 빛나게 만든 것 같은 느낌이었다. 아버지의 눈은 조금 더 깊어졌고, 풍부한 감정이 느껴졌으며, 푸른빛도 짙어졌다. 피부에서는 광채가 났다. 피에르는 아들의 안색이 어둡다는 걸 알아챘다.

"낯빛이 창백하구나. 누가 보면 네가 유령인 줄 알겠다."

"어제 잠을 잘 못 잤거든요……."

"나는 간밤에 한 순간도 눈을 붙이지 않았단다. 그게 저 위의 세계에서 놀라운 점 가운데 하나지. 잠으로 자기 삶의 3분의 1이나 잃어버릴 일이 없는 거야!"

두 사람은 수년 전부터 함께 회원으로 있던 라발쉬르르락 골프클럽의 첫 번째 출발 코스에 올라섰다. 피에르는 다른 회원들이 못 알아보도록 그렉 노먼 스타일의 커다란 밀짚모자와 선글라스를 착용했다. 5월 아침의 쌀쌀한 날씨 덕에 피에르의 복장이 이상해 보이진 않았다. 그리고 그는 긴팔의 터

틀넥 스웨터를 입었다. 추위를 많이 타는 골퍼의 컨셉으로, 심지어 그는 가을에 끼는 장갑을 끼고 있었다. 그것도 양 손에…….

피에르는 죽기 직전 핸디 8을 자랑했다. 그 나이대의 남자로서는 훌륭한 수준이었다. 대개는 해야 할 일들에 밀려 연간 30회도 경기를 하지 못하기 때문이다. 그 아들인 샤를의 경우는 핸디가 4(76타)였으나, 그의 경우는 아버지보다 골프를 더 자주 칠 수 있었다. 대학 교수의 유독 긴 여름휴가 기간 덕분이다.

그런데 피에르는 아들에게 골프에서 얻을 수 있는 훌륭한 교훈을 깨닫게 해주었다.

155야드의 파 3 인 코스의 두 번째 홀에서, 그는 생애 첫 홀인원을 기록했다. 물론 그에게 '생애'라는 말을 쓸 수 있을지는 모르겠지만 말이다.

게다가 그는 버디 7개를 해서 총 63타을 기록했다. 그의 인생(?) 최고의 경기였다. 이 사실을 깨달았을 때, 피에르는 "내가 내 나이를 쳐버렸다!"라며, 골프 쪽에서 익히 알려진 표현으로 탄성을 내질렀다. 이는 그리 쉽게 나올 수 있는 상황이 아니기 때문에, 대개 독보적으로 뛰어난 선수들에게서나 있을 법한 일이었다. 아버지에게 맞서려다 처참하게 깨진 아들은 78타라는 나쁘지 않은 점수를 기록하는 데 그쳐야 했다.

실로 샤를의 완벽한 참패였다. 아버지의 훌륭한 성적을 어떻게 설명할 수 있을까?

진짜로 살아 있을 때보다 더 세게 치지는 않았던, 그러나 240야드라는 꽤 훌륭한 거리를 뽑아낸 피에르가 다음과 같이 설명했다.

"내 생애 처음으로, 나는 '몰입한다'는 말이 무엇을 뜻하는지 알게 됐다. 이는 그저 머릿속에 아무런 의심이 없는 상태, 이상적인 타구가 무엇인지 알고 그저 이를 실행하는 것에 해당한다."

믿을 수 없을 정도로 잘 뻗어가는 샷을 날리던 그가 중간에 물러선 것도 이 때문이었다. 피에르는 마치 어린아이처럼 행복해했다. 매번 샷을 날리는 중간 중간, 피에르는 아들과 이런저런 수다를 떠는 것을 빼먹지 않았다. 더없이 훌륭한 골프장이라는 근사한 배경을 뒤로 한 채, 피에르는 아들에게 이렇게 이야기했다.

"내 우상인 레오나르도 다빈치에게서 한 번 더 네가 배웠으면 하는 게 있단다. 레오나르도 다빈치의 유명한 〈수첩〉에는 이런 이야기가 있지. '구름이 어떻게 형성되고, 어떻게 흩어지는지 기술해보라. 이는 수증기가 대지의 수분에서 공기로 증발되도록 만드는 한 과정이며, 안개가 생기는 이유이기도 하고, 대기가 짙어지도록 만드는 이유이기도 하다. 시각에 따라 하늘의 파란 정도가 달라지는 것도 이 때문이다. 코를 훌쩍이는 것도, 하품을 하는 것도 어떤 것인지 설명해보고, 균형 상실, 경련, 마비, 추위로 인한 오한, 발한, 피로, 배고픔, 졸림, 갈증, 욕구에 대해 설명해보라. 딱따구리의 언어에 대해서도 기술해보라……' 놀랍지 않으냐?

이 훌륭한 정신의 소유자에 견주어보면, 우리는 모두 아무런 질문조차 제기하지 않은 채 그저 먹고 자고 돈을 지불하는 데 만족하며 하루하루 살아갈 뿐인 몽유병 환자 같은 상태가 아니더냐?

그러니 우리도 저 위대한 레오나르도 다빈치처럼 자기 분야에서 끊임없는 호기심을 발휘하도록 하자꾸나. 레오나르도 다빈치처럼 세상에서 가장 호기심이 뛰어난 사람이 되는 거다.

어떤 사람은 왜 웃을 수 있었고, 어떤 사람은 왜 눈물을 흘리는지, 저들을 불안에 떨게 하고 저들의 마음을 사로잡은 게 무엇인지 깨닫도록 해라.

아마 스스로를 위로하기 위해서인지도 모르겠다만, 흔히들 자신의 성공에서보다 실패에서 더 많은 걸 배운다고 이야기한다. 어쩌면 맞는 말일지도 모르겠다. 하지만 네가 절대적으로 꼭 해야 할 한 가지는 바로 다른 사람들의 성공에 대해 호기심을 갖는 것이다. 내가 어떻게 성공할 수 있었는지 잘 생각하고 그 이유를 깨달아야 한다. 나는 병적인 호기심이나 질투심 섞인 호기심, 아무 짝에도 쓸모없는 호기심을 말하는 게 아니다. 그게 아니라 내가 말하는 건 '똑똑한' 호기심이다. 셜록 홈즈가 되어 돋보기를 꺼내어 든 뒤, 다른 사람들의 성공에 대해 분석하고, 그 비결을 깨닫고 이해하며, 저들을 성공에 이르게 한 원칙을 발견하거라. 결코 이러한 호기심이 잠들도록 해서는 안 된다.

모든 걸 알고 싶어하는 사람이 되거라. 매사에 질문을 제기하고, 무엇이든 답을 찾으려 애쓰는 사람이 되도록 해라.

흔히들 하는 말로, 어떤 소설책의 성공은 설명할 수 없다고도 하고, 또 예측도 불가능하다고 이야기한다. 할리우드 영화에 대해 종종 하는 이야기와도 비슷하다. 누구든지 그 무엇에 대해서 아무 것도 알 수가 없다는 말이다.

하지만 그게 정말 사실일까? 만일 그게 맞는 말이라면, 어떤 작가들은 어째서 다른 작가들보다 더 큰 성공을 거두는 걸까?"

"그거야 재능……이 있으니까요."

"맞는 말이다. 하지만 재능이 저절로 터득되고 계발되는 것이더냐?"

"그건 잘 모르겠어요."

"그 반대를 확신해야 한다. 즉, 재능이란 저절로 터득되고 계발되는 게 아니라고 확신해야 하는 거지. 소크라테스는 이렇게 말했다. '인간은 개선될 수 있다'고. 재능 역시 그렇단다. 사람들 말마따나 문체가 곧 사람이다. 네가 스스로 존재를 보다 완벽하게 개선시켜 나가면, 너는 소설가로서 자동으로 실력이 완벽하게 다듬어질 수 있다. 위대한 피카소가 이야기했듯, 한 사람의 예술가는 그가 만들어낸 작품으로서 위대함을 얻는 게 아니다. 그의 존재로써 위대함을 얻는 것이다. 그러니 어떤 분야든 성공의 원칙이 있다고 확신하거라. 그리고 끊임없이 그 원칙을 찾으려 노력해야 한다. 그렇게 해서 체계적인 성공의 원칙을, 너만의 방법을 만들어 가도록 해라. 크게 성공을 거둔 사람들은 거의 모두 자기만의 방식을 갖고 있단다.

젊은 시절, 나는 J. W. 매리어트 호텔을 세운 J. W. 매리어트를 무척 존경했더랬지. 이 사람은 (혹은 그 자손들은) 무에서 시작하여 지금 전 세계 3천 개에 가까운 호텔 체인을 소유하고 있단다. 이 호텔 사장의 아들이 얼마나 놀라운 비밀을 이야기했는지 아니? '사람들은 우리가 일처리를 할 때 '매리어트 방식'을 고수하는 것을 비웃는다. 하지만 호텔 분야에서 일한 경험이 있다면, 우리가 업무 처리 방식을 백과사전식으로 총괄 정리해둔 안내서에 대해 그리고 우리가 아주 사소하고 세밀한 부분까지도 정리해둔 것에 대해 쉽게 알 수 있다. 30분도 안 돼서 호텔 객실을 청소하는 방식을 66가지 단계로 정리하여 설명한 안내서이기 때문이다. 어쩌면 우리는 일을 처리하는 방식에 대해 약간 광적으로 집착하는 경향이 있는지도 모르겠다. 하지만 우리 모두에게 모든 것에 대한 나름의 처리 방식을 갖고 있다는 건 지극히 자연스러운 일이며, 이는 당연한 논리적 귀결이다. 만일 네가 지속적인 어떤 결과를 얻고자 한다면, 거기에 이르는 방식이 무엇이 될지 결정해야 하며, 글로써 이를 구체적으로 기술할 수 있어야 한다. 그리고 이를 실제 상황에 적용하고, 더 이상 개선할 부분이 아무 것도 없을 때까지 계속해서 개선시켜 나가야 한다.' 객실을 청소하는 66가지 단계라니, 놀랍지 않으냐? 그 정도에 이르려면 머리가 조금은 미쳐야 하는 게 아닐까? 누구나 할 수 있는 객실 청소 같이 지극히 단순한 일을 하는 데 최고의 노하우를

얻기 위해 레오나르도 다빈치 같은 수준의 호기심이 필요한
건 아니다. 나는 매리어트 호텔의 이 같은 광기에 존경을 표
한다. 그 광기가 이 호텔의 성공과 무관하지 않다는 점에 대
해 의심할 사람은 아무도 없을 것이다.

　사람들이 종종 하는 말이지만, 나 또한 반복해서 이야기해
주고 싶구나. 신께서는 지극히 사소한 부분에 깃들어계신다.
신은 어느 곳이든 존재하니, 당연한 말 아니냐고 할 수도 있
다. 그러나 사람들은 신께서 '지극히 사소한 부분'에 존재한
다는 사실을 종종 망각한다. 그게 바로 성공의 비결임을 잊는
것이다. 이 사소하지만 귀중한 부분에 대해 대부분의 사람들
이 관심을 갖지 않는 이유가 뭐라고 생각하느냐? 저들은 이런
세세한 부분들에 눈길조차 주지 않을 뿐더러, 설령 이를 본다
하더라도 이 부분들이 그저 '세세한 부분'들에 지나지 않는
다고 생각하고 만다. 그렇게 흥미롭지가 않다는 것이다. 그건
저들이 그렇게 흥미를 갖지 않았기 때문이다. 저들에게 그걸
요구하는 건 무리였을 것이다. 저들이 그토록 귀히 여기는 오
랜 습관에 너무도 위배되는 처사다. 하지만 그 때문에 저들은
결코 부자가 될 수 없다. 저들은 그동안의 습관에 문제를 제

기해봐야 하는 것 아닐까?

남들과 달라져라. 남들과 구별되는 네가 되어야 한다. 위대한 문호 빅토르 위고는 '한 마리의 사자가 남을 따라할 경우, 그건 그저 원숭이일 뿐이다.'라고 이야기했다. 그러니 독창적인 사람이 되어야 한다. 남들과 다른 너만의 독창성이 있어야 해.

하지만 독창성에도 여러 가지 종류가 있단다. 가장 으뜸이 되는 독창성이 뭔 줄 아느냐? 그건 바로 네 자신이다. 독창적으로, 너답게, 네 꿈의 끝까지 가보거라. 독창적으로, 너답게, 그 누구도 네 기를 꺾지 못하게 하거라. 데카르트의 말처럼, 네가 살아가는 시대의 모든 고정관념을 떨쳐버려라.

네가 선택한 직업에서도 그리 하도록 해. 스스로 새로운 것을 배우렴. 한 사람의 자유로운 사상가로서, 그게 바로 스스로에게 할 수 있는 가장 가치 있는 일이 아니겠니?

피카소는 이렇게 말했단다. "젊어지는 데는 오랜 시간이 필요하다." 그러니 네 젊음을 되찾도록 노력하거라. 그래야 네 진정한 독창성을 찾을 수 있단다.

네가 되찾으려고 애쓰는 젊음이란, 어린아이와 같은 새로운 시선으로 모든 걸 바라보는 것이란다. 스스로 실패할 수 있다는 사실을 모르는 만큼 더 과감히 뛰어들 수 있는 게지. 그건 뛰어난 아이가 아닌, 평범한 아이라도 누구나 할 수 있는 일이란다.

이는 곧 삶에 '예스'라고 말하는 것이다. 실패라는 단어의 정의도, 성공이라는 단어의 정의도 모르니까, 당당히 예스라고 말하며 나설 수 있는 것이다. 이러한 무지라면 정말 훌륭하지 않으냐?

진정 젊다는 건, 그 어떤 나이라고 해도, 과거에 그 어떤 실패를 경험했다 해도, 또 제아무리 빚이 많고 부족한 게 많으며 주위로부터 온갖 좌절과 만류의 소리를 듣는다 하더라도, 과감히 뛰어드는 것이다. 미지의 세계를 향해 쉽사리 파고드는 것이며, 첫키스만큼이나 가장 중요한 첫걸음을 내딛는 것이고, 결코 뒤를 돌아보지 않으며 결코 멈춰서지 않는 것이다.

그러니 보다 젊은 네가 되도록 해라. 어린아이와 같은 호기심을 되찾고, 모든 걸 새롭게, 신비롭게 바라봐라. 성공하는 것 못지않게 중요한 건 바로 네가 스스로 즐기는 것이란다!

또한 너는 기회를 잘 포착해야 한다. 성공하고 싶다면, 기회를 잡는 법을 배우도록 해라. 기회가 왔을 때는 물론 이를 잘 보는 것도 중요하지만, 그보다 더 중요한 건 기회가 오도록 상황을 만드는 것이란다. 그리고 네 포부를 발판으로 악착같이 매달려 두 눈을 똑바로 뜨고 확실하게 기회를 잡아두어야 한다.

기회를 잡으려면 미래를 내다볼 줄 알아야 하고, 치밀해야 한다. 기회란 종종 네가 기대하지 않았던 형태로 위장을 하며 마치 너를 시험하고 네 통찰력을 시험해보려는 듯 찾아오기 때문이지.

다른 사람들이 보지 못하는 걸 보도록 해라. 다른 사람은 눈앞에 두고도 보지 못하는 걸, 너만은 계속해서 지켜보고 있다가 이를 잡아내도록 해. 네 정신이 깨어 있는 상태라면, 그리고 네가 계속해서 기회를 찾아 헤매는 상태라면, 그런 기회가 존재한다고, 그것도 정말로 무한히 풍부하게 존재한다고 확신한다면, 그런 너라면 분명 남들이 보지 못하는 그 기회를 볼 수 있을 게다. 저들의 빈곤함은 네 눈에만 보일 거야.

통찰력을 길러라. 네 육감도 길러야 한다. 가장 중요한 걸 잊지 말거라. 바로 '행동'하는 것이다. 그리고 특히 행동은 신속해야 한다. 번개 같은 성공을 원한다면 번개 같이 움직여야 한다. 하나의 기회는 마치 파도가 밀려오는 모래 위에 쓴 메시지와도 같다. 네가 너무 기다리고 그 즉시 뛰어들지 않는다면, 바람과 파도가 그 메시지를 지워버리고 말 것이다. 그리고 너는 여전히 빈곤한 상태일 것이고, 다른 누군가가 네 대신 부를 얻을 것이다."

두 사람이 그렇게 고무적이고 훌륭한 대화의 장을 펴던 끝에, 한 가지 불명예스러운 상황이 찾아왔다. 샤를의 로커가 비워진 것이다. 두 사람이 로커룸에 도착했을 때, 직원 하나가 샤를의 로커에서 그의 이름이 쓰인 명함판을 빼서 휴지통에 막 버리고 있었다. 샤를은 직원이 자리에서 멀어진 뒤 로커 앞으로 갔다. 차마 보이고 싶지 않았던 모습인 만큼 더더욱 가슴이 아팠다.

"사람들, 행동 한 번 빠르군요!"

"그게 바로 삶이란다."

샤를은 자기 이름표를 주워든 뒤, 아버지가 다정한 시선으로 바라보는 가운데, 이를 주머니에 집어넣었다. 로커룸 입구에서 두 남자가 비닐봉지를 들고 있었다. 로커 안을 비우기 위해서였다.

샤를의 로커는 아버지의 로커 바로 옆에 있었다. 샤를은 옷을 갈아입었고, 피에르 역시 평상복으로 갈아입었다.

이어 꽤 빠른 속도로 로커가 비워졌다. 두 사람은 서로 신발 사이즈가 같았기 때문에, 피에르는 자기 신발을 아들에게 건네주었다. 물론 샤를 역시 이를 받아들였다. 뿐만 아니라 아버지의 수건, 오래된 점수표, 장갑, 크림 등도 모두 물려받았다.

아버지는 열쇠도 하나 건네주었다. 비밀 금고의 열쇠였다.

이를 본 샤를이 아버지에게 말했다.

"열쇠가 하나 있네요."

"그렇단다."

"이게 좋은 거예요? 아니면 제가 이걸 버리는 게 더 나은 거예요?"

"갖고 있거라. 같이 은행에 갈 거다."

"아, 정말요?"

샤를은 복잡한 심경으로, 일단 아버지가 시키는 대로 했다. 샤를은 열쇠를 주머니에 넣은 뒤, 그날 일과가 다 끝났기 때문에 굉장한 서글픔을 느꼈다. 샤를은 생각했다.

'아버지가 안 계신 내 삶은 저 로커처럼 그렇게 비워지겠구나……'

비워진다. 영원히……. 복잡한 아들의 표정에서 쉽게 그 생각을 읽을 수 있었던 아버지가 말했다.

"너무 슬퍼하지 말거라. 아직은 내가 여기 있잖니."

"그건 알아요. 하지만 내일 떠나실 거잖아요."

"그러니 우리는 자신들의 꿈을 이루고 스스로 좋아하는 일을 할 수 있을 때까지 세상의 모든 시간이 다 자기 걸로 남아 있을 거라 착각하는 사람들 대부분이 범하는 그런 실수는 하지 말자꾸나."

로커룸을 떠나기 직전, 피에르는 거울을 바라본 뒤, 미소를 지어보였다. 그리고 선글라스를 바로잡아 쓴 뒤 말했다.

"못생긴 걸로 유명했던 살아생전보다 지금 내 모습이 더 나은 것 같은데?"

"그런 말씀 마세요. 사람들이 그렇게 애기한 건 다 아버지를 시기해서 그런 거예요. 저는 늘 아버지가 잘생겼다고 생각했는걸요."

"고맙구나. 하지만 젊은 시절 내 얼굴이 자기 어머니 밖에 예쁘다고 말해주지 않을 그런 얼굴이었던 건 사실이다. 심지어 우리 어머니조차도 내 얼굴을 좋아하지 않으셨지……. 하지만 아무렴 어떠냐. 그러고 보니 네게 성공의 중요한 요소 가운데 하나를 얘기해줘야 할 것 같구나. 어쨌건 네 경우에는 그게 꽤 중요할 것 같아서 말이지……."

장애를 이용하라

　젊은 시절, 나는 못생긴 외모 때문에 많이 괴로웠단다. 거울 속에 있는 내 얼굴을 바라보는 것은 참기 힘든 고문 중에 하나였지. 하지만 거울보다도 더 끔찍했던 것은 바로 다른 사람들의 시선이었어. 내 어머니의 시선, 내 친구들의 시선은 참기가 더 힘들었지. 시간이 지나면 차츰 나아질 거라 생각했지만, 사람들은 나를 못난이라고 부르는 것에 익숙해지더구나. 쉰 살이 넘어서도 사람들은 내 등 뒤에서 "저 사람 정말 못생겼다. 백만금이 있어도 소용없을 것 같아. 저 남자의 여자는 대체 어떤 사람일까?"라고 수군거리더구나. 얼굴에 대한 고민은 하지 않아도 될 나이가 됐는데 말이야. 그 나이에 화려한 외모라는 게 있을 리도 만무하고 말이지…….

사람들은 네 어머니에 대해서도 수군거렸단다. 그리고 네가 빈소에서 본 젊고 예쁜 여자들에 대해서도……. 그 여자들은 네 어머니가 일찍 세상을 떠난 후 기분 전환을 위해 만났던 여자들이지.

등 뒤에서 수군거리지 않는 사람들이 속으로 무슨 생각을 하고 있는지 쉽게 짐작이 가고도 남았단다. 난 사람들의 생각을 맞출 수 있는 특별한 능력이 있기 때문이었지. 이건 못생긴 사람들만의 은밀한 특권이라고 생각해. 또 사람들의 마음을 꿰뚫어보는 혜안은 내 성공의 열쇠 가운데 하나였지.

다시 말해 사람들이 무슨 생각을 하는지 속내를 읽고, 그 사람이 쓸모가 있는지 파악하며, 위선적이거나 나약한 사람인지, 게으르거나 부정한 이득을 취하는 사람인지, 혹은 반대로 쓸모 있는 사람인지 알 수 있었기 때문에 내 주위에는 늘 좋은 사람들이 많았단다.

나는 그리스의 선박왕 아리스토텔레스 오나시스의 전기를 읽은 적이 있단다. 이 사람은 삼촌에게서 빌린 350달러를 가지고 사업을 시작했다. 그 역시 타고난 미남은 아니었지. 그런데 그의 전기를 읽다보니 이런 대목이 나오더구나.

"나를 잘 봐라. 나는 그리스의 신에게서 물려받은 게 아무것도 없지만, 못생긴 외모 때문에 속상해하며 시간을 허비하지는 않았다. 그 누구도 자신이 생각하는 것만큼 그렇게 못생기지 않았다는 점을 잊지 말라."

이 부분을 읽고 나니 힘이 생기더구나. 내가 과연 그렇게 못생겼을까? 가만히 생각해보니 그건 주관적 시각일 뿐이었어. 볼테르가 말했듯이, 사실 두꺼비에게 아름다움이란 두꺼비다운 것이 아니더냐?

이쯤에서 한 가지 짚고 넘어갈 부분이 있다. 잘생기지 않았다는 것은 사소한 문제에 해당한다. 대개는 대수롭지 않게 넘어가며, 남의 얼굴에 굳이 관심을 갖지 않는다. 다른 사람들의 얼굴을 일일이 쳐다보며 다닌다면, 저녁때 쯤 목에 상당한 통증이 느껴질 것이며, 산책을 하는 것이 오히려 피곤한 일이 되고 말겠지. 따라서 잘생기지 않았다고 해서, 그게 곧 못생겼다는 말과 같은 것은 아니란다. 잘생기지 않은 사람이 곧 무조건 사람들의 이목을 끌고, 수군거리며 손가락질해대는 그런 흉물스러운 모습은 아니라는 것이다.

그렇다면 네 백만장자 아버지는 정말 못생겼을까? 확실한 것은 깎아놓은 조각상처럼 잘생긴 내 형에 비하면 나는 못생긴 축에 속했다는 점이다. 형제간에 외모 차이가 너무 심해 심지어 한 핏줄에서 나온 형제가 맞느냐고 의심을 살 정도였지. 형과의 상당한 외모 차이는 나를 괴롭혔고, 내가 얼마나 못생겼는지 금세 입증해주었지. 더욱이 가장 끔찍했던 것은 어머니께서 형에 대한 편애를 전혀 감추지 않으셨다는 거야. 집에서 형은 모든 호사를 누렸고, 좋은 건 모두 형의 몫이었지. 이 점에 대해 나는 오랜 기간 서운하게 생각했단다.

하지만 이제는 어머니께 어떤 식으로든 감사하는 마음을 전하고 싶단다. 당시 나는 거의 병적으로 내 이름을 돋보이게 하려고 노력했던 것 같다. 만일 내가 형처럼 어머니가 귀하게 여기는 자식이었다면, 과연 그렇게 튀어 보이려고 노력을 했을까?

내 모든 성공은 추한 외모와 형에 대한 어머니의 편애 덕분이 아닌가 싶다. 만일 모든 걸 다시 시작할 수 있다면, 내가 과연 형과 자리를 바꿀 것 같으냐? 물론 아니란다. 어머니에게 사랑을 듬뿍 받으며 정신이 깨어나지 않은 상태로 잠든 채 살아가던 형의 삶보다는 내 삶이 훨씬 매력적이고 흥미로웠기 때문이지. 잘생겼지만 겉멋만 잔뜩 들어갔던 형은 마음만 먹으면 세상의 모든 여자를 자기 여자로 만들 수 있었다. 그러나 자기 힘을 들여 이뤄낸 것은 아무 것도 없었어. 형은 늘 무의미한 삶을 살고 있었고, 내가 성공한 것에 대해 항상 질투심을 느꼈지. 삶이란 참 신기하지 않으냐?

여기에 덧붙이고 싶은 말은 못생겼다는 게 곧 성공을 보장해준다는 건 아니라는 점이다. 이와 반대로 잘생긴 것 또한 성공에 걸림돌이 된다는 말도 아니다. 성공한 사람 중에 못생긴 사람들은 많다. 반면 뛰어난 외모의 소유자였던 레오나르도 다빈치, 플라톤, 리스트만 해도 인생에서 크게 성공하지 않았더냐?

나는 이제 못생긴 내 얼굴을 사랑한다. 그 얼굴은 더없는 내 훌륭한 친구였고, 충직한 내 동반자였단다. 내가 죽을 때까지 내 곁을 떠나지 않았으니까.

내게 못생긴 얼굴은 성공으로 이르게 해주는 통행증 같은 역할을 해주었단다. 부의 세계로 들어가는 출입국 사무소에서 내게 "당신은 못생겼소?"라고 물었을 때, 나는 당당히 "네!"라고 대답했다. 그러자 그 직원은 내게 신분증도 요구하지 않은 채 입국을 허락했지. "들어가도 좋소"라고 말이야.

성공의 비결이란 다양한 수단을 써서라도 원하고자 하는 바를 얻어내는 게 아닐까 한다. 사람들이 네게 레몬을 건네주면, 그걸로 레모네이드를 만들어라. 절대 두 손 놓고 가만히 있으면 안 된다. 어떤 상황에서든 모든 것에서 이점을 찾아내도록 노력해라. 그 어떤 시련과 역경이 있더라도 말이야.

능력이 뛰어난 사람들은 엄청난 장애물이 있더라도 이를 극복하고 놀라운 결과를 만들어냈단다. 네가 좋아하는 위대한 작곡가 베토벤을 떠올려보거라. 한 사람의 음악가로서 청각 장애보다 더 심한 장애가 어디 있겠느냐? 한창때의 나이에 그와 같은 일을 겪었다는 게 얼마나 잔인한 일이란 말이냐. 그럼에도 베토벤은 훌륭한 걸작을 만들어냈단다. 귀가 불편했는데도 위대한 곡을 남겼던 거지.

나폴레옹 힐이 말했던 걸 기억하렴.

"모든 패배, 모든 불행, 모든 실패는 그 안에 같은 수준의 특권이라는 씨앗을 내포하고 있다. 혹은 그보다 더 큰 특권이 그 안에 내재되어 있을 지도 모른다."

이 말은 그의 책《나의 꿈 나의 인생》에 나오는 것이란다. 이 책은 네가 반드시 읽어야 할 필독서지. 모든 분야에서 다 유용한 책이지만, 특히 소설가 같이 미래가 불확실한 직업이라면 더더욱 유용한 책이거든.

겉으로는 불리해 보이는 상황이라도, 모든 것에는 반드시 성공의 기회가 내재되어 있다는 사실을 유념해라. 이는 네 시련을 유익하게 만들어줄 것이며, 운이 따르지 않고 곤경에 빠지더라도 네 스스로 희망을 찾도록 해줄 것이다. 희망의 불빛이 점점 옅어지고 모든 걸 포기하고 싶은 충동이 들 때도, 시련과 좌절을 겪을 때도, 이러한 생각이 머릿속에 있으면 희망의 끈을 놓지 않을 수 있단다. 네가 겪는 그 어떤 실패도, 네 앞을 가로막는 그 어떤 장애나 실망도, 네가 성공을 거둘 수 있게 해주는 추진력이 될 수 있단다.

방금 전 내가 한 말을 증명해줄 만한 이야기를 짧게 덧붙이고 싶구나. 내가 죽기 얼마 전 어느 날 밤, 나는 신기한 꿈을 꾸었단다. 네게 이 얘기를 들려주는 이유는 그즈음에 이 꿈을 꾼 게 우연은 아니었기 때문이야. 꿈에서 나는 어떤 무덤 속에 누워 있었는데, 몸에 감각이 전혀 느껴지지 않았어. 물론 나는 죽은 상태가 아니었지.

그때 내 주위에는 키가 크고 잘생긴 남자들이 있었는데, 이 사람들에게는 은은한 빛이 나고 있었어. 그때 나는 이 사람들이 영혼의 인도자라는 걸 깨달았단다. 그 가운데 한 사람이 내게 단호하면서도 근엄한 목소리로 이렇게 말했단다.

"우리는 네게 고통을 줄 것이다. 네게 상당한 좌절감과 난처한 상황을 안겨줄 생각이다. 그건 네가 이를 감당할 능력이 되기 때문이며, 네가 보다 빨리 성장하길 원하기 때문이다. 너와 관련한 일을 하는 게 우리에게 주어진 업무이며, 너에 대한 신의 애정이다. 그러니 이 모두를 잘 이해하고 낙심하지 말라. 반대로 이 상황을 즐기도록 하라. 이 같은 시련을 통해 너는 내적 재능과 자질을 얻을 것이기 때문이다. 앞으로 지금껏 네가 경험하지 못한 행복보다 무한히 더 큰 행복이 너를 찾아올 것이다."

샤를, 네게 들려주는 이 꿈 이야기가 네게 유용하게 쓰일 수 있으리라 생각했다. 힘겨운 순간이 닥칠 때마다 이 말을 떠올리며 곰곰이 생각해보거라.

이번에는 삶에 관한 이야기를 네게 해주고 싶구나. 절대 잊어서는 안 되는 것들과 절대 놓쳐서는 안 되는 것들에 대해 이야기해주려 한다.

가장 중요한 걸 잊지 마라

"1518년, 레오나르도 다빈치가 사망하기 1년 전에 쓴 수기 가운데 도식이 그려진 한 페이지에는 '기타 등등'으로 끝나는 구문이 있었다. 여기에는 놀라운 메모가 하나 붙어 있었다. 그 내용은 'perche la minesstra si fredda'로, '수프가 식었기 때문에'라는 뜻이었다.

샤를, 아무리 위대한 인물이라고 해도, 깊은 성찰의 세계에 몰입해 있던 상황이라도, 그들은 단순한 삶의 현실에 대해서도 잊지 않는단다. 그건 너 또한 마찬가지야. 네 꿈이 아무리 크다고 해도, 또 네 계획이 아무리 거창하다고 해도, 네게 가장 중요한 게 무엇인지 결코 잊어서는 안 된다. 간단히 말하면 가장 중요한 건 바로 네가 사랑하는 사람들 그리고 너를 사랑하는 사람들이란다.

네가 인생에서 성공을 거둔다고 하더라도, 사랑이 없거나 네 곁에 동반자가 없는 삶은 공허한 삶이나 다름없다는 사실을 잊지 말거라. 내가 네 어머니에게 했던 실수를 너는 되풀이하지 말아야 한다. 나는 성공과 명예에 정신이 나갔었고, 내가 어느 정도 재산을 모은 후에는 내 주위를 맴돌았던 여자들에게 넋이 빠졌지. 너무도 섬세했던 네 어머니를 고통 속에서 죽어가도록 방치했단다. 그렇게 해서 나를 자유롭게 만들고 싶었던 거야. 자신의 사랑이 나를 부담스럽게 만든다고 생각했으니까.

나는 네 어머니를 잃은 슬픔에서 결코 회복될 수 없었다. 네 어머니가 남기고 간 빈자리를 지울 수 없었어. 나는 성공했다는 소리를 들을 수 있을지 모른다. 하지만 내 삶에서는 결코 그렇지 않았단다. 내가 유일하게 진심으로 사랑했던 여자를, 나를 진심으로 사랑해주었던 유일한 여자를 실망시켰기 때문이지.

하지만 저 세계에서 네 어머니는 내가 흘린 눈물을 지켜보았을 것이고, 내가 수년 간 독수공방하며 네 어머니에게 보낸 기도를 들었으리라 확신한다. 어제 저녁, 네 어머니가 나를 기다렸다고 사람들이 말해주더구나. 그래, 네 어머니가 나를 기다리고 있었어. 내일 저녁 성당 돔 천장을 통해 떠나고 나면, 거기서 네 어머니를 다시 만날 예정이다."

샤를도 어머니를 잃은 상심이 아주 컸다. 그런 어머니가 저 세상에서 아버지와 함께 지낸다는 말을 듣고 샤를은 주체할 수 없는 기쁨을 느꼈다.

그와 동시에 샤를은 또 다른 슬픔을 느꼈다. 그것은 방금 전 아버지가 상기시켜준 대로, 내일이면 아버지가 떠날 것이기 때문이었다. 이번에는 영영 돌아오시지 않는 것이다.

피에르에는 아들에게 당부의 말을 전했다.

"너도 클라라에게 이 아버지 같은 실수를 저지르진 말거라. 나는 클라라가 너를 진심으로 사랑하고 있는 걸 안단다. 그러니 그 애와 결혼하도록 하렴."

샤를은 아버지의 말을 따르는 게 어려울 것 같다고 생각했
다. 클라라가 이번에는 진심으로 자기 곁을 떠난 게 확실하
기 때문이었다.

"네가 사랑하는 여자에게 나 같은 실수는 저지르지 말도
록 해라. 그렇지 않으면 레오나르도 다빈치가 했던 말처럼,
결국 네 삶에서도 '죽이 식어버렸다'고 말하게 될지 모른다."

예기치 않은 수표 한 장

장례식 다음 날, 샤를은 자신의 아파트에서 아버지와 만나기로 약속했다. 클라라가 장례식에 참석하겠다고 약속했기 때문에, 피에르는 둘 사이에 아무런 일이 없다고 생각했다. 두 사람이 헤어졌을 거라는 의심은 추호도 하지 않았던 것이다. 아니면 아들을 배려해서 그런 척을 하고 있었는지도 모른다.

사실 지금과 같은 몸 상태에서 피에르는 많은 것들을 알 수 있었고, 사람들의 머릿속을 잘 읽어낼 수 있었다. 그렇지 않았다면, 피에르가 이 아름다운 처녀의 손을 계속 잡고 있던 상황을 어떻게 설명할 수 있을까. 그가 클라라에게 "다시 만나서 정말 기쁘구나, 클라라"라고 말했을 때, 이는 그저 겉치레나 빈말이 아니었다. 진심에서 우러나온 말이었다.

클라라는 피에르를 보고 깜짝 놀랐다. 아버지가 살아 돌아오셨다던 샤를의 말은 허튼소리가 아니었다. 클라라 역시 이를 인정해야 했다. 샤를의 아버지와 닮은 모습에 더 멋져진 모습으로 몸에서 광채가 나는 이 혼령을 보고 클라라는 아연실색했다. 피에르는 분명 그렇게 현실에서 존재하고 있었다. 클라라 역시 그가 '살아있다'는 걸 부인할 수 없었다.

다만 클라라가 피에르의 얼굴을 알아보기까지는 적지 않은 시간이 필요했다. 물론 그가 친숙한 옷을 입고 있기는 했지만 말이다. 그 옷은 클라라도 예전에 본 적이 있는 옷이었다. 고급 모직으로 된 우아한 정장이었다. 옷 색깔이 현재의 상황과 다소 어울리지 않은 데도 그랬다. 피에르가 입고 있던 옷은 검은색도 아니고, 그렇다고 어두운 계열의 색상도 아닌, 하얀색에 가까운 밝은색이었다.

클라라는 피에르가 사람들의 눈에 띄지 않고 장례식장에 들어갈 수 없을 것이라고 생각했다. 장례식에 참석한 사람들은 모두 검은 옷을 입고 있었기 때문이었다. 그리고 자신의 장례식에 참석하는 고인이라니……. 상황이 좀 이상하긴 했다.

아버지를 다시 본 샤를도 놀라기는 마찬가지였다. 물론 클라라보다야 그 놀라움이 적었지만, 한층 더 젊어진 아버지의 모습 때문이었다. 아버지는 전날보다 더 밝고 환한 모습이었다. 못생긴 얼굴의 흔적도 거의 완벽하게 사라졌다. 물론 못생긴 얼굴이 나쁘다는 건 아니다. 아버지의 솔직하고 명쾌한 설명처럼, 그 얼굴 나름대로의 중요한 역할이 있었다. 하지만 이제는 타의 추종을 불허하던 그 못생긴 얼굴이 사라졌다. 아버지는 미남형 얼굴이었고, 살아생전 사람들이 그렇게도 놀려대던 파란 눈은 두 개의 태양처럼 반짝였다. 그 태양과 같은 눈빛이 사람의 마음을 따뜻하게 녹여주었고, 마음을 훤히 비춰주며 이렇게 큰 소리로 외치는 듯했다.

"너무 진지하게 생각하지 말라. 그 무엇도 그렇게 심각한 건 없다. 아무것도 중요하지 않다. 그러니 네 스스로 즐겨라. 인생은 하나의 게임이다."

장례식에 걸맞게 검은 옷을 차려입은 샤를과 클라라는 우아한 흰색 양복 속에서 멋진 모습을 뽐내고 있는 피에르를 에스코트했다. 그리고 샤를의 아파트에서 나온 후 충직한 외젠이 기다리고 있던 리무진에 올랐다.

"외젠, 은행으로 가지."

피에르가 명령했다.

"예, 사장님!"

"아란훼스 협주곡을 틀게나."

"알겠습니다!"

외젠은 늘 그랬듯이 씩씩한 어조로 대답했다. 그리고 지나가는 말로 피에르에게 감사의 말을 전했다.

"사장님, 아이들이 감사의 뜻을 전해달라고 합니다. 아이들은 제가 사장님께 받은 2만5천 달러를 무척 감사하게 여기고 있어요."

피에르는 환한 표정을 지으며 껄껄 웃었다. 그의 호탕한 웃음과 못생긴 얼굴은 피에르를 상징하는 트레이드 마크였다. 물론 지금은 그의 은밀한 과업이 완수되고 모든 시련과 장애가 사라져버렸듯이 못생긴 얼굴도 사라지고 없지만 말이다.

"외젠. 아이들에게까지 모든 걸 말해줄 필요는 없었는데. 하하."

그렇게 말하면서 피에르는 아들을 돌아보며 함박웃음을 지었다. 샤를은 잘 모르겠다는 듯 샐쭉한 표정을 지었다.

협주곡의 유명한 기타 연주 부분이 리무진에 울려 퍼지자, 피에르가 큰소리로 말했다.

"더 크게 틀게나, 외젠! 더 크게! 안 들리잖나!"

외젠이 볼륨을 높이는 동안 피에르는 두 눈을 지그시 감고 머리 위로 두 팔을 올려 오케스트라를 지휘하는 시늉을 했다. 이번에는 기타와의 은밀하고 흥미로운 대화가 시작된 것이다. 클라라는 놀란 표정으로 옆에 앉아 있는 피에르를 바라봤다. 그녀는 약간 겁을 먹은 표정이었다. 그녀가 알고 있던 피에르는 얼마나 특이한 사람이란 말인가!

샤를은 잠시 골똘히 생각에 잠겼다.

'내 아버지는 지금껏 내가 만난 사람 가운데 가장 멋있게 미친 사람이다. 사실 저런 모습의 아버지는 한 번도 본 적이 없었다. 이제 열두 시간 후면 아버지는 여기에 없겠지. 그때가 되면 아버지께서는 정말 돌아가시는 거야. 아니, 엄밀히 말하면 돌아가시는 건 아니지. 이제는 이해할 수 있게 됐으니까. 하지만 어쨌든 아버지는 저 세상으로 다시 떠나실 테고, 이번에는 영원히 돌아오지 않겠지. 내게 주어진 이 선물은 오늘

밤 열 시에 마법이 풀리니까…….'

샤를의 눈에 촉촉한 이슬이 맺혔다. 클라라는 '당신 아버지, 미친 거 아냐?'라는 표정으로 샤를을 쳐다보았다. 그런데 샤를의 눈이 촉촉이 젖어 있는 것을 보고는 연민의 감정이 일어났다. 그가 자기 때문에 우는 것인지, 아니면 곧 헤어질 아버지와의 이별 때문에 우는 것인지 알 수는 없었으나, 어쨌든 샤를의 손을 꼭 잡아주었다.

〈랑제 공작부인〉이란 작품에서 발자크는 이 미묘한 느낌에 대해 사실적으로 묘사했다.

"마음에서 가벼운 사건이란 있을 수 없다. 마음은 모든 걸 증폭시키는 능력이 있다. 마음은 14년 된 제국의 멸망과 한 여인의 장갑 한 쪽이 떨어진 것을 동일한 무게로 평가한다. 그리고 마음속에서는 항상 제국보다 장갑의 무게가 더 많이 나간다."

샤를에게는 (그 이유야 어쨌든) 클라라가 잡아준 이 보잘것없는 손 하나가 우주 전체보다도 더 무겁게 느껴졌다. 그의 마음속에서는 자신이 받지 못한 수백만 달러의 유산보다 클라라가 잡아준 손이 더욱 가치 있게 느껴진 것이다.

샤를은 함께 살던 여자에게 버림받은 남자가 그 같은 상황에서 궁금해할 의문 하나를 제기한다. 클라라는 과연 단순한 동정심에서, 타인에 대한 인간으로서의 연민 때문에 내 손을 잡아준 것일까? 아니면 자기가 생각을 바꿨다고, 다시 그의 곁으로 돌아오고 싶다고, 실은 이미 다시 돌아온 것이나 다름없다고, 지금 이렇게 리무진 안에 같이 있지 않느냐고, 그 손으로 자기 손을 잡아달라고 무언의 고백을 하는 것일까?

그의 심장은 어린아이처럼 두근거리기 시작했다. 열한 살 때, 처음으로 좋아했던 여자아이 레이몽드 우드의 손을 잡았을 때와 같은 떨림이었다. 그리고 그의 머릿속에는 맨 처음 그 같은 경험을 겪을 때 누구나 하는 생각이 자리 잡았다. 이 여자가 바로 내 인생의 동반자다. 우리는 결혼해야 한다!

샤를은 클라라를 바라보며 웃음을 지어보였다. 이 웃음에는 참으로 많은 것들이 담겨 있었다. 하지만 이를 일일이 설명하는 건 부질없는 짓이다. 사랑에 빠진 한 남자가 웃음을 지을 때, 그 안에 포함된 수많은 뉘앙스에 대해서는 익히 잘 알고 있지 않은가!

은행이 코앞에 보였다. 리무진이 은행 앞에 멈춰섰을 때도 차 안에서는 계속 아란훼스 협주곡이 흐르고 있었다. 피에르는 차에서 내려 길 위에 있는 민들레 한 송이를 꺾어 클라라에게 주었다. 그는 이 민들레가 마치 장미꽃이라도 되는 것처럼 수줍은 청년이 된 마음으로 클라라에게 건네주었다. 이어 피에르는 또 한 번 클라라를 대경실색하게 만들었다. 첫 등장에서부터 클라라가 놀란 것을 생각하면, 이번이 세 번째 놀란 모습일지도 모르겠다. 피에르가 그녀에게 "나와 춤을 추지 않겠나?"라고 말하며 손을 내밀었기 때문이었다.

"춤이요? 방금 춤을 추자고 말했나요?"

그녀의 의문은 더욱 커졌다. 이런 백주대로에서, 장엄하게 울려퍼지는 협주곡에 맞춰 죽은 사람과 함께 춤을 추다니……. 물론 지금 피에르의 모습이 송장 같은 외형은 아니었지만, 어쨌든 이미 죽은 사람이 아닌가.

클라라는 깜짝 놀라면서 샤를에게 도움을 청하려고 뒤를 돌아봤다. 그러나 샤를은 별일 아니라는 듯 어깨만 으쓱해 보일 뿐이었다. 그는 입술을 꾹 다문 채 이렇게 말하는 듯했다.

"아버지가 특이한 분이시라는 것, 클라라도 오래 전부터 알고 있었잖아?"

클라라는 우선 민들레꽃부터 받아들였다. 봄의 기운이 느껴지는 따뜻한 노란색은 클라라의 우아한 검은 원피스와 뚜렷한 대조를 이루었다. 앞서 아들과의 숱한 대화 속에서 드러났듯이 한평생 점진적 외교를 신봉해온 피에르는 이번에도 비집고 들어갈 틈새를 발견했다. 그는 춤을 권하는 고전적인 제스처로 왼손을 내밀며 이탈리어로 익숙한 멘트를 날렸다.

"자, 그럼……?"

클라라는 오래 전에 피에르와 춤을 춰본 적이 있었다. 그녀가 알고 있는 피에르는 춤에 일가견이 있는 사람이었다. 그의 주위에 여자가 많았던 것도 이와 무관하지 않았다. 여자들은 춤추는 걸 좋아하고, 춤을 잘 추는 남자라면 더욱 호감을 느끼기 마련이었다.

결국 클라라는 피에르가 내민 손을 수락했고, 피에르는 길 위에서 클라라의 손과 허리를 잡았다. 다소 생뚱맞기도 한 이 모습을 많은 사람들이 지켜보았다. 샤를은 물론 길을 가던 거리의 사람들, 은행 고객들도 모두 두 사람을 지켜봤다. 어떤 이는 이 모습을 보고 눈살을 찌푸렸고, 어떤 이는 웃음을 지었으며, 어떤 이는 놀라움에 입을 다물지 못했다.

　그때 젊은 연인이 서로 다투기라도 한 듯 은행 문을 나서고 있었다. 무척 빼어난 미모를 지닌 젊은 여자는 즉흥적으로 마련된 무대 위에서 우아하게 춤을 추고 있는 클라라와 피에르의 모습을 보았다. 그 모습에 너무도 감명을 받은 나머지 여자는 남자와의 싸움을 멈추고 그 자리에서 울음을 터뜨렸다. 순간 그녀는 자신의 남자친구가 얼마나 분위기가 메말라 있는 사람인지 깨달았던 것이다. 그러나 남자의 경우는 달랐다. 낭만이라는 것은 그저 여자들의 투정일 뿐이라고 여겼고, 물러터진 남자만이 로맨티스트 운운하며 여자들의 비위를 맞춰 주는 것이라고 생각했다. 아니면 오로지 여자를 침대로 데려가기 위해 그 같은 행동을 하는 것이라고 생각했다.

　하지만 남자 또한 이 예기치 못한 광경을 목격하고 어떤 감흥을 느꼈다. 다마스로 가는 길목에서 뜻하지 않게 예수와 마주친 뒤 크게 감명을 받았던 사도 바울과 비슷하게, 남자는 눈물을 머금고 여자를 바라봤다.

　여자는 남자가 흘리는 눈물을 보고 의아하게 여겼다. 남자가 눈물을 흘리는 모습은 생전 처음 보는 광경이었기 때문이었다. 물론 그가 이전에 딱 한 번 눈물을 흘린 적은 있었다. 남자가 응원하던 하키 팀이 예선에서 일치감치 탈락하자, 분노에 차 흘린 눈물이었다. 그런 무뚝뚝한 남자가 여자 앞에 무릎을 꿇자, 여자는 왠지 모르게 이 남자가 자신이 늘 꿈꾸던 남자가 되었다는 사실을 깨달았다. 무릎을 꿇은 남자가 여자를 올려다보며 말했다.

"진작 말을 하려고 했는데, 아직까지 바보처럼 말을 못했어. 내 아내가 되어줄래?"

여자는 그 자리에서 고개를 끄떡이며 좋다고 대답했다. 한 번도 아니고 세 번이나 '좋다'고 외쳤다. 우리가 살고 있는 인생에서 이처럼 아름다운 계획이 또 어디 있을까?

여자는 뛸 듯이 기뻐하는 표정을 지으며 무릎을 꿇고 있는 남자를 일으켜 세웠다. 남자는 자리에서 일어나면서 미래의 아내에게 입맞춤을 해주었다. 이게 꿈인지 생시인지 확인하기 위해서인지, 아니면 자신이 처한 상황에 대해 보다 정확히 이해하고 싶어서인지, 여자는 남자를 잠시 뒤로 밀면서 물었다.

"왜 갑자기 생각이 바뀐 거야?"

"나도…… 나도 잘 모르겠어……."

남자는 그렇게 말하면서 손가락으로 클라라와 피에르가 춤추는 모습을 가리켰다.

"바로 저 사람들 때문이야!"

이 광경을 지켜본 샤를은 믿기지 않는다는 듯 고개를 설레설레 흔들었다.

'아버지께서는 정말 대단해! 이 세상 사람이 아닌데도 사람들에게 영향을 미치고 있다니.'

그때 음악이 멈추었고, 피에르는 클라라에게 감사를 표했다. 그리고 샤를에게 말을 건넸다.

"이제 그만 가자꾸나."

피에르는 샤를의 손을 잡고 그를 은행으로 데려갔다.

"저는 여기서 기다릴게요."

클라라는 두 부자의 뒷모습을 물끄러미 쳐다보았다. 아버지가 아들의 손을 잡고 은행으로 들어가는 모습이 그녀의 눈에는 마치 사랑하는 연인의 모습처럼 보였다. 샤를은 은행으로 들어가기 전에 서로 부둥켜안고 있는 연인 곁을 지나치며 문득 이런 생각이 들었다.

'그래도 이 친구들은 운이 좋아. 저들은 곧 결혼을 하겠지만

나와 클라라는 이제 끝이야. 완전히 끝이라고!'

리무진 안에서 클라라가 자신의 손을 꼭 잡아주긴 했으나, 무언가 불길한 예감이 그를 엄습해왔다.

은행에 들어간 샤를은 아버지의 지시에 따라 은행 직원에게 개인 안전보관함이 있는 금고로 안내해달라고 부탁했다. 샤를은 골프 로커에서 찾은 열쇠로 금고를 열었다. 열쇠에는 63이란 숫자가 적혀 있었다. 샤를은 금고 안에서 봉투를 발견했다.

"이 봉투를 뜯어볼까요?"

금고실을 나온 샤를이 아버지에게 물었다.

"아니다. 그 봉투는 쓰레기통에 버리거라."

그러나 묘한 호기심에 사로잡힌 샤를은 봉투를 열어보았다. 봉투 안에는 낱장의 종이가 들어 있었는데, 은행이 발행한 일정 액수와 이름 그리고 서명인의 이름이 적혀 있었다. 우리는 보통 이런 걸 '수표'라고 부른다. 그렇다. 봉투 안에 든 종이는 피에르가 샤를에게 주는 수표였다. 물론 달랑 한 장의 수표이긴 하였으나, 거기에 적힌 금액은 그리 평범한 숫자가 아니었다. 실로 엄청난 금액이 적혀 있었다. 정말 조금도 예상할 수 없는 숫자였다. 거기에는 무려 5천만 달러라는 금액이 적혀 있었다. 틀림없는 5천만 달러였다.

샤를은 할 말을 잃었다. 그러나 샤를이 뭐라 감사의 말을 전하기도 전에 피에르가 먼저 입을 열었다.

"그 액수는 네 형이나 누나에게 남긴 유산보다 적은 금액이다. 하지만 현금이라는 장점이 있지. 그리고 어떤 면에서는 네 형이나 누나가 가진 유산보다 더 가치가 있을 수도 있다. 내가 살아 있을 때 그 둘에게 일임했던 회사의 운영 방식으로 보건대, 내 사후에도 크게 달라질 건 없어 보인다만……. 여하튼 이제 그건 내 알 바 아니지. 내가 생각했던 것보다 더 빨리 그곳을 뜨게 되서 말이야."

"진심이세요?"

"그래. 진심이란다. 진심이 아닌 사람들은 바로 그만큼의 수표가 없는 사람들이야. 네 나이라면 그 정도는 이미 알고 있어야 하는 거 아니냐?"

샤를은 아직 아버지의 말을 믿을 수가 없었다. 아버지는 자신을 갖고 노는 것이다. 아마 수표는 유효한 상태가 지났고, 수표가 인출된 계좌에는 돈이 들어있지 않을 거다. 샤를은 아버지가 지금 자신을 갖고 노는 것이라고 생각했다.

5천만 달러라……. 이 정도의 액수면 그의 삶에 얼마나 많은 영향을 미칠 수 있는 금액인가? 어느 날 갑자기 교수직을 그만둘 수도 있고, 그 후 조용히 소설 집필에만 매진할 수 있으며, 미래는 걱정하지 않아도 된다. 자신이 꿈꾸는 바를 모두 현실에서 이뤄가며 살 수 있는 것이다. 5천만 달러라면 그만큼 큰 액수다. 샤를은 마치 마술 주문이라도 외듯 5천만이라는 숫자를 계속 되뇌었다.

"정말로 제게 5천만 달러를 주시는 거예요?"

샤를이 물었다.

"아니다."

피에르는 진지한 표정으로 반박했다. 샤를은 아버지가 농담하고 있다고 여겼다. 아버지는 평생을 그렇게 살아오신 분이었다.

"그럼 대체 무슨 생각이신지……."

"네가 이 수표로 뭘 했으면 좋겠는지, 내 생각을 알겠느냐?"

"아뇨. 하지만 곧 있으면 알게 될 것 같아요."

“그래, 지금 얘기해주마. 그 수표는 내가 방금 전에 한 말들을 네가 믿지 않을 경우에 이를 금고에 넣어두고 사용했으면 좋겠구나.”

“하지만 아버지…… 저는 아버지처럼 살 수가…….”

“문제는 간단하다. 내가 널 설득시키지 못한 경우에만 네가 이 돈의 주인이 되었으면 좋겠다는 거야.”

“설득이라뇨? 어떤 걸 말씀하시는 거예요?”

“내가 너에게 유산을 물려주지 않은 것은 네가 잘 되길 바라는 마음에서였다는 것, 내가 조금 전 네게 가르쳐주었던 것은 이 돈을 합한 것보다 더 값지다는 것, 내가 말한 대로 따르면 너는 위대한 소설가도 되고 돈도 굉장히 많이 버는 사람이 될 수 있다는 것, 무위도식하거나 시체처럼 살지 않고 한 사람의 인간으로서 네 모든 잠재력을 실현할 수 있다는 것, 그걸 네게 설득시키지 못한 경우를 말하는 것이지…….”

샤를은 올가미에 걸린 느낌이었다. 모든 게 그저 꿈만 같은 얘기였다.

“아버지는 저를 이상한 선택의 기로에 서게 하시네요.”

“네 말대로 삶이란 늘 우리를 이상한 선택의 기로에 놓이게 만들지. 그건 곧 네가 아무 것도 깨달은 바가 없다는 뜻이다.”

속마음을 들킨 샤를은 혼란스러웠다.

“하지만 제가 두 가지를 다 할 수는 없잖아요. 그러니까 수표도 제가 갖고, 제 인생도 새롭게 시작하는 건 어때요?”

“그건 안 될 말이다. 내가 처음에 했던 말을 떠올려 보렴.

성공하려면 일단 굶주려야 한다. 네게 5천만 달러가 있으면 너는 굶주린 상태가 될 수 없어. 더욱이 네 힘으로 그 돈을 버는 동안 진정한 기쁨도 모를 테고, 그만한 돈을 가질 자격도 갖추지 못할 거야.

평생 한 번밖에 겪지 못할 훌륭한 경험을 박탈당하는 거야. ‘내가 내 힘으로 이걸 이뤄냈다, 그 누구도 날 도와주지 않았다, 나는 빈손에서 시작했다, 스스로 성취하는 것은 큰 만족감을 안겨주는 일이며, 그 무엇보다도 큰 부를 안겨준다.’ 이런 식의 말도 할 수 없는 거지.”

“하지만 전…….”

“나는 내가 옳다고 생각한다.”

샤를은 더 이상 반박할 말이 없었다.

아버지의 생각이 불만스럽고 실망도 컸지만, 샤를은 아버지의 생각이 옳다는 사실을 알고 있었다. 더욱이 아버지는 늘 옳은 말만 하였다. 다른 재능 가운데서도 늘 옳은 말을 하는 능력 덕분에 아버지는 많은 재산을 모을 수 있었다.

"제가 아버지의 말씀을 따른다면, 저는 이 수표를 어떻게 해야 하는 거죠? 찢어버려야 하나요?"

"아니지. 이 돈은 계좌에 남아 없어지겠지."

"자, 그럼……?"

샤를이 아버지의 말투를 흉내냈다.

"자, 그럼…….."

그러자 피에르도 웃으며 화답했다.

"나는 네가 이 돈을 간직하고 있다가 내가 좋아하는 재단에 기부했으면 좋겠구나. 몬트리올 생트 쥐스틴 병원의 소아 환자들을 도와주는 재단이란다."

"몇 백만 달러만 제가 갖고 나머지를 재단에 기부하면 안 되나요?"

피에르의 얼굴에는 미소가 스쳤다. 그는 다정한 손길로 아들의 얼굴을 톡톡 건드렸다.

"그건 아니란다. 모 아니면 도야. 그리고 네 결정에 도움이 될지는 모르겠지만, 네가 주려고 하면 할수록 더 많은 것을 얻게 된다는 사실을 잊지 말거라."

샤를은 아무 말도 하지 않았다. 아버지가 말한 뜻과 그 고귀한 가치에 대해서는 그 역시 인정하는 바였다. 하지만 그의 머릿속에는 5천만 달러를 갖고 자신이 할 수 있는 모든 일에 대한 생각뿐이었다. 학교도 그만둘 수 있고, 크고 아름다운 집으로 이사할 수 있으며, 여행도 갈 수 있고, 특히 아무 걱정 없이 자신의 첫 번째 소설 집필에 매진할 수 있었다. 요컨대 자유로운 삶이 보장되는 것이다. 철학에서 흔히 하는 말로, 'summum bonum' 즉 '최고의 경지'에 이를 수 있는 것이었다. 그러나 아버지는 하나의 답변, 하나의 결정을 내리라고 못 박았다. 샤를은 아버지에게 이렇게 말했다.

"아버지 말씀이 옳다는 건 알겠어요. 하지만 결정을 내리기 전에 시간이 좀 더 필요해요."

"6개월이면 되겠니?"

"6개월이요?"

"그래, 6개월이 지나면 이 수표는 쓸모없는 종잇조각에 불과할 거야."

샤를은 수표에 적혀 있는 날짜를 확인했다. 수표의 발행 날짜는 바로 오늘로부터 꼭 6개월 후가 유효 기간이었다. 아버지는 이미 모든 걸 예상하고 있었던 것이다. 사전에 미리 계획한 일이었다. 더욱 놀라운 것은 이 모든 과정이 당신이 세상을 뜨기 전 이뤄졌다는 사실이었다.

프러포즈

장례식이 진행되는 동안 아버지는 외젠의 리무진에 있었다. 샤를에게 아버지의 장례식에 참석하는 것은 신기한 경험이었다. 사실 피에르가 차에 머물러 있기로 결정한 이유는 쉽게 짐작이 가고도 남았다. 피에르가 젊었을 때의 모습을 되찾았다고는 하나, 사람들은 분명 그를 알아볼 것이었다. 더욱이 그의 얼굴에는 신기한 광채가 나고 있었고, 이런 모습은 사람들의 궁금증을 자아낼 게 분명했다. 피에르는 자신을 알아보는 사람들에게 일일이 전후 사정 설명을 하고 싶지 않았다. 그가 다시 이 세상에 돌아온 것은 오직 자신의 '실패한 아들' 때문이었다. 하지만 실패한 인생을 살고 있다고 해도, 그는 자식들 가운데 가장 뛰어난 아이였다. 피에르가 가장 사랑했던 자식이기도 했다.

샤를에게는 아버지의 출현이 신기한 경험인 동시에 고통스러운 경험이었다. 아버지는 살아 있는 모습으로 곁에 있긴 했지만, 그 순간에도 아버지의 시신은 무덤 속에 갇혀 있었다. 샤를은 흐르는 눈물을 주체할 수가 없었다. 장례식에 참석한 모든 사람들이 눈물을 흘렸다. 샤를의 형과 누나, 삼촌, 고모, 아버지의 수많은 여자 친구들도 눈물을 흘렸다. 아버지의 여자 친구들이 장례식 분위기를 띄워보려고 했으나 소용없는 일이었다. 피에르의 삶은 그렇게 끝이 났다.

클라라 역시 샤를의 품에 안겨 눈물을 쏟아냈다. 그러나 샤를은 앞으로 클라라를 볼 수 없을 것이었다. 장례식이 끝나면, 아니 클라라가 그동안의 애정을 생각해 그의 곁에 있어준 '특별 서비스'가 끝나면, 그녀의 모습을 다시 볼 수 없을 것이었다.

피에르의 어머니인 엘레오노르 여사 역시 눈물을 흘렸다. 빈소에서는 그녀의 상태가 좋지 않았기 때문에 울지 않았지만, 오늘은 달랐다. 기억력이 좋아져서 지금 이 상황을 잘 알고 있었으며, 지금 땅 속에 묻히는 시신이 자기 아들이라는 사실도 알게 됐다.

엘레오노르의 눈물은 다른 사람의 눈물과는 조금 달랐다. 아들의 시신이 땅속에 들어가는 순간 평소 아들을 많이 사랑해주지 못했음을 깨달았기 때문이다. 인생이란 늘 잔인하리만치 모순적인 법이다. 정작 자신은 그렇게 많이 사랑해주지 못했는데, 아들은 자신을 원망조차 하지 않고 용서까지 해주었다. 유언장에서 피에르가 어머니에게 유산을 남겨주지 않은 이유는 살아생전 피에르가 풍부한 연금을 어머니에게 지원해 주었기 때문이다.

장례식을 마칠 무렵, 무덤 위로 마지막 흙 한줌이 뿌려지고 영원한 작별의 의미로 장미 한 송이가 던져졌다. 뒤를 이어 십자가가 놓이고 사람들이 하나둘씩 빠져나갔다. 샤를은 이때가 아니면 다시는 클라라에게 하고 싶었던 말을 전할 수 없을 거라는 생각이 들었다.

"지금이 적절한 때가 아니라는 건 알아. 하지만 내가……클라라라는 한 여자와 결혼을 할 수 있을까? 사랑해……."

클라라는 놀란 빛을 감추지 못하며 샤를을 바라봤다. 조금 망설이는 듯 보이더니 클라라가 입을 열었다.

"샤를, 너무 늦었어요. 그건 당신도 알고…… 나도 알아요……."

"왜 늦었다는 거지? 나도 아직 혼자고, 당신도 혼자잖아. 당신 혹시……."

"그건 아니에요, 샤를. 다른 사람을 만나는 것은 아니에요."

샤를의 생각을 읽은 클라라는 불쾌감을 느꼈다. 샤를은 셔츠 안주머니에 넣었던 5천만 달러 수표를 만져보았다. 그는 클라라에게 그처럼 큰 금액의 수표를 가지고 있다는 사실을 고백하고 싶었다. 그렇게 되면 샤를의 선택은 이 돈을 물려받는 쪽으로 내려질 것이다. 선택의 여지가 없기에 약간 아쉬움은 남겠지만, 그래도 아버지보다는 클라라를 택하는 것이 현명하지 않겠는가? 아버지가 말한 의도는 알겠지만, 유감스럽게도 선택은 수표를 물려받는 쪽이 될 듯 싶었다.

누구나 자신이 사랑하는 사람을 생각하기 마련 아닌가. 자신의 가족, 주변 측근들, 특히 자신이 미치도록, 정신이 나갈 정도로 사랑하는 여자를 먼저 생각하는 것은 당연한 일이 아닌가. 그렇게 사랑하는 여자가 자신의 곁을 떠나갔단 말이다.
영원히 돌아오지 않을 생각으로 자신의 곁을 떠나려 하고 있
단 말이다.

샤를은 5천만 달러 수표를 클라라에게 보여주고 승부수
를 던져야 했다. 자신의 전부를 얻기 위해 자신의 전부
를 거는 게임을 하는 것이다.

하지만 샤를은 곧 생각을 고쳐먹었다. 지금껏 그녀와 지내
온 날들을 떠올려보니 클라라는 돈에 관심이 없는 것 같았다.
더군다나 클라라는 이처럼 큰돈에 유혹되지 않을 것이라는
생각도 들었다.
"아버지가 내게 유산을 한 푼도 물려주시지 않아서 그런 건
가? 내가 돈이 한 푼도 없는 작자라서?"
샤를이 물었다.
"샤를, 어떻게 그런 말을 할 수 있죠?"
대놓고 모욕을 당한 클라라는 곧바로 샤를의 품에서 떨어
졌다.

리무진 안에서도 두 사람 사이의 분위기는 침울했다. 피에르는 그런 분위기가 어쩔 수 없는 현상이라고 생각했다. 클라라는 시장에 가야 한다는 핑계를 대고 길모퉁이에서 자신을 내려달라고 말했다.

"이제 다시는 못 보겠죠?"

클라라가 피에르를 보며 물었다.

"내일 일이 어찌 될지 누가 알 수 있겠어?"

의미심장하게 피에르가 대답했다. 마치 그는 말하고 싶지 않은 무언가를 알고 있는 듯했다. 샤를은 피에르의 대답을 대수롭지 않게 넘겼다. 샤를은 자기만의 생각에 깊이 빠져 있었다. 그는 방금 전 클라라의 말에 충격을 받았다. "이제 다시는 못 보겠죠?"라고 했던 그녀의 말은 피에르에게 한 말이었다. 하지만 샤를에게는 그 말이 예사롭게 들리지 않았다. 샤를은 감히 클라라에게 같은 질문을 던질 수가 없었다. 무슨 답이 나올 지 너무도 뻔했기 때문이었다.

샤를에게 클라라가 오늘처럼 아름다워보인 적이 없었다. 고통이란, 특히 이별의 고통이란 아름다움을 더욱 커보이게 만드는 재주가 있다.

리무진에서 점점 멀어지는 클라라를 바라보는 샤를의 낮빛은 어두웠다. 그런데 샤를과 달리 아버지의 눈은 갑자기 촉촉이 젖어들기 시작했다. 이를 본 샤를은 깜짝 놀랐다. 물론 아버지가 클라라에 대해 각별한 애정을 갖고 있는 것은 맞았다. 하지만 3년 가까이 사는 동안 아버지가 클라라를 본 것은 열 번도 채 되지 않았다. 부자지간에 오래 전부터 자리 잡은 냉기류 때문이었다. 그런데 아버지는 왜 갑자기 슬퍼하는 것일까. 샤를은 곧 그 답을 들을 수 있었다.

"곧 있으면 만나게 될 내 아내 루이즈가 생각나는구나. 그렇게 오랜 시간이 흐른 뒤에 이제야 보게 되다니……. 이제야 내 삶이 비로소 의미를 갖게 되는 것 같아. 모든 게 다시 제자리로 돌아가는 거지.

어린 시절의 중요함

"시골집으로 가세. 마지막으로 그 집을 보고 싶네."

클라라를 리무진에서 내려준 후 피에르가 제안했다.

노인들은 보통 이런 식이다. 생의 마지막 순간이 다가오면, 이들은 자신의 삶에서 가장 중요했던 장소나 사람을 한 번 더 보고 싶은 향수에 젖어든다. 일종의 이별 의식이다.

사실 피에르는 그런 노인들의 상황과는 달랐다. 이미 그는 죽은 상태에서 뒤늦게 자신의 작별 의식을 행하지 않았던가…….

시골집은 근사한 멤프레마고그 호숫가에 위치해 있었다.

한 시간 반 정도는 족히 가야 하는 거리였다. 피에르는 리무진을 타고 시골집으로 가는 도중에 아들을 위해 이야기보따리를 풀어냈다.

"플라톤이 했던 말, 기억나니? 그 이름에 걸맞은 모든 철학적 구조는 그 안에 그 자신의 모순을 내포하고 있다는 말……."

"그럼요. 유명한《편지들》에 있던 말이잖아요."

"그래. 그리고 이런 모순은 내 성공 철학에서도 적용이 되지."

"벌써부터 두려워지는데요."

피에르는 웃음을 지었다. 그러고는 공상에 잠긴 듯 몽롱한 표정을 지으며 말했다.

"어제 하늘나라에서, 뭐 일단은 그곳을 '하늘나라'라고 부르자꾸나. 그곳에서 나는 웅장하고 멋진 대성당 앞에 서 있었다. 이탈리아 건축가 브루넬레스키가 만든 피렌체 대성당과 같은 착각이 들더구나. 이 성당은 그보다 더 아름다웠고, 붉고 푸른 대리석은 광채로 둘러싸여 있었다. 성당 앞 광장에서 한 남자가 내게로 다가왔는데, 남자의 나이는 이십 대 청년으로 보였고, 외모가 아주 뛰어났지. 지금까지 내가 하늘에서 만난 모든 사람들보다 더 잘생겼단다. 금발머리는 어깨에 닿을 것 같았고, 파란 두 눈은 마치 빛을 머금은 우물 같은 느낌이었어. 대가의 눈과 같은 위엄이 느껴졌단다.

그의 옷차림은 르네상스 시대의 한 사람 같았어. 그가 내게 이렇게 말하더구나. '당신이 아들에게 한 말은 좋은 내용이다. 하지만 그에게 가장 중요한 부분에 대해 말하는 걸 잊지 말라'고. 그러고는 주머니에서 오래된 로마 시대 금화를 꺼냈는데, 거기에는 카이사르의 얼굴이 선명하게 새겨져 있었단다. 그리고 이 멋진 남자는 유명한 한 마디를 했지. '카이사르의 것은 카이사르에게, 신의 것은 신에게 돌려줘야 한다'고 말이야.

나는 이 남자가 누구인지 짐작이 갔단다. 나는 속으로 '예수님이구나!'라고 속삭였지. 순간 나도 모르게 무릎을 꿇었어. 그는 내 머리를 쓰다듬어 주었고, 매우 다정하게 웃었지. 그는 내게 이렇게 말했단다.

'일어나시오. 잘못 생각하셨소. 나는 당신이 생각하는 그 분이 아니오.'

'그럼 당신은 누구신가요?'

'누구라고 생각하시오?'

나는 잘 모르겠다고 실토했지. 그의 근엄하면서 잘생긴 얼굴에 감탄한 나머지 나는 할 말을 잃어버렸어. 그 남자는 내게 이렇게 말하더구나.

'나는 수년 전부터 당신이 생각해오던 바로 그 사람이오. 당신이 당신 아들에게 끊임없이 그 사상을 깨우치게 하려는 사람, 당신의 우상, 바로 그 사람이오……'

그때 나는 깨달았지. 뭐라 형언할 수 없는 엄청난 감정이 북받쳐 올라왔단다. 나는 말을 더듬으며 소리쳤지.

'당신은…… 레오나르도 다빈치로군요!'

'바로 맞췄소.'

'어떻게 내게 이런 영광이……'

'어떤 존재에 대해 단순히 생각하는 것만으로 그 사람을 무조건 당신 삶으로 끌어들일 수 있다고 생각하시오? 나에 대한 당신의 감탄과 존경의 마음이 나를 감동시켰던 거요.'

'하지만 저는 그렇게 대단한 사람이 아닌 걸요. 당신에 비하면 저는 정말 아무 것도 아닙니다.'

그러자 다빈치는 나에 대한 걸 모두 알고 있다며 이렇게 말하더구나.

'그런 소리 마시오! 당신 자신을 폄하하지 마시오. '나는 그렇게 대단한 사람이 아니다'라는 말에서 부정형을 모두 빼버리시오. 부정적인 것은 모두 악마의 관할이요, 긍정적인 것은 모두 인생과 영혼에 속하는 것이오. 언제나 '나는 대단하다'고 말하면서 당신 스스로를 존중하고, 자신의 참된 본성과 하나된 사람이 되시오. 방금 전 당신은 아들에게 위대함에 대해 장시간 설교를 하지 않았소? '위대한 새가 곧 체체로 산에서 첫 비상을 시작할 것이다. 온 세상을 경이로움으로 가득 채우고, 온갖 신문 지면을 그에 관한 명성으로 가득 채우며, 이 위대한 새는 자신이 본디 태어났던 둥지에 영원한 영광을 가져다줄 것이다.'라고 말이오.'

다빈치는 자신의 말을 스스로 완벽하게 재현하더구나. 물론 6백 년 전에 이런 생각을 글로 남긴 적이 있지만 말이야. 확실히 저곳에서의 시간은 이곳과 다르단다. 다빈치는 정말 훌륭한 천재라고 생각한다. 그는 또 이렇게 덧붙이더구나.

'이리 오시오. 당신에게 보여줄 게 있소.'

나는 그와 함께 성당 안으로 들어갔단다. 외부만큼이나 내부도 훌륭한 곳이었지. 저 하늘나라에서도 순례자나 진리를 탐구하는 사람들이 많았단다. 사실 얼마 전부터 깨닫게 된 사실인데, 이 세상은 마치 하나의 거대한 사원과도 같더구나.

젊은 시절의 다빈치는 나를 커다란 강당으로 데려가더구나. 그 안에는 나무로 된 커다란 조각상이 있었는데, '비트루비안 맨'을 표현한 어떤 기계의 한 종류 같았지. 팔과 다리는 네 개씩 있었단다. 나는 그것을 본 순간 다빈치가 저곳에 가서도 예전과 마찬가지로 계속 훌륭한 기계를 제작하고 있었음을 깨달았지. 그가 그림도 계속 그렸는지는 잘 모르겠는데, 차마 그것까지 물어볼 용기는 안 나더구나.

다빈치는 내게 '잘 보라'고 말한 후 왼손으로 손짓을 했다. 저 하늘에서도 그는 왼손잡이더구나. 내가 생각했던 대로, '비트루비안 맨' 뒤에는 또 다른 사람이 있다는 걸 알게 됐다. 완벽하게 동일한 인물이지만, 완벽하게 감추어진 또 다른 인물이지. 오직 팔과 다리만 겉으로 표현된 일종의 쌍둥이인 셈이야. 하지만 감쪽같이 숨겨져 있어서 나머지는 밖으로 드러나질 않는단다. 믿기지 않겠지만 믿어야 해. 사실 그 어떤 전문가도 이 같은 생각을 해본 적이 없었어. 이 위대한 예술가의 관습 때문에 함부로 발설하지 못했겠지. 두 번째 비트루비안 맨은 이를 가리고 있던 첫 번째 비트루비안 맨에게서 자유롭게 벗어났단다. 두 번째 비트루비안 맨은 정말로 첫 번째 비트루비안 맨과 똑같이 생긴 쌍둥이더구나. 키뿐만 아니라 얼굴도 똑같았어. 다만 그에게서는 첫 번째 비트루비안 맨에게 있던 수많은 주름이 없었고, 그보다 훨씬 더 젊은 모습이었지. 갓 스무 살쯤 되어 보였어. 그때 다빈치가 내게 이렇게 말했지.

'성공하고, 승리하고, 수백만 달러를 벌어들이고…… 이건 아무 것도 아니오. 야망도, 부와 영광에 대한 목마름도, 이는 우리 스스로의 문제점을 바로잡으며 보다 완벽한 존재가 되도록 도움을 주는 수단일 뿐이지. 우리가 경험한 모든 실패와 패배, 이뤄지지 못한 꿈들은 신께서 우리에게 보내주신 축복과도 같은 거요. 그 목적은 단 하나, 우리가 그 같은 진리를 깨달을 수 있도록 하는 거라오. 과거의 빚과 자신의 결함과 약점, 스스로의 단점과 더불어 실제 삶에 뛰어드는 인간은 첫 번째 비트루비안 맨과 같소. 그는 주름이 지고 늙은 얼굴을 하고 있다오. 연금술사들이 말하는 '구 인간'이지. 이어 그 자신의 위대함을 발견하고, 스스로의 완벽하지 못한 모습을 모두 떨쳐버린 인간, 빛을 모두 털어버린 인간은 두 번째 비트루비안 맨이고. 즉 연금술사들이 말하는 '신 인간', 즉 새로 다시 태어난 인간을 말한다오. 두 번째 비트루비안 맨은 자신의 젊음을 되찾고, 다시 어린아이가 되었소. 비밀은 바로 이거요. 다른 건 없어. 그러니 당신 아들에게 가서 다시 어린아이가 되라고 전해주시오'라고 말이야.

아버지가 그렇게 다빈치에 대해 말하는 동안 그들은 어느새 시골집에 도착했다. 정말 매력적인 집이었다. 샤를은 최근 몇 년간 이곳에 발을 들이지 않았다. 칠팔 년 만에 오는 것 같았다. 어쩌면 더 오래됐을 수도 있다. 마지막으로 이곳에 온 게 언제였는지도 잘 기억이 나지 않았다. 그건 샤를이 이 집을 좋아하지 않아서가 아니었다. 오히려 그 반대였다. 어린 시절 샤를은 여름방학마다 매번 이곳에서 휴가를 보냈고, 주말마다 이곳을 찾았다. 그래서 그는 이 집에 대한 남다른 추억을 간직하고 있었다. 하지만 아버지의 뒤를 따르지 않겠다고 결심한 후, 그는 차츰 형과 누나와의 왕래를 끊었고, 크리스마스나 부모님 생일 등 꼭 모여야 하는 자리가 아니면 얼

굴을 비추지 않았다. 가족들이라면 지긋지긋하다고 한 앙드
레 지드의 독설 수준까지는 아니지만, 크게 상황이 다른 것
도 아니었다.

피에르는 그저 집 주위를 맴돌기만 할 뿐 아무 말도 하지
않았다. 어쩌면 아무런 걱정 없이 마법과도 같은 시간을 보
낸 그 시절을 떠올리고 있는지도 몰랐다. 피에르 자신도 젊었
고, 아이들도 어렸으며, 아내도 아직 살아있던 그 시절에 대
해……. 그곳엔 아직 아내의 흔적이 많이 남아 있었다. 가구나
장식물, 전구에서 젖병까지 자기 손으로 직접 골랐던 게 바로
피에르의 아내였다. 아내의 넋은 집안 곳곳에 깃들어 있었고,
집안 물건에도 아내의 흔적이 느껴졌다. 오래된 그랜드 피아
노도 그 중 하나였다. 매일 저녁, 피에르의 아내는 그곳에 앉
아 피아노를 연주했다. 피에르는 음악광이었고, 아내는 훌륭
한 음악가였다. 아내는 뛰어난 기교와 풍부한 감성으로 드뷔
시를 연주했다. 그 모습을 보노라면 마치 드뷔시가 먼 조상이
라도 되는 듯했다. 그 외에도 라벨, 쇼팽, 슈베르트 그리고 남
편이 열광하는 베토벤의 곡도 훌륭히 연주했다.

샤를은 벅찬 감동 속에 말없이 아버지를 지켜봤다. 아버지

는 거실에서 꽤 오랜 시간을 지체했다. 거실의 커다란 창문은 호수 쪽을 향해 나 있었다. 침묵을 깨고 피에르가 말했다.

"정원으로 가보자꾸나."

정원은 무척 아름다웠다. 피에르는 정원의 자갈길을 지나 호숫가로 갔다. 그는 오랫동안 잔잔한 수면 위를 물끄러미 바라봤다. 그동안 샤를은 정원을 거닐면서 어린 시절의 추억을 떠올렸다.

샤를은 갑자기 눈살을 찌푸렸다. 무언가 다르게 느껴졌다. 정확히 뭐라고 말하기는 힘들지만, 정원에는 그가 알아보지 못하는 무언가 있었다. 샤를은 아버지가 자신을 왜 이곳으로 데려왔는지 이제야 알 것 같았다.

단순히 옛 시절에 대한 향수 때문이 아니었다. 어린 시절의 추억이 깃들어있는 이 시골집에 자신을 데려온 이유가 있었다. 그래서 아버지는 다시 어린 아이가 되어야 하는 중요성을, 레오나르도 다빈치와의 신기한 만남에 대해 이야기했던 것이다.

중요한 결심

샤를과 피에르는 다시 웨스트마운트의 집으로 돌아왔다. 5
천만 달러 수표에 대한 나름의 결정을 내린 샤를은 아버지와
헤어진 후 생트 쥐스틴 병원으로 찾아갔다.

샤를은 용기 있는 행동을 하고 싶었다. 아버지의 철학에 대
한 믿음과 아버지가 믿어준 자신의 위대함과 재능에 근거한
행동이었다. 아버지가 이곳에 있는 동안 아버지와 함께 모든
일을 완수하면, 아버지는 자신을 자랑스러워할 뿐만 아니라
당신의 아들이 좋은 결정을 내린 것에 매우 흡족해할 것이다.

그러나 막상 병원 접수계 앞에 서자, 샤를은 의구심에 사

로잡혔다.

아버지가 말했던 것처럼 자신이 대단한 사람이 아니라면? 훌륭한 소설가가 되지도 못하고, 재산을 모으지도 못한다면? 자신은 완전히 패배자가 되고 말 것이다. 만일 아버지가 자신을 잘못 봤다면 어찌할 것인가.

결국 자신이 철학 교수를 선택한 것은 운명이 그에게 정해둔 직업이기 때문이 아니었을까? 그에게는 훌륭한 소설가로서의 찬란한 미래가 예정된 건 아니지 않을까? 사실 그는 단 한 편의 소설도 탈고한 적이 없었다. 그가 시도했던 서너 편의 소설은 30페이지를 채 넘기지 못했다. 그게 샤를의 절대적 한계이며 현실이었다. 샤를은 간신히 그 정도의 분량을 채울 수 있을 뿐이었다. 그는 책 속의 등장인물과 줄거리, 문체 등 소설에 필요한 요소들에 자신이 없었으며, 자신의 재능에도 확신이 서지 않았다.

병원 접수대 앞에 선 샤를은 주머니 안에 있는 수표를 꺼내 물끄러미 쳐다보았다. 수표는 아직 이서를 하지 않은 상태였다. 샤를은 호흡을 가다듬고 주머니 안에서 펜을 꺼내들었다. 그리고 접수대 위에 수표를 올려놓았다.

5천만 달러는 그의 돈이었다. 샤를에게는 이 돈을 가질 권
리가 있었다. 훔치거나 나쁜 짓을 해서 얻은 돈도 아니지 않
은가.

"뭐 필요하신 거 있으세요?"

병원 접수계원이 물었다.

"방문하고자 하는 아이의 병실 호수를 잊어버리신 건가요?"

"아닙니다……."

샤를은 수표를 주머니 속에 집어넣고 도망치듯 그곳을 빠
져나왔다. 접수계원은 눈살을 찌푸리며 영문을 모르겠다는
듯 어깨를 으쓱거렸다.

샤를이 웨스트마운트의 집에 돌아왔을 때, 아버지가 보이
지 않았다. 샤를은 외젠에게 달려가 물었다.

"아버지는 어디 계시죠?"

“한 시간 전에 떠나셨는데요.”

“떠나요? 어디로요?”

“그건 저도 잘 모르겠어요……. 그게 저…….”

외젠은 왠지 무척 슬프고 당황한 기색이었다. 샤를에게 무언가를 숨기려는 듯했다.

“말해보세요.”

“사장님께서 제게 마지막 작별 인사를 고하셨습니다.”

“아저씨께 작별 인사를 고하셨다고요?”

샤를은 마치 외젠이 무슨 중죄라도 지은 것처럼 성난 목소리로 물었다.

샤를은 충격에 빠졌다. 평생을 그렇게 살아왔듯이, 이번에도 샤를은 아버지에게 무관심했다. 당연히 아버지가 곁에 있으리라 생각했던 것이다. 그는 아버지와의 마지막 순간을 최대한 이용해야 했다. 하지만 이제 아버지를 다시 볼 수 없을 것이다. 저녁 때 성 요셉 성당에서 보기로 한 약속은 이뤄지지 않을 것이다…….

아버지는 처음 만났을 때보다 약해진 상태였다. 전날에도 조금 힘들어했는데 이번에는 그 상태가 더 심각해진 것이다.

더 이상 여기 있을 수 없을 정도로 몸이 약해져서 지상에서의 흥미로운 체류 기간을 연장할 수가 없게 된 것이다. 어머니와의 재회도 빨리 하고 싶기 때문에 돌아가신 게 아닐까.

크게 상심한 샤를은 아버지의 모습을 조금이나마 다시 되찾고 싶은 마음에 아버지의 서재에 들어갔다. 그곳은 아버지가 돌아가신 후로 차마 발길을 할 수 없던 곳이었다.

아버지의 서재에서 무언가를 발견하다

아버지의 서재는 어린 시절 샤를이 꽤 좋아하던 장소였다. 사춘기 때도 샤를은 그곳을 아주 좋아했다.

아버지의 서재에는 늘 근엄하면서도 신비로운 분위기가 감돌았다. 그곳에 들어서면 약간의 두려움과 함께 묘한 기분이 들었다. 친구들과 함께 숨바꼭질을 하고 놀 때면, 그는 가끔 아버지의 서재에 숨기도 했다.

이곳은 아버지가 외출하고 나면 샤를이 즐겨 찾던 은신처였다. 아버지는 집을 떠나 있는 경우가 많았기 때문에 샤를은 아버지의 서재에서 자주 뒹굴 수 있었다. 샤를은 종종 아버지의 의자에 앉아 고개를 뻣뻣이 들고 배를 쑥 내민 채 입술을 앞으로 삐죽 대면서 근엄한 사장인 척하고 놀았다. 실로 왕좌와도 같은 그 자리에서 샤를은 자신이 세상에서 제일 존경하고 사랑하며 더없이 우러러보던 사람을, 그의 이상형이면서 인생 전체를 대신할 수 있는 사람을 흉내 내며 놀곤 했다.

상상의 궁전으로 뒤바뀐 현실적인 공간에서, 샤를은 한 손으로 전화기를 쥔 채 아버지 흉내를 내곤 했다. 아버지의 근엄한 표정으로 한껏 무장한 샤를은 전화를 걸어 지시를 내리는 척했고, 종종 거칠게 수화기를 내려놓았다. 아버지의 그런 모습을 자주 봤기 때문이었다. 샤를은 아버지처럼 멋진 사업가 흉내를 냈다. 하지만 현실에서 그런 일은 일어나지 않았다…….

샤를은 아버지와 등을 지고 철학 쪽으로 전향했다. 때로는 후회도 했다. 사실 그는 철학을 연구한 것이 아니라 철학을 가르쳤다. 물론 이상주의자였던 그는 현실이 이럴 줄 몰랐었다. 학생을 가르치는 일이란 게 늘 즐거움을 주는 건 아니었다. 사람들은 상상을 하기가 힘들겠지만, 이는 한없는 좌절감을 겪게 하는 일이자, 상당히 고역이기도 했다.

뚜렷한 목적이나 방향도 없이 수업을 듣는 학생들도 많고, 수업 내용은 귀담아듣지 않은 채 하품하고 조는 학생들도 태반이었다. 한 해 한 해 시간이 갈수록, 학생들의 나이는 더 어려졌다. 하지만 샤를이 더 젊어질 리는 없었다. 그렇게 세월이 흘러 나이가 들어간다는 사실은 누구에게나 충격이다. 우리도 이제 '늙는' 것이다.

바로 그 순간, 샤를은 아버지와 함께 더 많은 시간을 보낼 수 있었음을 뒤늦게 깨달았다. 삶의 무의미한 일들을 뒤로 하니 아버지의 죽음과 더불어 찾아온 괴로움의 시간이 떠올랐다. 샤를은 아버지와의 만남을 중요하게 여겼지만, 자신의 불찰로 인해 소중한 시간을 놓쳐버렸다. 또한 자신의 인생에서 가장 사랑한 여인인 클라라와의 소중한 시간 역시 놓쳐버리고 말았다.

아버지 서재 벽면에는 커다란 책장이 놓여 있었다. 거기에는 철학책은 물론 소설책, 역사책, 위인전기가 꽂혀 있었다. 피에르는 위인들의 훌륭한 삶을 좋아했다. 그는 늘 삶의 불가사의한 측면에 대해 관심의 끈을 놓지 않았다. 마치 아인슈타인이 그런 것처럼……

벽에는 화려했던 그의 생애를 보여주는 사진들도 있었다. 퀘벡 및 그 외 지역의 사람들과 함께 찍은 사진도 있었고, 업계 사람들, 예술가들, 유명인들과 함께 찍은 사진도 있었다. 물론 매력적인 머리칼을 휘날리는 베토벤의 커다란 초상도 걸려 있었다. 전설적인 추한 외모 속에서도 빛을 발하는 소크라테스의 커다란 초상도 있었다. 서재에는 무척 훌륭한 오디오 시설도 구비되어 있었다.

샤를은 오디오가 있는 곳에 음반 케이스가 열려 있는 걸 보았다. 카라얀이 지휘한 베토벤 교향곡 9번의 음반이었다. 이건 우연 아닌 우연이었다. 샤를은 아버지가 그토록 좋아하던 베토벤의 곡을 들으면서 이 세상을 떠났을 지도 모른다는 생각을 했다. 아버지는 베토벤을 본받으며 평생을 살아왔다. 아버지의 비서에 따르면, 점심을 먹고 서재에 들어간 아버지는 바닥에 쓰러져 있었다고 했다. 아버지는 당신이 무척 좋아한 음악을 들으며 돌아가셨다. 베토벤의 9번 교향곡은 아버지가 저 세계로 들어가는 출입증 같은 것이었으리라…….

여기까지 생각이 미치자, 샤를은 무언가 조금 위안이 되는 걸 느꼈다. 샤를은 위대한 작곡가가 남긴 마지막 교향곡을 튼 뒤, 잠시 공상에 빠졌다. 그러고는 꿈 많던 어린 시절로 돌아가 아버지의 책상에 앉았다. 이 책상은 18세기 프랑스 양식의 오래된 고가구로, 꽤 값이 나가는 집기였다. 자리에 앉은 샤를은 어머니의 아름다운 초상화를 훑어봤다. 어머니가 돌아가신 뒤에도, 아버지는 이를 책상 위에 고이 간직하였다. 처음 심장 발작을 일으킨 후 아버지는 적잖이 놀랐었다. 아마 곧 세상을 떠날 날이 머지않았다는 생각에서였을 수도 있고, 저쪽 세계의 상황을 알게 돼서 그랬을 수도 있다. 그런 상황을 겪고 난 후, 피에르는 자신의 모든 여자 친구들을 돌려보냈다. 그리고 자기만의 특이한 의식에 들어갔다. 바로 아내인 루이즈 드뷔시를 위한 의식이었다. 자신의 과오에 대해, 한 여자의 남편으로서 수없이 저지른 부정한 과거에 대해 뉘우치는 듯 보였다.

하인들은 서재에서 음악을 듣고 있는 피에르의 모습을 자주 목격했다. 특히 그는 바브라 스트라이샌드의 〈메모리즈〉를 많이 들었다.

루이즈 드뷔시 역시 피에르 만큼이나 음악을 사랑했다. 사업을 통해 재산을 모을 생각이 없었다면, 피에르는 아마 교향악단 지휘자가 됐을 지도 모른다. 그는 천성적으로 맨 앞에 서서 남을 이끌고 지휘하는 사람이 되기를 좋아했기 때문이었다.

즐기며 일을 해서 돈을 벌어라.

한없이 파고들어라.

이성적으로 생각하라.

샤를은 아버지가 한평생 사람들 앞에서 지겹도록 설파하던 슬로건을 떠올리며 향수에 잠겼다.

루이즈 드뷔시는 우아하고 늘씬하며 기품이 넘치는 금발의 여인이었다. 하지만 무척 여린 사람이기도 했다. 루이즈 드뷔시에게 피에르는 유일한 존재 이유이자 삶 그 자체였다. 피에르도 이 사실을 알고 있었다. 그래서 그녀의 향수에 잠기고, 그녀에게 죄의식을 느꼈으며, 이토록 놀라운 변신을 한 것이다.

샤를은 아버지가 세상을 떠나기 전에 오래된 앨범을 꺼내 보았다는 걸 뒤늦게 알았다. 가죽으로 된 예쁜 양장 앨범이었다. 샤를은 이 앨범을 보고 싶은 유혹을 참을 수가 없었다. 앨범 속에는 부모님의 아름다운 결혼사진이 들어 있었다. 두 사람 모두 무척이나 젊고 아름다웠으며, 로맨틱한 분위기가 느껴졌고, 앞으로의 꿈과 희망에 가득 차 있는 모습이었다. 이 모든 것이 너무도 아득하게 느껴졌다. 자식들이 어렸을 때의 가족사진도 있었다. 지금은 모두 사라지고 없는 그 옛날의 풋풋한 모습이었다. 휴가나 여행을 갔을 때 사진도 있었다. 앨범 안에는 한 사람의 모든 인생이 한 편의 영화처럼 담겨 있었다. 이 사진들은 참으로 별 것 아닌 듯 보이면서도, 어떻게 보면 이보다 더 대단할 수가 없었다.

샤를은 삶이 참으로 빨리도 지나간다는, 지극히 평범한 생각을 해보았다. 물론 샤를보다 먼저 다른 수많은 사람들이 했을 생각이다. 하지만 다른 사람의 삶이 아닌 그 자신의 삶이라면 왠지 조금 덜 평범하게 느껴지는 법이다. 삶은 너무도 빨리 지나간다. 그리고 추억 외에 아무것도 남지 않는다. 그리고 그 추억이란 것도, 항상 분홍빛인 것만은 아니다.

그의 부모님은 돌아가셨다. 이제 어린 시절의 그런 순수한 즐거움은 결코 없었다. 그의 형과 누나, 샤를은 그들과도 화해를 해야겠다는 생각이 들었다.

어쨌든 지금의 상황은 예전과 조금 달라진 게 문제였다. 이제 형과 누나는 한푼도 없는 자신을 더 싫어할 터였다.

샤를은 앨범을 덮었다. 마치 그의 인생 전체를 덮는 것 같은 느낌이었다. 아버지의 서재 안에서는 웅장한 합창 교향곡이 흐르고 있었다. 순간 샤를의 얼굴에 미소가 번졌다. 나뭇가지로 투명 교향악단을 지휘하던 아버지의 광기 어린 모습이 떠올랐기 때문이었다. 아버지의 뒤를 따르던 꼬마들은 어른들이 자신들처럼 미친 듯이 즐거워하는 것을 보고 무척 신기하고 재미있어 했다. 나이가 많은 어른이었기에 꼬마들은 더욱 신선한 재미를 느꼈을 것이다.

샤를은 서재 안에서 약병을 발견했다. 이걸 왜 진작 보지 못했을까? 샤를은 약병 표면에 적힌 글씨를 읽었다. 이 약은 아버지가 수년 전부터 복용하던 혈압약이었다. 그런데 약병을 뜯은 흔적이 없었다. 샤를은 약병에 적혀 있는 날짜를 살펴봤다. 아버지가 심장 발작으로 쓰러진 다음날 제조된 약이었다.

이것은 곧 아버지가 한 달간 약을 복용하지 않았다는 뜻이었다. 어떻게 당신의 건강에 이처럼 소홀히 할 수가 있는가. 아니, 이게 정말 건강을 소홀히 해서 생긴 일일까? 죽기로 결심한 아버지의 남모르는 속마음은 아니었을까? 혹은 죽기 한 달 전 저쪽 세계를 아버지가 이미 알아서 생긴 일일 수도 있다. 당신이 가야 할 때가 왔다는 확신 때문일 수도 있다.

샤를은 약병을 책상 위에 올려놓았다. 그는 결코 그 답을 알 수가 없을 것이다. 그리고 이에 대해 감히 아버지께 여쭤보지 못할 것이다. 하지만 아버지를 마지막으로 다시 보게 된다면, 저녁 때 니로다와의 신기한 만남이 정말로 일어난다면…….

잠시 지나간 추억에 잠겨 있던 샤를의 눈에 책 한 권에 들어왔다. 아버지의 책상 위에 어지럽게 놓여 있던 책들 가운데 한 권이었다. 샤를은 이 책이 이곳에 있다는 사실에 무척 놀랐다. 그 책은 다름 아닌 피터 우스펜스키의 《위대한 가르침을 찾아서》였다.

샤를은 아버지가 전혀 생각지도 못할 만큼 특이한 사람이라고 생각했다. 이렇게 전문적인 책을 읽는 사업가라니, 이런 생뚱맞은 사람이 또 어디 있는가? 그는 또 한 가지 사실을 깨달았다. 자신은 아버지에 대해 아는 게 정말 없었다는 점이었다. 아버지는 사업가였던 동시에, 이 시대의 로맨티스트였고, 여자 다루는 기술도 남달랐다. 또한 박애심도 넘치는 분이었다. 특히 어렵고 힘들게 살아가는 사람들을 위해서는 발

벗고 자선을 베풀었다.

　무엇보다도 아버지는 진정한 철학자였다. 한 사람의 진정한 철학자……. 이는 아버지를 가장 잘 표현해줄 수 있는 말이었다. 평범함과 진부함이 대세가 된 시대에서 무척 보기 드문 부류의 사람이었다. 아버지는 정말 자유로운 사상가가 아니던가. 사람들의 편견이나 선입관을 비웃고, 자기만의 사고방식을 정립하여 그 자신의 행동 규칙을 정하고, 나름의 철학을 세우는 그런 자유 사상가였다. 그리고 모든 걸 알고 싶어 하고, 경험하고 싶어 하며, 모든 걸 정복하려고 했던 사람이었다. 왜 이런 사실을 진작 알지 못했을까? 진작 이를 알았더라면, 아버지와 얼마나 흥미로운 대화를 나눌 수 있었을까.

　책을 펼쳐 본 샤를은 아버지가 손으로 주석을 달아놓은 416페이지를 주목했다. 그곳에는 아버지가 붉은 색으로 밑줄까지 쳐 두었다. 문득 무언가가 머리를 스쳐갔다. 아버지가 이 책을 남겨 두었다면, 그건 우연이 아닐 것이다…….

　그게 사실이든 아니든 샤를은 그 책을 탐독했다. 마치 그 부분이 아버지에 관한 무언가를 자신에게 알려줄 것만 같았다. 책에서 밑줄을 그어놓는 곳은 대개 감명 깊게 읽은 부분이 아닌가. 그 부분에는 다음과 같은 글이 적혀 있었다.

"객관적 예술과 주관적 예술이 서로 다른 것은 전자의 경우 예술가가 '실제로' 창작을 하며 자신이 의도한 바를 행한다는 점이다. 이때의 예술가는 자신의 작품에 자신이 원하는 느낌과 생각을 집어넣는다. 작품이 관객에게 미치는 영향은 명확하다. 관객들은 저마다 물론 자신의 수준에서 작품을 받아들이되, 작가가 이들에게 전달하고자 했던 것과 동일한 느낌 및 생각을 전해 받는다."

샤를은 이 글을 완전히 이해하지 못했다. 그렇다고 이 글의 의미를 전혀 모른다는 뜻은 아니었다. 일부 학생들의 말마따나 무슨 말인지 모르겠는 '초현실적인' 내용이었다. 하지만 그 다음 단락을 읽으면 좀 더 명확해질 것이다.

붉은 색으로 밑줄이 그어진 곳의 여백에는 마치 조약돌로 가는 길을 표시해 둔 엄지왕자의 경우처럼 같은 색 잉크로 꾹꾹 눌러 찍은 점선이 듬성듬성 이어지며 418페이지로 넘어가고 있었다. 그리고 여기에서도 한 단락이 똑같이 선명한 붉은 색 잉크로 밑줄 표시가 되어있었다.

"음악이라는 한 가지 예시밖에는 못 들 것 같은데, 완전히 객관적인 음악은 내부 음계를 바탕으로 하고 있다.”

　내부 음계라……. 곰곰이 생각에 잠긴 샤를의 이마에는 깊게 주름이 패었다. 이 내용이 무슨 상황을 말하는지 도통 알 수가 없었던 샤를은 호기심에 이끌려 다음 부분을 읽어 내려갔다. 아울러 아버지는 쓸데없는 형이상학적 작품을 단편적으로 받아들이는 사람은 아니라는 확신도 있었다.

　샤를은 곧 문맥의 의미를 파악할 수 있었다. 여기에서 말하는 것은, 사람에게 영향을 줄 수 있는 위대한 음악이 그 사람을 변화시키고 달라지게 만들 수 있다는 점이었다.

　그 외에도 밑줄이 처져 있는 부분을 정신없이 읽었다. 아버지가 마치 자신에게 몇 가지 지표와 어떤 중요한 메시지를 남겨둔 것 같았기 때문이다. 그 부분의 내용은 이랬다. “음악으로 예리코 성채를 함락시킨 이야기는 객관적 음악의 전설이다.” 그리고 조금 더 떨어진 곳에서는 “오르페우스가 가르침을 위해 음악을 사용했다”고 적혀 있었고, 끝으로 마지막 부분에는 이런 내용이 적혀 있었다. “예술은 단순히 하나의 언어가 아니다. 이는 그보다 훨씬 더 큰 무언가다.”

　특히 오르페우스와 관련한 부분의 여백에는 아버지가 써둔

글자가 있었다. 모든 게 석양빛에 더욱 아름답게 빛나듯이 아버지의 글씨 또한 그 죽음으로써 더욱 미화되어 보였는데, 그 글자는 바로 '베토벤 94'였다.

베토벤 94라…… 과연 이게 뭘 의미하는 걸까?

아버지와의 이별

아버지를 빨리 보고 싶은 마음에, 샤를은 약속 시간보다 일찍 성 요셉 성당에 도착했다.

니로다와 아버지는 아직 도착하지 않았다. 샤를은 성당 안의 단출한 의자에 자리를 잡고 앉았다.

샤를은 별의별 생각에 사로잡혔다. 만약 아버지가 오지 않는다면? 아버지가 저 세상으로 영영 떠나서 오늘 이 자리에 오지 않는다면? 아버지가 기력이 쇠해지고 몸도 약해져서 어머니를 만나보고 싶은 향수에 사로잡혀 그렇게 가버린다면? 어찌됐든 이는 아버지의 권한이다.

아버지는 이미 이곳으로 내려와 당신의 마음을 보여주지 않았던가. 전쟁으로 얼룩지고, 빈곤과 기아 문제에 허덕이는 이 험한 세상에 내려온 것은 정말 감사할 일이다. 의심 많은 토마 사도와도 같이 샤를의 눈에는 아직 의심스러운 부분이 있었지만, 어쨌든 아버지는 그에게 위대함으로 찾아가는 길을 보여주었다.

시간은 어느덧 밤 10시 10분……. 여전히 니로다나 아버지의 모습은 나타나지 않았다. 샤를의 얼굴은 점점 시무룩해져 갔으며, 불안감에 안색이 변해갔다. 특별한 이유가 있다 해도 그날 오후에 아버지를 혼자 내버려두지 말았어야 한다는 생각이 가슴을 파고들었다.

특별한 이유라…… 이 대목에서 그는 머리를 쳤다. 샤를은 그 이유를 알아냈다. 아버지가 약속 장소에 나오지 않는 진짜 이유를 알아낸 것이다. 온몸이 빛으로 이루어진 아버지는 무엇이든 볼 수 있으며, 그의 깊은 속마음까지도 꿰뚫어볼 수 있었다. 아버지는 오늘 오후 병원에서 어떤 일이 있었는지 알고 있었고, 그가 수표 이서와 기부를 거부한 것에 대해서도 알고 있었다. 그런 아들의 모습에 실망해 저 하늘로 영영 돌아간 것이다. 두 번이나 실패한 아들…… 이제 더는 실패할 기회도 없는 아들…… 영원히 돌이킬 수 없는 실패의 길을 가게 된 아들…… 그런 아들에게 실망한 나머지 결국 저 하늘로…….

그 순간 샤를은 지금껏 한번도 느껴보지 못했던 외로움을 경험했다.

샤를은 자리에서 일어났다. 그는 집으로 돌아갈 생각이었다. 완벽하게 고독한 그만의 공간, 초라하고 보잘 것 없는 삶의 공간, 아버지도 클라라도 없는 그 공간으로……. 그러고 보니 그는 두 번이나 버려진 처량한 신세가 되지 않았는가.

자리에서 일어난 샤를은 봉헌실을 지나갔다. 봉헌실은 소중한 사람의 치유를 바라는 기도에서 상처 받은 영혼의 안식을 위한 기도에 이르기까지, 온갖 기도들을 위한 등잔이 있는 곳이었다. 벽에는 연령대별로 다양한 사이즈의 목발들이 걸려 있었다. 브라더 앤드류의 기적으로 치유된 환자들의 목발이었다. 봉헌실 앞에 도착하자 성당 문이 천천히 열렸다. 샤를은 거지 니로다가 도착한 것이라고 생각했다.

'우주의 서열상으로 봤을 때, 그의 나이가 엄청나게 많아 우주의 특혜를 받을 수 있다고 했던가…….'

그곳에는 많은 사람들이 있었다. 적어도 스무 명쯤은 되어 보였다. 샤를은 이 사람들이 어른이 아닌 어린아이라는 사실을 확인했다. 이 아이들은 맑고 순수한 목소리로 아름다운 화음을 만들어내며 베토벤 교향곡 9번 4악장 '환희의 송가'를 부르고 있었다. 샤를은 아름다운 노래에 한 번 감동을 받았고, 어린이 합창단의 성가에 또 한 번 감동을 받았으며, 아이들 목소리의 순수함과 섬세함에 또 다시 감동을 느꼈다.

기쁜 마음으로 '환희의 송가'를 부르면서 몇몇 아이들은 이상한 놀이를 하고 있었다. 사실 그 아이들 중 몇몇은 작은 손을 가지고 마법사 같은 손놀림으로 어린이용 목발을 해체했다. 한때 그 아이들이 짚고 다녔을 목발이었다. 샤를은 이를 보면서 문득 이런 생각이 들었다. 그곳에는 니로다가 지상으로 데려온 아이들도 있었다. 며칠간, 혹은 몇 시간이나마 이곳에 머물 수 있도록 해준 것만으로도 그 아이의 부모는 충분히 감사하고도 남을 것이다. 암이나 다른 갑작스런 삶의 불행으로 느닷없이 자식을 떠나보낸 부모의 상처를, 잠시나마 보는 아이들의 얼굴 이외에 그 무엇으로 위로할 수 있겠는가……

당혹스럽고 감격스러운 마음으로 아이들이 있는 곳으로 다가가던 샤를은 이 아이들이 보통 아이들이 아니라는 걸 깨달았다. 아이들은 모두 망자의 신분이었다. 이 세상 사람이 아니었던 것이다. 아이들은 광채로 빛나는 혼령의 몸을 하고 있었다. 그의 아버지와 똑같이 말이다.

그때 한쪽 끝에서 한 남자가 들어왔다. 어둠 속에서도 샤를은 그게 누구인지 금방 알아보았다. 바로 니로다였다. 아이들은 니로다가 모습을 드러내자마자 노래를 멈추고 하던 놀이를 그만두었다. 그러고는 서둘러 수상한 거지 니로다의 곁으로 앞다투어 달려갔다.

아이들이 가고 난 자리에는 대여섯 개의 목발이 널브러져 있었다. 목발의 존재는 마치 피에르의 추한 외모와도 비슷한 느낌이었다. 우리가 지니고 있는 장애와도 같은 것이었다. 아이들은 그렇게 목발을 그 자리에 남겨둔 채 홀가분한 마음으로 떠나갔다. 아이들이 남기고 간 것은 이것만이 아니었다. 아이들은 함께 놀던 놀이 상대도 남겨두고 떠났다. 아이들이 있던 무리 가운데서 유일하게 혼자 어른이던 그 사람이 환하게 그 모습을 드러냈다. 샤를은 그가 누구인지 어렵지 않게 알아볼 수 있었다. 그는 바로 피에르였다. 아버지는 몇 시간 전보다 더 멋있는 모습이었고, 그때보다 더 환한 광채로 빛나고 있었다.

샤를은 아버지에게 달려가 그를 꽉 껴안았다. 아버지가 살아 계실 때는 그렇게 아버지를 안아본 적이 별로 없었다.

"다시는 안 오시는 줄 알았어요!"

샤를은 아버지에게 속마음을 털어놓았다. 두 사람은 오랜 시간 함께 손을 붙잡고 서로의 얼굴을 쳐다보았다. 둘은 세상에 둘도 없는 친구처럼 환한 미소를 지어보였다. 오랜 기간 멀리 떨어져 지낸 어린 시절 친구를 되찾았을 때의 벤허가 이와 비슷하지 않았을까?

그때 깔깔 웃고 떠들고 장난치는 아이들에 둘러싸인 니로다가 말했다.

"거기 둘, 늦었어요……."

니로다는 손으로 시계를 툭툭 치는 시늉을 했다. 그는 시계를 차고 있는 척했지만, 사실 그에게 시계는 몇 세기 전부터 이미 필요 없는 물건이었다. 레니에 부자가 급히 그 앞으로 달려왔다.

"어디 있었어요?"

니로다가 물었다.

"저는 10시 15분 전부터 와 있었어요."

"내가 돔 지붕이라고 하지 않았나요!"

니로다는 나름 친절하게 잘라 말했다.

샤를은 자신의 실수를 깨달았다. 샤를은 맨 처음 만났던 성
당에서 니로다와 아버지를 기다리고 있었던 것이다. 거긴 노
트르담 사제단의 소박한 문지기 브라더 앤드류가 성 요셉에
게 처음으로 예배를 드리기 시작한 곳이었다. 반면 피에르는
아무런 설명도 없었고, 아무도 그에게 이유를 묻지 않았다. 니
로다가 명령했다.

"날 따라 오세요. 시간이 없어요."

그는 두 부자를 대성당으로 데려갔다. 아이들은 두 명씩 짝
을 맞춰 손을 잡고 따라갔다. 아이들은 노래를 부르기 시작했
는데, 이번에는 구노의 '아베 마리아'를 불렀다. 이는 일찍이
세상을 떠난 어머니를 만나러 갔기 때문에 부르는 노래일까,
아니면 이 세상 모든 아이들의 어머니인 마리아를 위해 부르
는 것일까? 알 수 없는 일이었다. 샤를과 그의 아버지는 이 신
기한 행렬의 마무리를 장식했다. 커다란 돔 천장 아래에서, 모

두 빠른 걸음으로 지나갔다. 샤를의 입장에선 저들의 속도가 엄청나게 빠르게 느껴졌다.

우선 아이들이 먼저 떠나기로 했다. 아이들은 대부분 둘씩 짝을 지어 서로 손을 잡고 있었다. 조금 전 행렬을 할 때와 비슷한 모습이었다. 형제자매든 혹은 오래된 친구 사이든 모두들 그렇게 둘씩 짝을 지어 서 있었고, 니로다는 이들에게 다가가 아이들의 미간 사이를 손으로 짚은 뒤 말했다.

"날 보거라. 그리고 이 빛을 기억하라. 이 빛을 기억하라!"

니로다는 아이들의 뺨을 살짝 치며 "잘 가거라!"라고 인사를 건넸다. 마치 어린 천사처럼 공중으로 부양한 아이들은 돔 천장으로 빨려 들어가는 듯 이내 모습을 감추었다. 마지막으로 피에르의 차례였다.

샤를은 아버지와의 이별이 두려웠다. 정말로 두려웠다. 하지만 그게 삶이지 않던가. 이제 그에게 주어진 사흘간의 시간이 다 되었다.

지난 사흘간, 샤를에게 많은 이야기를 해주었던 피에르는 이 순간만큼은 짤막하게 말했다.

"내가 너에게 말했던 것을 잘 기억하거라. 네가 얼마나 대단한지 잊지 말고, 네 능력을 낭비하지 말거라. 이게 바로 네가 너에게 물려주는 유산이다. 레오나르도 다빈치의 마지막 충고를 잊지 않도록 하렴."

"만일 제가…… 길을 찾지 못하면요?"

"네 할머니가 네가 가야 할 길을 보여주실 거야."

"그건 말이 안 돼요. 할머니는 알츠하이머병에 걸리셨다고요."

"그게 바로 증거다. 네가 어릴 적 놀았던 정원에 할머니와 함께 가 보거라. 나는 이제 떠나야 할 시간이란다."

피에르는 니로다 쪽을 돌아보며 이제 떠날 준비가 되었다는 신호를 보냈다. 니로다는 피에르가 어른이긴 하였으나 어린 아이들을 다룰 때와 마찬가지 방식으로 그를 다뤘다. 하지만 피에르에게만은 조금 다른 방식이었다. 피에르의 정수리 위에 왼쪽 주먹을 올려놓고는 다른 쪽 손도 주먹을 쥐어서 이 왼쪽 주먹을 쳤다. 니로다는 이렇게 말했다.

"당신은 이제 떠날 준비가 되었소."

피에르는 정말로 떠날 준비가 되었다. 하지만 샤를은 아니었다. 곧 피에르의 몸집이 계속 작아지기 시작하더니, 일곱 살의 어린 아이 크기에서 잠시 멈추었다. 그는 잠시 묘한 웃음을 짓고는 니로다가 방금 전 두드렸던 그곳에 오른손 검지를 갖다놓았다.

"사랑한다, 아들아."

"저도 아버지를 사랑해요."

"그럼, 행운을 빈다."

피에르의 몸은 서서히 공중 위로 떠오르기 시작했다. 경이로운 아이의 모습이 된 그는 앞서 먼저 간 아이들처럼 돔 천장으로 사라졌다.

샤를은 생각했다.

'이제 모든 게 다 끝났어. 다 끝났다고. 이제 다시는 아버지를 볼 수 없을 거야.'

샤를은 니로다를 돌아봤다. 이제 성당에 남아 있는 사람은 니로다와 샤를, 둘 뿐이었다.

"실은…… 당신이 조금 원망스러워요."

샤를은 속마음을 털어놓았다.

"날 원망한다구요? 하지만 당신이 내게 부탁한 소원을 들 어드렸잖아요?"

샤를은 그의 말을 인정하며 대답했다.

"그건 사실이에요. 하지만 이제 저는 아버지가 전보다 더 그리워지게 됐어요. 사실 사흘 전까지 저는 아버지에 대해 아 는 게 없었어요. 그저 제 아버지일 뿐이었고, 그 깊은 속마음 까지는 모르는 사람이었죠. 하지만 이제 저는 제 아버지가 어 떤 사람인지 알게 됐죠. 아버지께서 얼마나 깊고 폭넓은 정신 의 소유자인지도 알게 됐고, 아버지의 광기 어린 모습에 대해 서도 알게 됐어요. 아버지는 이제 제 최고의 친구가 됐어요. 그런데 저는 그런 분을 잃어버렸어요……."

샤를은 고개를 푹 숙였다. 그는 아버지와의 이별의 아픔을 참을 수가 없었다. 니로다는 말이 없었다. 그는 사흘 전 빈소 에서 사용했던 구슬을 다시 주머니에서 꺼냈다.

"당신에게 선물을 하나 더 주겠소."

"선물을 하나 더 주신다고요?"

샤를은 니로다가 아버지를 또 다시 되살아나게 하려는 모 양이라고 생각했다.

"당신 아버지께서는 살아생전 생판 모르는 사람들에게도 선처를 베풀어서 저 하늘에 있는 그의 가방 안에는 아직 뭔가 남아 있기 때문이오."

"아……."

니로다는 유리구슬 위로 몸을 숙여 그 안을 들여다보았다. 구슬 안이 다시 움직이기 시작했다. 구슬 안은 처음 봤을 때처럼 신비로운 연기가 일어나기 시작했다. 니로다 앞으로 다가간 샤를은 구슬 안에서 새하얗고 커다란 탁자를 보았다. 탁자 중앙에는 하얀 원반 같은 게 놓여 있었다. 그 가운데는 분홍색 대리석 기둥이 솟아 있었는데, 그 위쪽에 금으로 된 아름다운 손목시계가 걸려 있었다. 샤를은 실망감에 젖어들었다. 그는 아버지의 모습을 다시 보게 될 것으로 기대했던 것이다.

구슬 안에는 여러 명의 남자들이 보였다. 이들은 모두 열 명쯤이었는데, 벌거벗은 아이가 이들이 모여 있는 위로 솟아올랐다. 아이는 두 살 정도 되어 보였다. 머리는 곱실거리는 금발로, 무척 귀여운 아이였다. 두 뺨은 포동포동했고, 허벅지도 통통했다. 남자들은 시계를 뺀 뒤, 이를 다른 두 기둥 쪽으로 집어던졌다.

이게 무슨 상황인지 알 수 없던 샤를은 눈썹을 씰룩거렸다. 도대체 이게 무엇을 의미한단 말인가? 니로다가 말했다.

"3년 후 같은 날, 당신은 집에서 잔치를 벌일 일이 생길 겁니다. 그 잔칫날에 당신은 열두 명을 초대하게 될 거예요. 하지만 그 중 한 사람은 시계가 없을 겁니다. 하얀 식탁보가 깔린 커다란 테이블 가운데에는 케이크 하나와 촛대 두 개가 있을 텐데, 다른 열한 명의 사람들에게 그 사람들의 시계를 빼서 가운데에 올려놓아달라고 부탁하세요. 그리고 이 시계들이 모인 한가운데 당신 아버지께서 유산으로 물려주신 시계를 올려놓으세요."

니로다는 더 이상 말이 없었다. 샤를은 고개를 끄덕였다. 그러고는 곧 놀라운 사실을 깨달았다.

'니로다는 그 일까지 알고 있었어. 아버지께서 내게 주신 시계까지 말이야! 그것을 어떻게 알았을까?'

샤를은 니로다에게 자세히 캐묻고 싶었다. 이 모든 상황이 조금 이상하기도 했고 약간 알쏭달쏭하기도 했기 때문이었다. 그러나 니로다는 냉담했다.

"뭘 그렇게 궁금해 하는 거죠? 내 말을 믿을 수 없는 건가요?"

샤를은 고개를 숙였다. 마치 잘못한 만큼의 벌을 받고 있는 듯했다. 니로다의 그 같은 경고에도 불구하고, 샤를은 사흘 전 빈소에서 처음 만난 이후 줄곧 궁금했던 질문을 과감히 던졌다.

"당신은 대체 누굽니까?"

니로다는 샤를이 기대했던 것과 전혀 다른 대답을 했다. 현명한 자들이란 대개 그런 법이다. 현명한 자들이 우리가 기대했던 답을 내놓는다면, 그 사람은 진정 현명한 자가 아니다. 아니면 우리가 저들과 비슷한 사람일 수도 있다.

"사람의 정신 상태에는 여러 가지가 있습니다. 이 세상에 존재하는 사람들의 수만큼이나 다양하지요. 하지만 그 가운데 가장 대표적인 네 가지만 말씀드리겠습니다. 그게 앞으로 삶의 방향을 잡는 데 도움이 될 겁니다. 먼저 첫 번째는 멍한 상태입니다. 당신 아버님 말씀대로, 자기 자신이 살아 있다는 사실을 자각하지 못하는 사람들이 많지요. 일종의 자고 있는 상태이기 때문입니다. 자기도 모르게 스스로의 능력을 외면해버립니다(샤를은 속으로 '이 사람도 이걸 알고 있구나'라고 생각했다). 그 다음은 산만한 상태인데, 이 상태에서는 정신이 한 자리에 고정되어 있으나 별로 오래 지속되지 못합니다. 그리고 이런 사람들의 삶은 마치 하나의 나뭇가지에서 다른 나뭇가지로 힘겹게 움직이는 한 마리 연약한 새와 같은 형태지요. 그렇게 무한 궤도를 돌다가 결국엔 지쳐버리고 불안에 떨기 마련입니다. 자신이 어디로 가야할지, 또 자신은 어디에서 온 것인지 결코 알 수 없기 때문이죠. 이는 지금 시대를 살아가는 사람들 대부분의 정신 상태라고 보시면 됩니다.

그 다음은 집중 상태인데, 이런 상태에서는 하나의 문제에 대해 오랜 기간 정신을 쏟는 게 가능합니다. 이 정신 상태는 자신이 선택한 분야에서 상당한 성공을 거두고 엄청난 부를 모을 수 있습니다. 특히 고요와 환희를 얻을 수 있지요. 마지막은 모든 근심과 걱정, 모든 생각의 흔들림이 없어지는 상태입니다. 그렇게 되면 어른의 정신 상태가 어린아이의 정신 상태 같이 되고, 쉽사리 성공을 거둘 수 있지요. 그가 손을 대는 모든 게 황금으로 변한다고 보시면 됩니다. 이런 정신 상태의 사람들은 다른 사람들이 천천히 여유를 갖고 해도 못할 일을 무척 빠른 시간 안에 해낼 수 있습니다. 천재라는 표시지요. 또한 이런 사람들은 걸작을 만들어내기도 합니다. 과거에 어떻게 지내왔고 어느 정도로 순수하느냐에 따라 더러는 우리가 '기적'이라고 부르는 걸 이뤄내기도 하지요. 항상 사랑하는 마음을 간직하며 평온과 즐거움 속에서 살기 때문입니다. 정신이 최종적으로 완성된 상태인 셈이죠. 전문 용어로는 '니루다'라고 합니다. 이와 비슷한 제 이름도 거기서 나온 거죠. 드넓은 정원에서 마주치는 사람들을 위해 조금이나마 보여드리는 제 정신 상태라고 할 수 있습니다. 사실 저는 신의 정원사입니다. 그게 제 직업이지요. 저마다의 의식 상태에는 이렇듯 하나의 정신 상태가 필요합니다."

니로다는 잠시 이야기를 멈췄다가 다시 덧붙였다.

"만일 당신이 이 네 번째의 상태에 도달하면, 당신은 나나 당신 아버지처럼 될 수 있습니다. 어쩌면 그보다 더 나은 상태에 이를지도 모르죠. 그리고 아버지의 빈자리에서 느껴지는 슬픔도 치유할 수 있습니다. 당신이 꿈꾸는 훌륭한 소설가가 될 수도 있어요. 스스로의 능력이 부족하지 않을까 하는 두려운 마음을 떨칠 수 있으니까요. 당신이 그러한 상태에 이르면, 당신은 그 누구라도 될 수 있으며, 모든 걸 이해할 수 있고, 당신의 마음은 우주처럼 드넓어질 겁니다. 더 이상 외로움도 느끼지 않을 수 있습니다. 사실 그곳에서는 타인이라는 개념이 없으니까요.

그 같은 상태가 되면 당신은 스스로 원하는 걸 하게 되고, 이는 곧 신이 원하는 일이 될 겁니다. 모든 건 신의 의지로 생기니까요. 하지만 시간을 낭비하지 마십시오. 가방만 잔뜩 싸놓고 여행을 하기도 전에 세상을 떠나는 사람처럼 쓸데없는 일을 하다 길을 돌아가며 헤매지 마십시오. 저들은 거창한 계획만 잔뜩 세워놓고 정작 이를 실행하기도 전에 저 세상으로 떠나고 맙니다. 그 계획이란 다름 아닌 자기 자신에 대해 알고 행복해지는 계획이죠. 부디 신의 은총이 함께하길 바랍니다.”

이 말을 듣고 난 샤를은 또 다시 놀랐다.

‘이 사람은 내 꿈이 소설가라는 것을 알고 있잖아?’

샤를은 그에게 질문을 더 하고 싶었으나, 그는 이미 눈에서 점점 멀어져가고 있었다. 니로다는 마지막 작별 인사를 고했고, 샤를은 더 이상 그를 잡을 수가 없었다. 이미 그는 샤를을 위해 상당히 많은 걸 해주지 않았던가?

흔히들 불행은 혼자서 찾아오지 않는다고 이야기한다. 사실 이는 인생을 그렇게 분홍빛으로만 보지 않는 사람들이 내

뱉는 말이다. 이 사람들은 행복해질 기회, 부자가 될 기회를
보지 못한다. 하루에 세 번씩이나 자기 눈앞에서 지나가는 그
기회를 말이다.

아마 샤를의 생각도 늘 그랬던 것 같다. 불행이 겹쳐 온다고
생각했던 것이다. 적어도 최근 며칠부터는 그랬다. 하지만 그
의 집에는 놀라운 소식이 그를 기다리고 있었다.

클라라의 고백

그것은 바로 클라라였다. 클라라가 돌아온 것이다. 그녀의 모습은 마치 이 세상 사람이 아닌 것처럼 아름다웠다. 그녀는 왜 돌아왔을까? 샤를은 갑작스런 그녀의 등장에 의구심을 품었다.

클라라는 거실 소파에 앉아 깊은 생각에 빠져 있었다. 마치 꿈을 꾸고 있는 듯한 모습이었다. 그녀는 어떤 꿈을 꾸고 있는 걸까? 자신의 꿈? 아니면 샤를과 함께 두 사람으로서의 꿈? 샤를은 그녀에게 다갔다.

"당신……."

샤를은 하마터면 '당신, 뭐 놓고 간 거 있어?'라고 물을 뻔했다. 하지만 그건 너무 비관적인 발언이었다.

"샤를, 얼굴이 창백해보여요. 괜찮아요?"

"아버지가 돌아가셨어. 앞으로 다시는 아버지를 못 뵐 거야……."

클라라는 자리에서 일어나 그를 안아주었다. 이런 그녀의 행동은 과거 함께 살았던 사람으로서 동정과 연민의 행동일까?

"클라라, 당신은 정말 착한 여자야. 이렇게 힘든 상황에서 당신이 날 위로해준 것을 난 평생 잊지 못할 거야."

"샤를, 내 말 잘 들어요. 내가 다시 돌아온 것은 당신이 장례식에서 했던 말, 만일 그 말이 진심이라면 그에 대해 괜찮다는 말을 들려주려 온 거예요. 하지만 당장은 아니에요. 그러니까 내 말은 오늘 밤 당장은 아니라는 거죠. 내일도 물론 아니고……. 하지만 6개월 후까지는 아니에요."

"클라라, 그게 무슨 소린지……."

"우리 결혼 문제 말이에요."

"내 프러포즈를 받아들인 거야? 정말이야?"

"그래요. 하지만 난 아이를 갖고 싶어요. 그건 10년 후가 아니라……."

"그거야 당신이 원한다면 오늘 밤이라도 할 수 있지."

"나는 정말 아이가 갖고 싶어요……."

샤를은 젊은 신부를 들어 올리듯이 두 팔로 클라라를 들어 올렸다. 그리고 그녀를 침실로 안고 가서 침대 위에 내려놓았다. 클라라는 빠르게 옷을 벗었고, 샤를 역시 그에 못지않은 속도로 옷을 벗었다.

"당신에게 보여줄 게 하나 있어."

샤를이 말했다.

"얼른 보여줘요!"

클라라가 애교를 떨며 말했다.

"그게 아니라……."

샤를은 재킷 주머니에서 5천만 달러 수표가 들어있는 봉투를 꺼내 클라라에게 내밀었다. 클라라는 검은색 브래지어와 그에 잘 어울리는 팬티만을 입은 채 봉투를 받아들었다. 샤를이 건네 준 봉투를 열어 본 클라라는 놀라움에 소리를 질렀다.

"세상에, 5백만 달러예요!"

"5백만 달러가 아냐. 잘 읽어봐. 0을 하나 덜 읽었어. 5천만 달러 수표야."

"5천만 달러요……?"

클라라는 다시 수표를 바라봤다. 굳이 숫자로 적혀있는 금액에서 0의 개수를 다시 확인할 필요는 없었다. 수표의 총액이 글자로도 쓰여 있었기 때문이다. 숫자와 달리 글자는 잘못 볼 염려가 없다. 샤를의 말은 거짓이 아니었다. 클라라는 두 눈을 크게 떴다. 도무지 믿어지지가 않았다. 샤를의 아버지는 정말로 부자가 아닌가! 그의 아버지는 자신이 생각했던 것보다 훨씬 돈이 많은 사람이었다. 샤를의 아버지는 이렇게 엄청난 금액의 수표를 서명할 수 있을 정도로 엄청난 부자였다. 아직도 충격에서 헤어나지 못한 클라라가 물었다.

"당신 아버지는 당신한테 유산을 물려주지 않은 걸로 아는데요."

"나도 그런 줄 알았어. 하지만 아버지가 얼마나 사람을 잘 속이는 분인지 알잖아. 아버지는 나를 깜짝 놀라게 해줄 일을 따로 준비해두셨던 거지. 지난번에 우리가 함께 은행에 갔을 때 있잖아. 그때 우리가 은행에 갔던 것은 이 수표 때문이었어."

"그 말은 곧 우리가 부자라는 뜻이네요. 그것도 아주 엄청 난······!"

클라라는 수표를 팔랑팔랑 흔들면서 말했다.

"정말 흥분되는데요? 더 이상 못 참겠어요. 샤를, 우리 어서 사랑을 나눠요!"

샤를은 그런 클라라의 흥분 상태를 공유할 수 있는 상태가 아니었다.

"별로 마음에 들어 하지 않는 분위기네요······. 무슨 일이에요?"

"아버지께서 이 수표를 주긴 했는데, 난 이 수표를 은행에 예치시킬 수 있어. 그런데 이건 아버지가 내게 내린 일종의 시험 같은 거야."

"시험이요?"

"응."

샤를은 이 수표에 담겨진 이야기를 클라라에게 차근차근 말해주었다. 클라라는 처음엔 놀라움이 없지 않았지만, 실망하는 기색이나 역정을 내진 않았다. 심지어 그런 아버지의 뜻에 반박하지도 않았다. 샤를은 모든 설명을 마치고 클라라의 판결을 기다렸다.

"나는 어떻게 하면 좋을까?"

샤를이 물었다.

"당신이 정말로 하고 싶은 건 뭔데요?"

샤를은 클라라의 지극히 현명하고 사랑스러운 질문에 무척 놀랐다.

"나는 말이야, 이 돈을 전부 기부하는 것에 당신이 반대하지 않는다면…… 그리고 남은 시간 동안 그 돈이 없다고 날 원망하지만 않는다면…… 당신이 빈털터리 남편을 곁에 두어도 아무렇지만 않다면……."

"당신 아버지가 옳다면 내 남편은 빈털터리가 되지 않을 거예요. 그리고 당신 아버지가 늘 옳았다는 사실은 당신도 나도 잘 아는 사실이에요. 당신은 훌륭한 소설가가 될 거예요. 앞으로 우리는 부자가 될 거고, 보다 중요한 것은 당신이 원하는 게 바로 글쓰기라는 거죠. 그건 당신의 꿈이에요. 설령 그게 잘 안 되더라도, 그러니까 내 말은…… 아픈 곳을 괜히 후벼 파려고 이런 얘길 하는 게 아니라, 5천만분의 1 정도의 확률로 일이 잘 안 될 경우를 말하는 거예요. 여하튼 일이 잘 안

풀리더라도, 나는 문제가 되는 부분을 해결하려고 할 거예요. 그게 세상의 끝은 아니니까요. 그렇게 하면 당신은 적어도 노력했다는 말은 할 수 있을 거예요.”

“지금 한 말 진심이야?”

“그럼요!”

“나는 마지막으로 아버지를 기쁘게 해드리고 싶어. 적어도 내 인생에 한 번은 아버지를 기쁘게 해드리고 싶은 거야. 지금껏 살아오면서 늘 아버지를 실망시켰거든. 이게 그동안의 내 잘못을 만회할 수 있는 마지막 기회인 것 같아. 그리고……..”

샤를은 말을 채 끝마치기도 전에 눈물을 흘리기 시작했다. 그리고 이어 울먹이는 가운데 이렇게 덧붙였다.

“미안해…… 이렇게 울지 않고서는 아버지에 대한 이야기를 할 수가 없어. 나는 지금도 아버지께서 돌아가셨다는 생각이 들지가 않아. 물론 사람들은 내 말이 틀렸다고 할 거야. 아버지는 이제 이 세상 사람이 아니라고, 이미 돌아가시고 없다고…… 이제 나는 다신 아버지를 볼 수 없을 거라고…….”

클라라는 자리에서 일어나 샤를에게 수표를 내밀었다.

“이 돈, 난치병 아이들에게 기부하기로 해요.”

수표를 받아든 샤를은 이를 방바닥에 집어던졌다. 그 순간이 무척 감격스러웠다. 그리고 속으로 이렇게 생각했다. 세상 그 어떤 여자도 내게 이 같은 사랑의 마음을 보여줄 것 같진 않다고.

'클라라는 있는 그대로의 내 모습을 사랑해주는 여자다. 그녀는 내가 꿈을 이루길 원한다. 그녀는 나를 정말 사랑한다……. 그리고 내 어리석음으로 인해 이렇게 좋은 여자를 잃을 뻔하지 않았던가……. 클라라는 내 운명의 여자다.'

두 사람이 삶을 함께하며 침대를 같이 쓰고, 서로의 열정과 고민을 함께 공유해온 게 벌써 3년 전부터이고, 그동안 수백 번도 더 사랑을 나눴지만, 둘은 그날 밤만큼 이렇게 달콤하면서도 열렬히 관능적으로 사랑을 나눈 적이 없었다. 그날 밤은 두 사람의 인생 최고의 밤이었다.

수수께끼의 실마리가 풀리다

아직 축배를 들기에는 일렀다.

샤를은 몇 년 전부터 소설 쓰는 작업을 차일피일 뒤로 미뤄왔다. 클라라와 환상적인 밤을 보내고 난 뒤 잠에서 깨어난 샤를은 그녀가 자신을 전적으로 지지해주고 있는 상황에서도, 이 5천만 달러를 기부하는 게 선뜻 내키지가 않았다. 그의 삶에서 늘 꼬리 같이 따라다니던 불안감, 스스로의 미래와 그 자신의 가치에 대한 의심과 회의가 더욱 증폭되기 시작했다. 특히 평온한 마음으로 기부를 하려면, 먼저 아버지가 남기고 간 알쏭달쏭한 수수께끼의 열쇠를 찾아야 할 것 같았다. 그 열쇠는 레오나르도 다빈치와의 기이한 만남과도 관련이 있었고, 베토벤과도 연관이 있었다. 베토벤 94. 뭔가 중요한 정보로 보이던 메모. 무엇보다 결정적으로 기술하고 있는 그 단락의 여백에 아버지가 매우 훌륭한 정자체로 적어두셨던 그 메모. 거기에는 분명 베토벤 94라고 적혀 있었다. 이게 대체 뭐란 말인가.

클라라와의 예기치 못한 재회 이후 샤를은 주방에서 모닝커피를 앞에 두고, 그녀에게 질문을 던졌다.《위대한 가르침을 찾아서》에 쓰여 있던 것처럼 베토벤 이름과 함께 94라는 숫자를 적고 클라라의 의견을 물었다.

"클라라, 이걸 보고 무슨 생각이 들어? 아버지가 어떤 책의 여백에 써 두신 건데, 이게 아버지께 뭔가 중요한 의미였던 것 같아서."

클라라는 곰곰이 생각을 하고 있지만, 사실 옷차림이 단출하기 때문에 샤를의 이야기에 집중하기 힘든 상황이었다. 희고 밝은 캐미솔 위로 어깨가 다 드러났고, 캐미솔 안에는 아무 것도 입지 않은 상태였다. 또한 팬티만 입은 게 전부여서, 화두를 던져놓고 딴 생각 하고 있는 샤를을 탓하긴 힘든 상황이었다. 하물며 그녀의 가슴 라인이야 더 말해 무엇하랴…….
어쨌든 그런 클라라 앞에서 샤를의 생각은 완전히 다른 데
가 있었다.

클라라는 잠시 생각한 후 사랑스러운 어깨를 으쓱해보였
다. 어딜 봐도 깊이 생각한 것 같지는 않았다. 하지만 이렇게
짧고 순간적인 단순한 발상은 종종 문제의 해결책을 찾아내
고 중요한 결정을 내리는 최선의 방법이 된다. 클라라는 곧 어
린아이같이 귀여운 목소리로 자신의 생각을 말했다.

"9번 교향곡 4악장을 말하는 게 아닐까? 그게 당신 아버지
가 가장 좋아하던 교향곡 아니었어?"

그녀의 대답은 샤를에게 적잖이 당혹감을 안겨줬다. 샤를
은 미친 사람처럼 자리에서 벌떡 일어났다. 그리고 클라라의
이마에 입맞춤을 한 뒤 소리쳤다.

"사랑해, 클라라! 당신 정말 최고야! 사랑해!"

샤를은 빠르게 침실로 향했다. 샤를 역시 거의 옷을 입고 있
지 않은 상태였기 때문이다. 그의 머릿속에서는 무언가 다급
함이 느껴졌다. 이렇게 다급한 마음에는 성공을 보장해주는
요소들이 가득 들어 있는 듯하다.

"샤를, 당신 어디 가려고 그래요. 오늘 아침은 나와 같이 먹기로 했잖아!"

클라라가 말했다.

"잠깐만!"

샤를은 그렇게 말하면서도 클라라 쪽은 돌아보지도 않았다. 잠깐이라…… 클라라는 샤를의 말을 믿지 않았다. 그와 너무 오랜 시간을 같이 살았던 탓이다. 물론 사랑의 약속은 약속이었다. 더욱이 지난밤 클라라가 해준 게 너무 많아서 잠결에 감사의 표시로 했던 약속이 아닌가. 클라라는 별 수 없다는 듯 다시 어깨를 으쓱해 보이며 체념했다.

샤를은 자신의 이마를 쳤다. 자신은 얼마나 바보 같았던가!

베토벤 94, 그렇다! 베토벤 교향곡 9번 4악장! 전날 봉헌실에서 몸에서 광채가 흐르던 신비로운 아이들이 아버지를 둘러싼 채 해맑게 부르던 노래가 바로 4악장, '환희의 송가'였다.

아이들은 그에게 힌트를 준 것이었다. 삶이란 종종 그런 식이다. 우리 눈앞의 금쟁반 위에 작은 종잇조각들을 모두 얌전히 내려놓는다. 그리고 이를 다시 붙이기만 하면 전체 그림이 보이고, 그렇게 결국 우리의 운명이 보이는 것이다. 정확히 그 이유를 말할 수는 없었지만, 샤를은 무언가 중요한 퍼즐 조각 하나를 맞춘 것 같았다.

샤를은 엘레오노르 할머니를 만나야 할 것 같았다. 아버지가 마지막으로 한 말도 그것이었다. 어느 누구나 마지막에 하는 말은 늘 중요하지 않은가.

옷을 다 입은 샤를은 할머니에게 전화를 걸었다. 몸도 좋지 않고 기억력도 점점 희미해져갔지만, 할머니는 시골집에서 정신이 멀쩡한 시간을 보내고 있었다. 다행히 할머니는 시중을 들어주는 하녀가 있었기 때문에 건강이 호전되고 있었다. 하녀를 부릴 수 있었던 것은 피에르의 관대한 배려 덕분이었다. 할머니에게 아버지는 전혀 배은망덕한 아들이 아니었다. 물론 그런 아들이 될 수도 있었다. 애초부터 발을 잘못 들여놓아 하찮은 복수를 하겠다고 자기 삶을 망치는 사람들이 얼마나 많은가. 냉담한 어머니와 일찍이 가버린 아버지를 생각하면, 피에르도 충분히 그런 사람이 되고도 남을 상황이었다.

그러나 피에르는 그와 다른 길을 갔다.

샤를은 허둥지둥 할머니 댁 전화번호를 눌렀다. 할머니는 귀가 잘 안 들리고 걸음도 매우 느렸다. 젊은 사람들은 대개 험한 난관 따위는 닥치지 않을 거라 지레 생각하고, 자신의 건강이 악화되는 일은 오지 않을 거라 생각한다. 아니, 건강이 악화된다고 해도 그렇게 심하지 않을 것이라고 생각한다. 하지만 그 같은 삶의 시련은 누구에게나 닥쳐오기 마련이다.

할머니 집에서는 한참이나 전화벨 소리가 울려야 했다. 결국 스무 번째 전화를 걸었을 때, 비로소 할머니가 전화를 받았다. 수화기에서 할머니의 약간 떨리는 듯한 목소리가 들려온 것이다.

"여보세요? 누구세요?"

"할머니, 저예요! 샤를!"

"샤를 누구요?"

드디어 통화가 시작되었다! 그리고 이 통화에서 샤를은 할머니의 옛 기억을 끄집어내야 한다. 과거에 있었던 어떤 진실에 대해, 어떤 비밀에 대해 파헤쳐야 한다. 하지만 할머니는 지금 제정신이 아니었다. 장례식 하루 전날, 할머니는 잠시 제정신을 찾았다. 하지만 그 때문에 할머니는 죽을 듯한 고통을 느껴야 했다. 자신의 아들이 세상을 뜬 모습을 묵묵히 지켜봐야 했기 때문이었다. 할머니가 가슴속에 담고 있던 아들에 대한 사랑이 너무도 뒤늦게 터져 나와 더더욱 가슴이 아팠다. 할머니로서는 최악의 순간이었다. 이 가련한 노인의 위태로운 의식 상태로서는 그날의 일이 더없이 끔찍했으리라.

"샤를이에요, 할머니 손자요!"

"아 그래요……."

샤를은 할머니가 자신을 기억하지 못하고 있다는 걸 깨달았다. 무척 답답하기도 했지만, 가슴 속 깊이 고통이 느껴졌다. 사실 우리가 종종 잊고 살아가지만, 기억이란 모든 존재의 근간이다. 따라서 이는 사람들 사이를 맺어주는 모든 관계의 기반이 되기도 한다. 또한 모든 애정 관계의 기반이기도 하다. 따라서 기억이 없다면 우리는 서로 남이나 다름없다. 기억을 가지고 있는 쪽에서 보면 이는 고문이 아닐 수 없다.

'괜찮아. 기억이 사라진 게 아니라 잘 떠오르지 않는 것뿐이니까. 할머니를 직접 가서 만나뵈어야겠다. 그럼 좀 달라지겠지. 할머니가 내 얼굴을 알아보실 거야.'

나이 든 사람들은 대개 방금 전의 일이나 최근의 일을 기억하지 못한다. 열쇠를 어디에 두었는지, 꼬박꼬박 챙겨먹던 약병은 어디에 있는지 기억을 하지 못하는 것이다. 약병은 전날과 똑같은 서랍에 있는데도 말이다. 하지만 예전의 일이라면 아마 기억을 하고 있을 것이다. 샤를이 원하고 있는 것도 예전의 기억이었다. 할머니가 간직하고 있는 예전의 기억들, 피에르가 할머니에게 보여주었을 비밀, 그걸 알고 싶은 것이었다. 할머니의 예전 기억을 되살리면, 문제의 실마리를 찾을 수 있지 않을까.

"할머니, 곧 찾아뵐게요!"

샤를은 그렇게 말하고 전화를 끊었다. 주방으로 간 샤를은 클라라에게 급히 시골집에 있는 할머니를 만나러 간다고 설명했다. 클라라에게도 함께 갈 것을 권했으나, 클라라는 혼자 집에 남아 있겠다고 말했다.

"근사한 아침상인걸!"

클라라가 비꼬았다.

샤를은 잠시 멈칫거리며 클라라를 쳐다보았다. 섹시하고 고혹적인 자태의 클라라는 샤를의 발길을 잡기에 충분했지만, 그는 일단 이 문제부터 해결을 해야겠다고 생각했다.

샤를은 클라라의 이마에 가벼운 입맞춤을 하고 집을 나섰다. 차에 오른 그는 시골집을 향해 미친 사람처럼 돌진했다. 물론 오디오에서 '환희의 송가'를 트는 일도 잊지 않았다. 수수께끼를 파헤치려는 시도는 이미 시작되었다.

할머니에게서 얻은 힌트

"샤를, 네 소식 들은 게 벌써 언제 일이냐? 요새 뭐 하고 지내는 게야?"

나이는 들었지만 아직 출중한 외모를 지닌 할머니는 이미 오래 전에 여자로서의 몸치장을 포기한 상태였다. 화장도 하지 않았고, 향수도 뿌리지 않았으며, 옷차림새에도 그다지 신경을 쓰지 않았다. 그럼에도 팔십 대의 할머니는 아직 매력을 간직하고 있었다. 아직도 젊은 몇몇 연하남에게는 관심과 선망의 대상이었다. 할머니의 그런 외양 못지않게 기억력도 생생하면 얼마나 좋을까.

이는 샤를이 늘 애석하게 여긴 부분이었다. 샤를은 나이 든 할머니를 자주 찾아뵙지 못한 것에 자책하고 있었다.

"할머니, 아버지께서 제게 할머니를 찾아뵈라고 말씀하셨어요. 할머니를 찾아가면 아버지께서 남긴 메시지를 할머니가 제게 알려주실 거라고요……."

"아니, 그런 거 없는데……."

할머니는 눈살을 찌푸리며 말했다.

"정말이에요? 아버지는 뭔가 있다고 말씀하셨는데. 아버지께서는 비상한 기억력을 갖고 계시잖아요."

"비상한 기억력이라고? 하지만 나를 보러 오는 건 기억하지 못하는 모양인데……."

"아버지께서 너무 바쁘셔서요."

샤를은 아버지를 두둔했다.

"애들은 늘 그렇게 말을 하지……."

할머니는 비록 알츠하이머 환자이긴 했으나, 의식은 멀쩡했다.

"아버지께서 마지막으로 할머니를 뵈러 오셨을 때, 저에 대한 이야기를 하지 않던가요?"

"마지막? 모르긴 해도 그게 아마 3년은 됐을 게다. 녀석이 300년 전에 이야기한 걸 다 기억할 만큼 내 기억력은 좋질 못해. 그리고 한 번 생각해 보렴. 오늘 아침에 전화해서는 나를 보고 싶다고, 급한 일이라고 하더니만 여기 오지도 않았잖니? 나보다 더 중요한 전화통화가 있는 게야."

그렇게 말하고 난 뒤 할머니는 말이 없었다. 샤를은 감히 할머니의 말을 부정할 수가 없었다. 이를 비난할 수는 더더욱 없었다. 이건 젊은 사람이든 나이 든 사람이든 누구나 싫어하는 상황이었다. 샤를은 난감한 표정을 지으며 속으로 괜한 시간 낭비를 하는 게 아닌지 고개를 갸웃거렸다. 할머니는 결코 아버지와 나눴던 대화를 기억하지 못하실 터였다.

그런데 갑자기 할머니가 눈물을 흘리기 시작했다. 전혀 예상하지 못한 일이었다. 샤를은 할머니가 우는 까닭을 알 수 없어 그냥 할머니를 내버려두었다. 잠시 후 할머니의 입에서 놀라운 발언이 튀어나왔다.

"내가 바보였어! 내가 바보였다고!"

할머니는 같은 말을 계속 반복했다. 할머니는 당신이 내뱉은 말을 무척 확신하는 듯했다. 무척 강한 어조로 말하면서도 거기에는 엄청난 자책과 원망이 섞여 있었다.

"녀석이 죽은 게 어제였는지 그제였는지 기억이 나질 않아. 이제는 날짜야 언제였든 별 상관없는 일이지만…… 이젠 너무 늦었어. 우리 불쌍한 피에르, 날 그렇게 좋아했는데……. 나는 그게 괴로웠어. 정말 너무도 괴로웠단다, 샤를. 왜냐하면 내가 녀석을 많이 사랑해주지 않았거든. 나는 늘 그 아이를 매정하게 대했단다. 내가 미쳤지, 내가 미쳤어. 한평생 나는 그 아이보다 형을 더 좋아했단다. 그 아이의 형은 잘생겼으니까…… 하지만 바보였지. 어리석었어. 인생도 실패하고 날 돌봐주지도 않은 불효막심한 놈이었지. 하지만 네 아버지는 내게 모든 걸 다 해줬어. 네 아버지는 날 부양할 의무가 없었어. 내게 빚진 게 아무 것도 없었지. 그런데도 내게 모든 걸 다 해줬단다! 그리고 이젠 너무 늦었다. 네 아버지는 세상을 떠나 저 땅 속에 묻혔어. 그 아이의 얼굴을 다시는 볼 수 없겠지. 네 아버지는 날 결코 용서하지 않겠지? 내가 대체 왜 그랬을까? 너는 젊으니까, 잘생기고 똑똑하니까, 너는 내 아들의 아들이니까, 내게 그 이유를 말해줄 수 있겠니? 너는 그 이유가 뭔지 아니?"

"그런 말씀 마세요, 할머니……. 아버지는 할머니를 무척 좋아했어요. 아버지는 제게 할머니의 좋은 점을 종종 말씀해 주셨는걸요."

그 말이 끝나자 할머니의 얼굴빛이 환해지면서 울음을 그쳤다. 그리고 마치 난생 처음 예쁘다는 말을 들은 열 살짜리 소녀처럼 되물었다.

"정말이냐?"

하지만 이것으로는 문제가 해결되지 않았다. 할머니는 또 다시 기분이 착 가라앉았다.

"샤를, 내가 별로 도움이 못됐다면 미안하구나. 그건 네 잘못이 아니란다. 내가 늙어서 그래. 나는 이제 너무 늙었단다. 피로도 빨리 오고, 다리도 많이 아파. 심장에서도 통증이 느껴지지. 나는 이제 나 자신도 못 알아볼 지경이 돼버렸단다. 네겐 이 모든 게 이상하게 들리겠지. 네가 얼마나 놀랄지 짐작이 가고도 남는다. 놀라움이라…… 그래, 이 단어가 적절한 것 같구나. 아침에 눈을 떴을 때, 네 자신이 늙었다는 사실을 지각할 때 얼마나 놀라운지 아느냐? 마찬가지로, 과거에 네가 할 수 있었던 모든 것들, 자전거 타기라든가 걷기라든가

술 마시고 웃고 여행하고 사랑을 나누었던 순간들, 이 모든 게 끝나버렸음을 깨달았을 때의 느낌이란, 이 모든 게 단지 추억에 지나지 않았다는 사실을 깨달았을 때의 느낌이 얼마나 놀라운지 아느냐? 용도도 모르는 약이 냉장고 가득 채워져 있는 걸 보고 나 자신에게 연민을 느꼈던 적이 한두 번이 아니었단다. 사람들이 나한테 몸 좀 챙기라고, 건강에 유의하라는 말이 귀찮았던 적도 한두 번이 아니었어. 건강이라……건강을 잃은 지 벌써 십 년도 더 되었단다. 우리 영감이 세상을 떠난 뒤로 건강이란 더 이상 내 삶에 없는 단어가 되었지. 우리 영감이 일부러 먼저 떠난 거라고 말할 수도 있을 게야. 그렇게 하면 내가 좀 더 빨리 영감 곁으로 갈 수 있을 테니까. 하지만 그게 뜻대로 잘 되지 않았단다. 신이 아무래도 날 잊어버리신 모양이야."

"할머니, 그런 말씀 마세요!"

샤를이 격렬히 반대했다.

"저희는 할머니를 사랑해요. 저희에겐 할머니가 필요하다고요."

그래도 할머니의 기분은 나아지지 않았다.

"머리가 돌고 있는 늙은이를 누가 필요로 한단 말이더냐? 내가 누굴 기다리는 건지, 누가 이미 가 버리고 없는지 알지 못하는 때가 허다하다. 전에는 악보도 없이 바흐 곡을 연주했는데, 이젠 쉽고 간단한 동요도 연주할 수가 없더구나. 너는 모를 게다. 젊은 사람들은 이런 걸 이해 못해. 너희는 늙는다는 게 서서히 살랑살랑 다가오는 거라 생각하지……."

샤를은 무슨 말을 해야 할지 몰랐다. 그때 문득 한 가지 생각이 떠올랐다.

"할머니, 이리 좀 와 보세요! 제게 좋은 생각이 있어요!"

샤를은 할머니의 손을 잡고 집을 나섰다. 할머니는 샤를의 팔에 이끌려 순순히 따라 나왔다. 할머니의 얼굴은 어린 시절의 예쁜 소녀처럼 기쁜 기색이 역력했다. 사실 우리에게는 결코 나이 들지 않고 우리 안에 오롯이 남아 있는 일부분이 있다. 물론 이는 우리가 간직한 모습 가운데 가장 아름다운 부분이기도 하다.

"할머니, '환희의 송가'를 연주해주세요."

할머니를 피아노 앞으로 데리고 간 샤를이 제안했다.

"환희의 송가?"

할머니는 그게 뭔지 모르겠다는 듯이 고개를 갸웃거렸다. 샤를이 입술을 삐쭉 내밀자, 할머니는 무척 흥분된 모습으로 피아노 의자에 앉으며 말했다.

"그야 물론 베토벤 곡이 아니냐?"

할머니는 피아노로 편곡된 '환희의 송가'를 능숙하게 연주했다. 열 소절 정도를 연주한 후, 할머니는 무언가가 떠오르는 듯 별안간 소리쳤다.

"그래! 그러고 보니 이제야 생각이 나는구나! 네 아버지가 말이다, 심장 발작이 있고 얼마 되지 않아 날 보러 왔었지. 그때 네게 봉투를 하나 주더구나."

"봉투요?"

"그래. 봉투 안에 종이가 들어 있었던 것 같은데……."

"그 봉투는 어디에 있어요?"

"그 봉투가 어디에 있냐고? 그걸 왜 나한테 묻는 거냐?"

이 대목에서 샤를은 엄청난 인내심이 필요했다.

"그 봉투를 어디에 넣어두었는지 생각 안 나세요?"

"글쎄다……."

할머니는 또 무슨 생각이 났는지 큰 소리로 말했다.

"내가 그 위에 앉았어!"

"그 위에 앉아요?"

할머니는 갑자기 벌떡 일어나더니 의자의 덮개를 열었다. 할머니는 그 안에서 봉투를 찾아내 샤를의 눈앞에서 자랑스레 흔들었다.

"할머니, 굉장해요!"

"나도 안다."

샤를은 서둘러 봉투를 열어보았다. 봉투 안에는 할머니의 말대로 종이가 한 장 들어 있었다. 얼핏 보아 양피지 같기도 했는데, 오래된 종이는 분명 아니었다. 샤를은 그 종이에 적혀 있는 아버지의 필체를 금방 알아보았다. 이 종이에는 그림도 그려져 있었는데, 그것도 아버지가 그린 그림이 분명했다. 사실 아버지는 그림에도 매우 뛰어난 재능을 지니고 있었다. 딱히 미술 수업을 받지 않았고, 큰 노력을 기울이지 않았는데도 그림을 잘 그렸다. "재주 있는 사람은 아무 것도 배우지 않은 상태에서도 모든 걸 알고 있다"는 몰리에르의 말은 틀린 게 아니었다.

그림은 붉은 색과 검은 색만 이용한 소박한 스타일로 그려져 있었다. 샤를은 먼저 일곱 명의 외형을 찬찬히 살펴보았다. 신기한 빨간 모자를 쓰고 있었고, 머리는 중세시대 책에서나 나올 법한 헤어스타일이었다. 이들은 돌로 만든 높은 벽 쪽을 보고 나팔을 불고 있었다.

이 그림을 보면서 샤를은 전율을 느꼈다. 《위대한 가르침을 찾아서》에서 아버지가 밑줄을 쳐 두었던 단락이 떠올랐기 때문이었다. 이 책에서 저자는 고대 나팔을 이용한 예리코 성채의 함락이 그 완벽한 예라고 했었다. 종이 위에는 그 밖에 다른 것들도 있었다. 왼쪽 구석에는 수많은 빛줄기가 쏟아져 나오는 태양이, 가운데에는 원반 같은 게 달린 막대기가 있는 샘터도 있었다. 특히 샘터 주위에는 사람들이 여럿 있었는데, 꽤 특이한 행동을 하고 있는 모습이었다. 남자와 여자들이 한 남자 앞에 길게 줄지어 있었는데, 남자는 신부 복장을 하고 금으로 된 높은 삼중관(교황이 특별한 행사에 쓰는 금관)을 쓰고 있었다. 그는 망치를 들고 남자의 머리 위를 쳤다. 남자는 줄 선 사람들 가운데 제일 앞에 있는 사람으로, 삼중관을 쓴 사람 앞에서 무릎을 꿇고 있었다. 그 뒤에는 함박 미소를 짓고 있는 한 아이가 있었는데, 손에 무언가를 들고 있었다. 얼핏 봤을 때, 샤를은 그게 컵받침 같은 것이라고 생각했다. 하지만 자세히 보니 그건 아이 자신의 두개골 파편이었다. 이 아이의 머리에는 정수리가 있어야 할 자리에 아무 것도 없었다. 이 신비로운 신체 부위는 성직자들이 삭발을 하는 부분으로, 이는 곧 저들이 하늘의 빛을 향해 열려 있다는 표시였다. 이는 철드는 시기를 표현한 것이라고 한다.

샤를은 전날 니로다가 아버지에게 했던 광경을 떠올리며 다시 한 번 전율을 느꼈다. 남자는 아버지의 머리 위에 주먹을 올려놓은 뒤 이어 그 위를 쳤다. 그림에서처럼 망치로 친 건 아니지만, 모양새는 똑같았다. 모든 게 이상했다. 이해할 수도 없었다. 이게 무슨 쓸모가 있는 건지 알 수가 없었다. 도대체 아버지는 왜 이처럼 알쏭달쏭한 그림을 그렸던 걸까? 그림 옆으로 문장 하나가 적혀 있었는데, 이 또한 그 의미를 알 수 없었다.

"어린 시절의 정원으로 가라. 샘터 가까이로 가서 낮의 속눈썹 천 개가 하나로 되는 걸 보라. 그리고 10. 23에 빛의 길을 따라 가라. 1. 4 경 비발디. 5. 22, 네 형과 누나 그리고 너를 파헤쳐라. 네 발 밑에 깔린 네 숨은 재능을 찾아내라. 신께

서 원하신다면, 그리고

여기에서 아버지는 '능력'이라는 단어에 강조 표시를 해
두었다.

암호 같은 내용에 당황한 샤를은 아버지의 메시지를 다시
한 번 읽어보았다. 그 안에 숨겨진 뜻을 알아내고 싶었다. 이
게 대체 무슨 메시지란 말인가? 아버지는 왜 이렇게 난해한
표현 방식을 사용한 것일까?

이제 영원히 두 눈을 감은 아버지는 약간의 기발한 발상과
엄청난 땀방울로 얻어진 게 아니라면 그 무엇도 가치를 지니
지 못한다고 생각했다. 이렇게 난해한 글을 남긴 것도 어쩌면
그런 아버지의 뜻이 반영된 게 아닐까?

샤를은 벽시계를 쳐다보았다. 10시 13분이었다. 샤를은 다
시 한 번 소스라치게 놀랐다. 무언가 뿌리칠 수 없는 직감으
로 느끼건대, 샤를은 왠지 앞으로 10분 후에 모든 일이 벌어

질 거라는 확신이 들었기 때문이다. 그의 직감이 맞는다면, 그
에게 남은 건 단 10분의 시간뿐이었다. 10분 안에 수수께끼의
열쇠를 찾아야 한다.

그의 인생을 결정지을 10분이 될 수도 있는 일이었다.

샤를 레니에, 다시 아이가 되다

그날 아침, 샤를은 클라라에게 무심코 던진 질문에서 적절한 방법을 찾아냈다. 이 알쏭달쏭 수수께끼 같은 문장을 엘레오노르 할머니에게 여쭤보는 것은 어떨까?

나이가 들긴 했어도 여전히 음악에 조예가 깊었던 할머니는 이 문장을 읽자마자 '1.4.비발디'에 주목했다.

"이건 비발디의 사계 같구나. 그리고 여기에 적혀 있는 1은 1악장인 봄을 말하는 거고."

"할머니 말이 맞아요!"

이것을 풀고 난 샤를은 모든 것이 10분 후에 벌어질 것임을 확신했다. 이제는 9분밖에 남지 않았다. 그리고 문장 속에 적혀 있는 '5.22'는 5월 22일을 뜻하는 것이었다. 그날이 바로 오늘이었다. 그러나 샤를은 아직 핵심을 찾지 못하고 그 주변을 배회하고 있었다.

할머니는 고민에 빠져 있는 샤를을 위로하면서 종이를 슬쩍 쳐다보았다. 그러고는 엷은 미소를 띠우며 이렇게 소리쳤다.

"네가 찾아 헤매고 있는 것을 여기서는 찾지 못할 게다."

"왜요?"

놀란 샤를이 물었다.

"여기 좀 보렴. '어린 시절의 정원으로 가라. 샘터 가까이로 가서'라고 쓰여 있잖니. 정원과 샘터는 저쪽에 있거든."

할머니는 약간 떨리는 손으로, 거실의 커다란 창문 너머 정원을 가리켰다. 거기에는 새들이 물을 마시는 곳이 있었다. 샘터 역할을 대신하는 곳이었다. 샤를은 다시 한 번 자신의 이마를 쳤다. 왜 아버지가 남긴 메시지의 앞부분을 제대로 읽지 않았던 것일까? 왜 상징적 의미만 찾으려고 애썼던 걸까? 필경 이는 그의 직업병 때문이리라. 철학자라는 직업적 특성상

왜곡하고 꼬아서 보는 습관이 있었던 것이다.

"할머니, 정말 대단하세요!"

샤를은 할머니의 이마에 입맞춤을 한 뒤 감사의 인사를 전했다.

"칭찬해줘서 고맙구나. 마들렌이랑 같이 차 한 잔 내어주랴? 네가 좋아하던 게 아니냐?"

"괜찮아요, 할머니. 지금은 됐어요."

샤를은 벽시계를 바라보았다. 이제 8분이 채 남지 않았다. 샤를은 서둘러 정원으로 갔다. 사실 할머니는 샤를이 어떤 중요한 문제로 골머리를 썩이고 있는지 잘 알지 못했다. 할머니는 샤를을 바라보며 이런 생각을 할 뿐이었다.

'요즘 젊은 애들은 시종일관 뛰어다니는구나!'

정원에서 새들이 물 마시는 곳으로 다가간 샤를은 지난번 아버지와 함께 왔을 때 눈여겨봤던 것을 주의 깊게 살펴봤다. 어딘가 달라진 게 있었다. 하지만 그게 무엇이란 말인가? 대체 무엇이 달라진 것인가? 샤를은 어서 그걸 찾아내야 했다. 시간이 많이 남아 있지 않았다. 샤를은 주위를 두리번거렸다. 그러다가 문득 여기에서 무언가 빠져 있다는 것을 깨달았다.

샤를은 그곳이 어디인지 알 것 같았다. 그곳은 새들이 물을 마시는 곳에서 몇 미터 떨어진 곳에 있는 덤불숲 앞이었다. 해마다 봄이 되면 이 덤불숲에서는 아직 여린 초록빛 새싹들이 눈에 띄었다.

그렇다. 예전에는 이 덤불숲 앞에 무언가 있었다. 지금 여기에 사라지고 없는 무언가 있었다. 그게 무엇인지는 곧 밝혀질 것이다.

샤를은 마르셀 프루스트의 《잃어버린 시간을 찾아서》 중 '스완네 집 쪽으로'의 유명한 도입 부분이 떠올랐다.

"하지만 마들렌을 한 입 베어 문 뒤, 과자 부스러기들이 입 안 곳곳으로 흩어지며 내 미각을 자극했을 때, 내 몸에서는 전율이 느껴졌고…… 맛있는 음식을 먹었을 때의 쾌감이 온 몸으로 퍼져나갔다. 대수롭지 않았던 내 삶은 인생의 희로애락을 되찾았고, 이와 함께 나는 해로울 게 없는 파국적 상황이라든가 덧없이 짧은 인생의 무상함에 대해서도 깨우쳤다. 나는 더 이상 내 자신이 보잘 것 없는 사소한 존재라는 생각을 하지 않았으며, 언젠가는 죽어 없어질 덧없는 존재라는 생각도 그만두게 되었다."

주인공 마르셀과 마찬가지로 샤를 역시 전율을 느꼈다. 방금 전 할머니는 그에게 차와 마들렌을 내어주겠다고 말했다. 어쩌면 프루스트의 이 유명한 소설 대목처럼 그 마들렌을 먹었을 지도 모를 일이었다. 삶은 또 다시 그의 코밑에, 그 모든 의미심장한 것들을, 엄지왕자의 하얀 조약돌 같이 지표가 될 수 있는 모든 것들을 늘어놓은 셈이었다. 샤를이 할 일이란, 단지 이를 똑바로 보고 그저 따라가기만 하면 되는 것이었다.

가만히 생각해보니 아버지가 그토록 자신에게 가르쳐주려고 했던 것은, 비록 그 표현 방식은 조금 달랐어도, 바로 이 소설 속 주인공처럼 '스스로가 보잘 것 없고 사소하며 덧없는 존재가 아니라고 느끼는 것'이었다. 어린 시절의 신비로운 숲 속에서, 아버지는 자신이 잊고 있었던 스스로의 능력에 대해, 자신이 되찾아야 할 신비로운 능력에 대해 역설하면서 그 점을 깨우쳐 주고 싶었던 것이었다. 어린 시절의 신비로운 숲 속에서…….

샤를은 덤불숲과 아버지가 남긴 종이를 번갈아 쳐다보았다. 그때 여러 장면이 스르르 떠올랐다. 신비로운 나팔 연주자들, 망치로 사람들 머리 위를 치며 사람들을 신비로운 세계로 인도하는 남자, 삼중관을 쓰고 신부 복장을 한 남자 앞에 줄지어 선 사람들, 남자 뒤에서 즐거운 표정으로 멀어지는 아이들, 어른에서 어린아이 것으로 바뀐 두개골 정수리……. 샤를은 이제야 이 아이에 대해 이해하기 시작했다. 아이는 천상의 망치로 정수리를 맞기 전에는 어른의 상태였다. 그러나 올바른 방향으로 줄을 선 가운데, 진정한 모험의 길에 접어들면서, 아이가 추구하는 방향은 결국 그 목적을 달성하고 아이의 삶은 비로소 의미를 찾았다. 아이의 변신이 이뤄진 것이다.

샤를은 아버지가 남긴 문장 가운데 다음 대목을 침착하게 읽어보았다.

"샘터 가까이로 가서 낮의 속눈썹 천 개가 하나로 되는 걸 보라. 그리고 10. 23에 빛의 길을 따라 가라."

그것은 샘터가 아니라 새들이 물을 마시는 곳을 가리키는 것이었다. 어차피 같은 것이다. 이건 확실히 제대로 찾은 게 맞았다.

낮의 속눈썹 천 개가 하나로 되는 것이라…… 낮의 눈…….

그렇다! 이집트인들에게 낮의 눈이란 곧 태양을 지칭하는 것이었다. 태양의 속눈썹 천 개라 함은 곧 태양의 빛줄기를 말하는 것이 아닌가. 10시 23분의 태양이었다……. 지금 시간이 얼마나 되었을까? 10시 20분. 이제 3분밖에 남지 않았다! 샤를은 호수가 있는 쪽을 바라봤다. 해가 비치는 곳은 호수 쪽이었다. 호숫가에 서 있는 떡갈나무 두 그루는 몸통이 잔가지 없이 곧게 높이 뻗어 시야를 가리지 않았다. 이 나무 사이로 태양이 훤히 드러나 있었다.

이제 비로소 감이 오기 시작했다. 기쁨에 도취된 샤를은 아이팟 헤드폰을 끼고 '환희의 송가'를 틀었다. 고막이 터질 정도로 볼륨을 높인 샤를의 모습은 마치 음악을 크게 틀고 정신 나간 사람처럼 즐거워하던 아버지의 모습과 비슷했다.

그는 새가 물 마시는 곳 주위를 미친 사람처럼 빙글빙글 돌았다. 그리고 큰 소리로 애원했다.

"베토벤! 나 좀 도와줘, 제발 부탁이야! 당신은 알지? 내가 찾아야 하는 게 뭔지, 내가 깨달아야 하는 게 뭔지, 당신은 알고 있잖아! 그걸 당신 음악 속에 넣어두었으니까! 그건 내 아버지도 말씀하셨고, 우스펜스키의 책에도 쓰여 있어. 아버지가 거기에 붉은 색으로 밑줄까지 쳐두셨어! 그러니 제발 내게 말해줘. 당신이 그게 뭔지 알고 있다는 거, 나도 다 안다고! 당신은 위대한 사람이잖아. 당신은 위대한 베토벤이라고. 난 그저 하찮은 대학의 하찮은 교수 나부랭이에 불과한 사람이라고. 자기 인생에서 아무 것도 이루지 못한 그런 사람이지. 하지만 당신은 천재잖아? 천재! 천재가 왜 태어나는데? 보통 사람을 도와주라고 태어나는 거잖아! 그러니까 날 도와줘. 당신은 날 도와줘야 해! 이렇게 빌게. 제발 부탁이야. 내겐 시간이 얼마 없어. 난 이번에도 실패하고 말 거라고. 그러니 신의 축복을 위해서라도 제발 날 도와줘!"

신의 조화였을까, 아니면 정말 베토벤이 그의 말을 귀 담아 들었던 것일까. 불현듯 어린 시절의 추억이 샤를의 뇌리를 스치고 지나쳤다.

샤를이 일곱 살 때, 그는 형과 함께 새들의 샘터 옆에서 놀던 적이 있었다. 그때는 형이 아직 어른이 되지 않았던 때였으며, 샤를에게는 최고의 친구였던 시절이었다.

그는 그때 형과 함께 모든 걱정 근심으로부터 벗어나 눈살 한 번 찌푸릴 일 없이 행복하게 놀았다. 어린아이에게 세상에서 제일 심각하면서 중요한 것은 노는 일이었다. 그러나 점점 어른이 되면서 우리는 이를 잊어버린 채, 이른바 '중요하다'고 하는 일들에 자신의 인생을 바친다.

샤를은 형과 함께 놀던 때를 떠올리며 그 놀이를 재현했다. 돋보기로 새들이 물마시던 곳을 덮고 있던 오래된 신문에 구멍을 내고 무늬를 만들며 태우고 놀았다. 바로 이런 놀이를 하면서 아버지가 말한 '낮의 속눈썹 천 개가 하나로 되는 것'이 뭔지 깨달았다. 그것은 바로 돋보기의 원리였다. 돋보기로 햇빛을 모아 하나로 만드는 것이었다.

그러나 태양빛은 진흙으로 뒤덮여 있는 돋보기에 잘 스며들지 않았다. 샤를은 샘터의 물을 가져와 커다란 돋보기를 정신없이 닦았다. 서둘러야 한다. 시간은 마냥 그를 기다려주는 게 아니다. 그의 아이팟에서는 여전히 '환희의 송가'가 흘러나오고 있었다. 신비롭고 장엄하면서도 너무도 아름다운 곡이었다. 삶이란 어느 날 갑자기 별 것 아닌 것처럼 느껴질 때가 있다. 아무리 중요한 일을 하더라도, 아무리 똑똑하고 솔직한 사람이라고 해도, 모든 게 별 것 아닌 것처럼 느껴질 때가 있다. 조잡한 뒷돈 거래, 멋모르고 열심히 쫓아가는 커다란 메달, 우리가 사랑이라고 부르는 가벼운 운동 등 모든 게 상대적으로 별 것 아닌 듯 느껴지고 아무런 가치도 없는 것처럼 느껴질 때가 있다. 제아무리 0이라는 숫자가 많이 달려 있다 하더라도, 맨 앞에 1이 없으면 여기에 목을 맬 이유가 없어지고 마는 수표처럼……

돋보기가 잘 닦이지 않자, 샤를은 셔츠를 벗어 이를 걸레로 사용했다. 그렇게 미친듯이 집중하는 그의 모습은 그 어느 때보다도 아름다웠다. 돋보기의 유리는 곧 깨끗해졌고, 원래의 투명함을 완벽하게 되찾았다. 샤를은 햇빛을 가리고 있었기 때문에 조금 뒤로 물러섰다. 그러고는 그곳에 돋보기를 갖다 댔다.

햇빛은 곧장 돋보기 위로 내리쬐었고, 돋보기를 통해 하나로 뭉쳐진 빛줄기는 샤를이 그토록 의아하게 여기던 덤불숲으로 향했다. 샤를은 종이에 적혀 있던 지침을 떠올렸다. '10. 23에 빛의 길을 따라 가라.'

마침 시간은 10시 23분을 가리키고 있었다. 그리고 거기에는 빛의 길이 생겨났다. 아버지가 남긴 메시지에서 예고한 대로, 환상적인 빛의 길이었다. 샤를은 덤불숲으로 다가갔다. 숲은 성서에 나오는 '(하느님이 모세에게 모습을 나타낸) 타오르는 덤불숲'처럼 환하게 빛나고 있었다. 샤를은 빠른 속도로 나뭇가지를 치웠다. 그리고 뒤늦게 깨달았다. 정원에서 없어진 게 무엇인지 깨달은 것이다. 그건 덤불숲에 가려져 있었다. 나뭇가지들이 제멋대로 무성하게 뻗어있던 터라, 그 안에 숨겨져 있었던 것이 보이지 않았던 것이다. 그것은 바로 세 개의 작은 동상이었다.

이 세 개의 사랑스러운 동상은 피에르가 아버지로서의 무한한 자부심을 가지고 자식들을 생각하며 세운 것이었다. 왼쪽에는 형의 동상이, 가운데에는 누나의 동상이, 맨 오른쪽에는 자신의 동상이 있었다.

어떻게 이걸 잊을 수 있었던 걸까? 돋보기를 통한 빛줄기는 누나의 동상 발밑 지표면을 내리쬐고 있었다.

"네 형과 누나 그리고 너를 파헤쳐라."

샤를은 형 동상의 발밑을 파기 시작했다. 손톱이 빠지도록 열심히 파헤쳤다. 5월의 대지는 아직 촉촉한 상태였다. 곧 형의 동상 밑의 땅속에서 작은 철제 상자를 발견했다. 샤를은 이를 보자마자 뚜껑을 열었다. 그 안에는 오래된 금화 하나가

들어 있었다. 이어 샤를은 누나의 동상 발밑을 파내고 비슷한 철제 상자를 찾아냈다. 여기에는 금화 두 개가 들어 있었다. 끝으로 자신의 동상 발밑을 파고 그 안에서 찾은 금화의 숫자를 세어 보았다. 금화는 아홉 개였다. 그리고 왠지는 모르겠지만, 문득 자신이 착각했을지도 모른다는 생각이 들었다. 그는 서둘러 다시 금화의 수를 세어보았다. 하지만 여전히 금화는 아홉 개밖에 없었다.

어쨌든 그건 중요한 게 아니었다. 정말로 중요한 건 아버지가 그에게 거짓말을 한 게 아니라는 사실이었다. 피에르는 세 자식의 아버지, 그것도 가장 재능 있는 아버지였다.

세 개의 동상 앞에 무릎을 꿇고 앉아있던 샤를은 진정 눈앞이 밝아지는 것을 경험했다. 그렇다. 불현듯 그는 지금까지 겪은 모든 일들의 경이적인 신비로움에 감동했고, 지금까지의 이 기묘한 모험에 압도당했다. 지금껏 철학자로서 지극히 이성적으로 바라본 시간의 개념이 얼마나 다른 것이었는지 깨달았다. 또한 아버지의 심오한 통찰력과 미래를 내다보는 능력에 놀랐으며, 아버지가 감수했던 그 위험에 대해서도 놀라움을 금치 못했다. 그는 모든 것이 사랑에서 비롯된 것이었음을 깨달았다. 그 무엇으로도 잴 수 없는 무한한 사랑이었다. 이는 아버지가 갖고 있는 최고이자 최대의 능력이었다. 그 즈음 '환희의 송가'가 끝나면서 그의 감정은 최고조에 이르렀다. 결국 이 모든 상황에 너무도 감격한 나머지, 기어이 눈물을 쏟아내고 말았다.

샤를은 불길 하나가 등을 타고 올라와 시뻘건 빛으로 자신의 머리를 가득 채우는 느낌을 받았다. 그리고 곧 손에 쥐고 있던 아홉 개의 금화를 바닥에 떨어뜨리며 털썩 주저앉았다. 마음은 뭐라 형언할 수 없는 기쁨으로 가득 차 있었고, 이마는 주름살 하나 없이 매끈하게 펴졌으며, 그 모든 근심으로부터 자유로워졌다. 샤를은 하늘을 쳐다보았다. 드넓은 하늘, 저 하늘을 아름답게 수놓은 신비로운 구름……. 샤를의 눈이 반짝 빛났다. 새롭고 경이로운 분위기가 그의 눈빛 속에서 찬란하게 빛나고 있었다.

샤를은 너무도 아름다운 모습이었다.

다시…… 아이가 되었다.

운명의 실현

다음날 오전, 찬란한 미래를 확신한 샤를은 클라라와 함께 환한 얼굴로 생트 쥐스틴 병원을 찾았다.

샤를은 병원 접수계 직원에게 5천만 달러짜리 수표를 내밀었다. 여직원은 눈살을 찌푸렸다. 수표의 적혀 있는 이 어마어마한 금액이 병원 이름으로 쓰인 게 아니었기 때문이었다. 샤를은 여직원에게 수표의 뒷면을 보여주었다. 거기에는 '생트 쥐스틴 병원을 위해'라는 글과 함께 그의 서명이 적혀 있었다. 모든 의심과 걱정이 사라진 서명이었다. 그의 아버지가 원했던 대로 말이다.

"잘 알겠습니다. 하지만 이 정도의 금액이라면 원장님을 직접 만나 뵙는 게 좋을 것 같은데요."

병원장 역시 수표 금액을 확인하고는 두 눈이 휘둥그레졌다. 그러고는 감격에 겨워 무한한 감사의 뜻을 전했다.

"만일 아버님께서 이 자리에 계셨다면 무척 대견해했을 겁니다."

더없이 적절한 발언이 아니던가! 샤를은 클라라를 바라보면서 지긋이 서로 웃음을 나누었다.

"이쪽으로 오시지요. 어떤 아이들에게 선행을 베푸신 것인지 직접 보여드리겠습니다."

원장은 클라라와 샤를을 아이들이 노는 커다란 실내 놀이터로 데리고 갔다. 그런데 이곳에서 조금 신기한 일이 벌어졌다. 원장이 아이들에게 샤를을 미처 소개하기도 전에, 그가 이 아이들에게 얼마나 큰 도움을 주었는지 설명을 하기도 전에, 아이들이 하던 놀이를 멈추고 그에게로 다가오는 게 아닌가! 어떤 아이들은 휠체어를 타고, 어떤 아이들은 목발을 짚고, 또 어떤 아이들은 혼자 힘으로 샤를 곁으로 다가왔다. 마치 샤를이 아이들의 친구라도 된 것처럼 기쁘게 그를 맞이한 것이다. 병원 원장은 놀라움을 금치 못했다. 지금까지 병원에서 오래 지내왔지만, 이런 광경은 한 번도 본 적이 없었다. 샤를이 무척 관대하게 보이긴 했지만, 그가 유명한 하키 선수도 아니고 셀린 디옹 같은 유명 가수도 아니지 않은가!

클라라 역시 놀라기는 마찬가지였다. 클라라는 샤를을 바라봤다. 그리고 샤를처럼 그녀 역시 흘러내리려는 눈물을 꾹 참았다. 행여 아이들의 행복하고 즐거운 시간을 망쳐놓을까 걱정이 됐던 것이다.

"당신 아버지가 옳았어."

클라라가 한 마디 내뱉었다.

"아버지는 항상 옳으셔."

샤를이 대답했다.

그때 실내놀이터 한 구석에서 카드놀이를 하고 있는 아이 세 명이 샤를의 눈에 띄었다. 이 아이들은 카드놀이를 하느라 다른 아이들처럼 자기 곁으로 오지 않은 것으로 보였다. 그리고 이 세 명의 아이들 중에서 샤를은 자신이 알 것 같은 한 아이를 보았다. 그건 바로 자신의 아버지였다.

일곱 살의 아버지는 어린아이의 모습으로 또래 친구들과

함께 재미있게 카드놀이를 하고 있었다. 아버지가 다시 살아 돌아오신 걸까? 샤를은 이를 확인하고 싶은 마음이 굴뚝같았다. 아버지를 다시 찾고, 말을 걸고, 꼭 껴안고 싶었다. 그때 원장이 그에게 몇 가지 질문을 하는 바람에 그럴 수가 없었다.

샤를이 다시 카드놀이를 하는 아이들 무리 쪽을 바라보았을 때, 그곳에는 두 명밖에 보이지 않았다. 샤를은 원장과 클라라에게 양해를 구한 뒤, 두 아이가 있는 곳으로 달려가 물었다.

"함께 있던 친구는 어디 갔니?"

"어떤 친구요?"

일곱 살 혹은 여덟 살 정도 되어 보이는 한 아이가 물었다. 아이는 머리카락 한 올 없었고, 눈썹도 찾아볼 수 없었다. 소아암을 앓고 있는 아이였다.

"너희들 여기서 셋이 놀고 있지 않았니?"

"아뇨, 저희는 둘이서 놀고 있었는데요."

옆에 있던 아이가 말했다. 이 아이는 소아암에 걸린 아이와 비슷한 또래로 보였는데, 큰 수술을 받은 후 회복기에 접어든 상태였다.

“아, 그래……”

실망한 샤를이 말했다.

“아저씨, 슬퍼보여요.”

소아암에 걸린 아이가 말했다.

“아니다, 난……”

아이는 카드놀이를 하던 테이블 위의 동전을 바라봤다. 그리고 잠시 고민하다 1달러를 쥐어 샤를에게 내밀었다.

“이거 가지세요. 아저씨에게 드릴게요. 이게 아저씨에게 행운을 가져다줄 거예요.”

“아, 정말 고맙구나! 이거 정말 감동인걸……”

그때 샤를은 정말로 대단한 감동을 느꼈다. 이 아이가 자신에게 너그러운 마음씨를 보여주어서가 아니라, 철제 상자 안에 있었던 금화 아홉 개가 떠올랐기 때문이었다. 어떻게 열 개가 아닌지 의아해하던 그가 아니었던가? 그런데 이 아이의 동전을 받고 나니 이제는 열 개가 된 셈이다.

아버지였다. 샤를은 이를 확신했다. 아버지가 자신에게 이같은 선물을 준 것이다. 5천만 달러 수표를 병원에 기부하라는 자신의 충고를 따른 감사의 뜻으로, 아들이 부친에게 보여준 애정에 대한 고마움의 뜻으로, 이렇듯 선물을 준 것이다.

이곳에 아버지가 있었다. 자신에게 1달러짜리 동전을 건네줌으로써 자신이 늘 거기에 있다는 사실을, 앞으로도 그의 곁에 있을 거라는 사실을, 그 자신의 심장이 뛰는 소리만큼이나 가까운 곳에 존재한다는 사실을 보여주고 싶었던 것이다.

다음 달, 샤를은 클라라와의 약속을 지켜 결혼식을 올렸다. 결혼식은 무척 간소했다. 약식으로 가볍게 올렸으나, 감정만은 그 어떤 화려한 결혼식 못지않게 충만했다.

행복은 혼자 오지 않는 법이다. 클라라가 곧 임신을 한 것이다. 장례식이 끝나고 얼마 지나지 않아 샤를은 공증인으로부터 아버지의 양복과 구두, 그리고 멋진 시계를 받았다. 그의 몫으로 남겨진 유산이었다. 샤를이 화에 못 이겨 챙겨가지도 않은 물건들이었다.

아버지의 유산이 담긴 상자를 열면서 샤를은 자신이 느꼈던 고통을 떠올렸다. 공증인의 집에서 유언장이 발표되던 그날의 반발심과 분노도 생각났다. 하지만 이제는 그 모든 일이 아득하게 느껴졌다. 이제는 모두 무의미한 일이었다. 샤를은 고개를 끄덕이며 입가에 환한 미소를 지었다.

샤를은 새로운 삶이 시작되었다는 의미로, 아버지의 양복을 입고 아버지의 구두를 신고 왼쪽 손목에는 아버지의 시계를 차고 결연한 마음으로 작업을 시작했다. 그가 쓸 만한 소설의 소재는 얼마 전 아버지와 함께 겪은 그 일밖에 없었다. 한 달이 채 안 되는 시간 만에 샤를은 소설을 탈고했다.

그의 책은 대단한 성공을 거두었다. 샤를은 이를 보며 생각했다.

'콕토의 말이 맞았어. 한 권의 책은 곧바로 그 역사가 생기든가 그렇지 않든가 둘 중 하나다.'

그의 소설책은 전 세계에서 300만 부 이상 팔려나갔다. 미국의 한 출판사는 그의 차기작 세 권에 대해 선인세로 500만 달러를 제안했다. 잠시, 아니 5초간 고민한 샤를은 이 제안을 흔쾌히 수락했다. 이 놀라운 쌍방 합의에 대해 약식으로 계약을 성사시킨 뒤, 출판사는 거액의 수표를 보내왔다. 비록 이 금액이 자신이 기부했던 금액보다 적긴 하지만, 이를 보며 샤를은 두 가지를 떠올렸다.

나는 이제 막 소설가로서의 내 인생을 시작하려는 단계다. 언젠가는 내가 그 5천만 달러를 손에 쥐게 될 것이다.

이 금액은 내가 느끼는 지금 이 기분과 비교를 할 수가 없다. 이 돈은 내가 번 돈이다. 더욱이 내가 좋아하는 일을 해서 번 돈이다!

아버지의 말은 결코 틀리지 않았다!

예언의 실현

니로다가 샤를에게 수수께끼 같은 예언을 한 지 꼭 3년이 지났다. 샤를과 클라라는 아들의 만 두 번째 생일을 축하하기 위해 작은 파티를 열어 친구들과 부모님을 초대했다. 그동안 클라라는 잘생긴 아들을 낳았는데, 아들의 이름은 볼 것도 없이 피에르 2세였다.

그때만 해도 샤를은 니로다의 예언을 잊은 지 오래였다. 오래된 약속이나 소원은 대개 머나먼 기억 저편으로 보내버리기 일쑤이지 않던가.

하지만 아들이 두 다리로 굳건히 서서 새하얀 케이크 위의 커다란 촛불 두 개를 끌려고 했을 때, 샤를은 불현듯 니로다의 말이 떠올랐다. 그가 자신에게 주겠다던 두 번째 선물, 열두 명의 손님이 올 것이라는 말…….

샤를은 온몸에 전율을 느꼈다. 그는 얼른 손님들을 세어 보았다. 이들은 니로다의 예언대로 정말 열두 명이다.

샤를은 이들에게 시계를 끌러 테이블 위 케이크 앞에 놓아 달라고 정중하게 부탁했다. 그들은 샤를의 부탁을 이상하게 여기면서도 순순히 따랐다. 다만 한 사람만이 자신은 시계를 차고 있지 않아 거기에 동참할 수 없을 것이라면서 사과의 뜻을 전했다. 이것도 니로다의 예언 그대로였다!

샤를은 시계를 한 줄로 늘어놓고 그 가운데 아버지의 시계를 올려놓았다. 그리고 아들인 피에르 2세에게 말했다.

"피에르, 네가 가장 좋아하는 시계를 하나 고르렴."

아들은 아버지가 왜 그런 질문을 하는지 그 이유를 알 수 없다는 듯 웃음을 지었다.

샤를의 아들은 한참을 망설이다가 예상과는 달리 샤를이 내민 시계의 바로 옆의 것을 집었다. 샤를은 실망감에 얼굴을 찌푸렸다. 니로다가 아이에게 이 같은 테스트를 하라고 한 이유를 짐작했기 때문이었다. 이는 티베트의 수도승들이 과거의 달라이 라마가 환생한 것으로 알려진 아이에게 치르는 테스트였다.

그러나 어린 피에르 2세는 눈을 찡긋하더니, 처음에 집은 시계를 내려놓고 샤를의 시계를 집었다. 그러고는 자랑스럽게 아버지를 돌아보며 함박웃음을 지었다. 샤를은 감동의 눈물을 흘렸다.

이미 모든 걸 알고 있었던 클라라도 기쁨의 눈물을 흘렸다. 샤를은 애써 벅찬 감동을 억누르며 아버지가 남겨준 시계를 찬 아들에게 다가가 떨리는 목소리로 이렇게 소곤거렸다.
"아버지, 맞죠?"

　주인공 샤를은 이 시대를 살아가는 30대의 자화상이다. 이 사회가 정해준 흔한 진로대로 학업을 마치고 사회에 진출하여 시키는 대로 일하고 주는 대로 월급 받으며 아무 생각 없이 쳇바퀴 굴러가듯 하루하루를 살아간다. 그러다 문득 생활에 치여 한쪽에 내려놓은 자신의 꿈을 생각하면 가슴이 먹먹해진다. 하지만 그 꿈을 실현할 자신도 용기도 없기 때문에, 결국 다시 꿈은 꿈으로 남겨둔 채 현실로 돌아간다. 머리는 꿈속에, 몸은 현실 속에 있기 때문에 잠에서 미처 다 깨지 않은 흐리멍덩한 눈빛으로 무의미한 일상을 반복한다.

　실제 백만장자로서 백만장자 시리즈를 쓰는 마크 피셔는 돈 버는 '기술'이나 '기법'을 알려주지 않는다. 다만 돈 버는 '마인드'와 '지혜'를 알려줄 뿐이다. 이 책에서도 마크 피셔는 '샤를'이라는 인물을 통해 평범한 사회인이 백만장자로 성공할 수 있는 가능성을 보여준다. 그에게 백만장자란 경제적 차원의 백만장자만을 의미하는 건 아니다. 백만장자 시리즈를 통해 마크 피셔는 일단 마음이 부자인 백만장자로 살 수 있는 법부터 알려주기 때문이다. 그리고 위인들의 성공 사례에 따라 어떻게 하면 그 시대의 주역이 될 수 있는지도 일깨워준다. 그에 따라 경제적인 부를 거머쥐는 건 부차적인 소득이다. 중요한 건 내 손에 거저 쥐어진 백만금이 아니라, 과감히 이를 뿌리치고 자기 손으로 백만금을 일궈내겠다는 용기와 자신감이다. 그리고 이게 막연한 객기가 되지 않으려면, 어린아이의 눈으로 바라보는 세상의 진리를 깨우쳐야 한다. 그게 바로 이 책의 주인공 '샤를'을 통해 저자가 전달하고자 하는 메시지다.

어릴 때부터 건강이 별로 좋지 않았던 마크 피셔는 돈보다 소중한 가치에 대해 남들보다 일찍 온몸으로 '체득'했을 가능성이 크다. 유년기부터 급성 관절 류머티즘에 시달리며 병치레가 잦았던 그는 자연히 물리적인 신체 활동은 별로 할 수가 없는 상황이었고, 따라서 청소년기부터 이미 책과 명상 등 정적인 활동에 파고들며 생각의 깊이를 더해갔다. 하지만 조급한 마음에 섣불리 시작했던 소설은 별로 성공을 거두지 못했고, 이후 생계를 위해 다른 직업을 전전하다 출판계에 몸을 담게 된다. 이어 주위의 권고로 '마크 피셔'라는 필명을 만든 뒤 소설가로서의 꿈에 다시 한 번 불을 붙인 그는 서른네 살에 《백만장자》를 써서 세계적인 성공을 거둔다.

딱히 타고난 재능도, 물려받은 재산도 없는 지극히 평범한 사람이었기에, 맨손으로 시작하여 성공의 '시크릿'을 몸소 깨우친 마크 피셔는 그의 작품 속 주인공과 같은 현대인들에게 그 누구보다 할 말이 많은 사람이다. 아직 피에르 레니에의 단계에 이르지 못한 이 시대의 수많은 샤를 레니에들을 자기만큼 행복한 삶의 주인공으로 만들기 위해 마크피셔는 자신이 좋아하는 글로써 인생 성공의 진정한 '시크릿'을 전달해주고 있다.

사실 세상에 돈 많은 사람은 많다. 하지만 돈도 많고 행복한 사람은 별로 없다. 심지어 돈과 행복이 서로 반비례 관계라는 공식도 성립하는 세상이다. 그래서 행복을 누리며 경제적으로도 풍족한 삶을 원하는 사람들에게 저자는 주인공 샤를의 백만장자 아버지 피에르의 입을 빌려 이렇게 얘기한다.

"잠에서 깨어나라. 그리고 아이의 마음으로 어른의 세계를 살아가라. 그러면 백만금과도 바꿀 수 없는 소중한 삶의 가치와 함께할 것이며, 백만금의 돈이 저절로 수중에 생길 것이다."

책을 읽고 난 뒤, 이 같은 저자의 메시지가 와닿는다면, 또 하나의 샤를 레니에를 피에르 레니에의 단계로 끌어올리고자 했던 저자의 의도는 성공한 셈이다.

책을 번역하면서 가장 크게 와닿았던 건 미처 잠에서 깨지 못한 채 관성적으로 하루하루를 살아가는 회사원의 모습이었다. 어쩌면 그 사람의 모습이 지금의 내 모습과 많이 겹쳐졌기 때문인지도 모르겠다. 사실 나 역시 잠이 덜 깬 상태에서 관성적으로 하루 하루를 살아가는 그 회사원과 다를 바가 없었다. 일이 하기 싫어지니 일하면서 틈만 나면 딴짓을 하게 되는데, 그렇게 정신이 산만해진 상태에서 좋은 번역이 나올 리 만무했다. 그래서 내가 이 일을 왜 선택했는지, 어떤 면이 좋아서 이 일을 직업으로 삼았는지 곰곰이 생각해본 뒤, 잠에서 깨어난 정신 상태로 마음을 다잡고 제대로 번역을 해보니 즐기면서 일하는 게 가능해졌다. 맨 처음 번역을 할 때 느꼈던 재미도 되살아났다. 캐나다 불어의 특성상, 책 자체도 프랑스 쪽 책보다 더 쉬운 편이긴 했지만, 지금껏 작업한 책들 중 최단시간에 제일 빠른 호흡으로 번역해낸 책이 바로 이 작품이었던 것 같다. 깨어 있는 정신으로 즐기면서 일을 한다는 게 어떤 기분인지 저자 덕분에 다시 한 번 깨달을 수 있었다. 독자들 역시 이를 깨달을 수 있다면, 지구 반대편에서 느긋하게 커피 한 잔을 즐기고 있을 마크 피셔가 또 한 번 흐뭇하게 웃음 지을 수 있지 않을까?

_ 배영란

인생의 고난에 고개 숙이지 마라

초판 1쇄 인쇄 | 2012년 6월 25일
초판 4쇄 발행 | 2012년 12월 5일

지은이 | 마크 피셔
옮긴이 | 배영란
펴낸이 | 박상진

펴낸곳 | 진성북스
출판등록 | 2011년 9월 23일
주소 | 서울시 강남구 대치동 944-25번지 진성빌딩 10층
전화 | (02) 3452-7762   **팩스** | (02) 3452-7761
홈페이지 www.jinsungbooks.com
ISBN 978-89-97743-03-2 13320